Australian Politics
in a Digital Age

Peter John Chen

Australian Politics
in a Digital Age

Peter John Chen

E PRESS

Published by ANU E Press
The Australian National University
Canberra ACT 0200, Australia
Email: anuepress@anu.edu.au
This title is also available online at http://epress.anu.edu.au

National Library of Australia Cataloguing-in-Publication entry

Author: Chen, Peter John.

Title: Australian politics in a digital age / Peter John Chen.

ISBN: 9781922144393 (pbk.) 9781922144409 (ebook)

Notes: Includes bibliographical references.

Subjects: Information technology--Political aspects--Australia.

                   Information technology--Social aspects--Australia.

                   Internet--Political aspects--Australia.

                   Information society--Social aspects--Australia.

                   Communication--Political aspects--Australia.

Dewey Number: 303.48330994

Cover image: Jonathon Chapman, *Typographic Papercut Lampshade*, http://www.flickr.com/
photos/jonathan_chapman1986/4004884667

Cover design and layout by ANU E Press

Contents

List of illustrations

List of figures

List of tables

About the author

Peter John Chen is a lecturer in media and politics at the University of Sydney. He holds a PhD from The Australian National University. His research focuses on the relationship between media and political processes, with a particular interest in new forms of communication. He also teaches and researches in the areas of public policy, Australian politics and social movements.

Peter is the author of numerous articles and chapters on the role of digital media in Australian political life, and the author of *Electronic Engagement: A Guide for Public Managers* (ANU E Press, 2007) and the co-author of *Electronic Democracy? The Impact of New Communications Technologies on Australian Democracy* (Democratic Audit of Australia, 2006). He is a member of the editorial boards of the *Journal of Information Technology & Politics* and the *International Journal of Electronic Governance*.

Photo courtesy of the University of Sydney

Acknowledgements

I would like to thank my research collaborators over the years: Dr Stewart Jackson Dr Jay Smith, Dr Lucas Walsh and Dr Ariadne Vromen. In addition, I'm indebted to the consistent, reliable and high quality work of my research assistant Elise Wood, the red pen of Anna Bardsley and the editorial assistance of Sam Vincent. Finally, I'd like to acknowledge the kind and useful comments of my reviewers, the Australian and New Zealand School of Government and ANU E Press for the publication of this book, supporting my choice of an open-licensing approach permitting derivative works.

For Jo.

Acronyms and jargon

AAP	Australian Associated Press
ABC	Australian Broadcasting Corporation
ABS	Australian Bureau of Statistics
ACMA	Australian Communications and Media Authority
AEC	Australian Electoral Commission
ALP	Australian Labor Party
ANZSOG	Australia and New Zealand School of Government
API	application programming interface
ascii	American Standard Code for Information Interchange (character encoding)
ATA	Australian Taxpayers' Alliance
AWiA	Australian Women in Agriculture
BBC	British Broadcasting Corporation
CMS	content-management system (software)
CSG	coal seam gas
DDOS	distributed denial-of-service
EBP	evidence-based policy
e-democracy	electronic democracy
FOIA	Freedom of Information Act
Gov 2.0	Government 2.0
hi-fi	high fidelity
ICT	information and communications technology
KISS	keep it simple, stupid
LOIC	Low Orbit Ion Cannon (software)
MMOG	massively multiplayer online game (software)
MP	member of parliament
NBN	National Broadband Network
NGO	non-government organisation
NPM	new public management
NSFW	not safe for work
NSM	new social movement
OECD	Organisation for Economic Co-operation and Development

OSMO	online social movement organisation
OSS	open-source software (licensing model)
PBB	political big brother (website)
PR	public relations
PRIA	Public Relations Institute of Australia
PSI	public sector information
Q&A	Question and Answer (television show)
ROFLMFAO	rolling on floor laughing my fucking ass off
RSPT	Resource Super Profits Tax
RSS	really simple syndication (web format)
SMO	social movement organisation
SMS	short messaging service (text messaging)
SNS	social networking service
SOL	Senator Online (party)
SOP	standard operating procedure
UGC	user-generated content
USB	universal serial bus (hardware)
WWW	World Wide Web
YRaW	Your Rights at Work

Chapter 1 — Contextualising our digital age

It becomes normal, if you do it enough. Everything does.

— Dr Philip Myman, 'Pilot', *Better off Ted* (Fresco, 2009, s01e01)

The Australian media landscape

Digital media has been increasingly making a mark on the practice of politics in Australia. In the days before the 2010 federal election, 'progressive' online public interest advocacy group GetUp! took a legal challenge to the Australian High Court. Based on concerns of its members that reforms to electoral enrolment laws made under the previous Coalition government had unfairly disenfranchised younger Australians in 2006, the group mobilised legal resources and supporters to successfully change the law. Similarly, the organisation forced the Australian Electoral Commission (AEC) to accept online enrolment, setting up an online system to aid in the registration of voters — a direct intervention in the management of elections (Hopewell, 2010). This group, which had formed only five years previously, suddenly became a significant voice in Australian electoral politics. GetUp! moved from a focus on media campaigns to actions which directly altered Australian electoral law, the operations of the AEC, and the electoral balance in a year that was marked by a knife-edge electoral contest.

The 2007 election was also marked by its use of digital media, this time from within the world of formal politics. Then Opposition leader, Kevin Rudd, was placed front and centre of a campaign employing a slick presidential-style website, and strong use of social networking services (SNS) and online video (Chen and Walsh, 2010). This marked the beginnings of political campaigning in Australia that employed direct video and 'social media' to target supporters and key groups, moving party campaigns further away from the mass-media strategies that dominated political campaigns since the 1960s. Additionally, this use of technology had other meanings for the electorate. Rudd's use of digital media emphasised his 'newness': not just a change of government, after a long period under Prime Minister John Howard, but a generational change from a man associated with talkback radio and television, to Rudd and his emphasis on information technology and the internet.

At the grassroots level we have also seen the way a range of applications of the internet have affected the political world. Increasingly Australians are accessing online media as a source of political information. This continues a process of the 'mediation' of politics: the tendency for the media to become pre-eminent in linking people and institutions in the modern political environment. This is not, however, simply a passive process of 'more TV politics'. People are empowered by the interactive nature of the technology to be more politically expressive in online forums, SNS and blogs. Political memes — viral ideas — move rapidly through a globalising online community. The speed of contemporary politics can be remarkable. A paternalistic and patriarchal comment by a Canadian police officer[1] in late January 2011 spurred a colourful protest in downtown Toronto in late April (BBC, 2011). By early May, similar 'slutwalks' were being undertaken in Melbourne (Craig, 2011) as a new generation of young women identify that the personal is political and attempt to reclaim words that control and interpellate women. The rapid movement of ideas and culture serves as a new reservoir for the knowledge and traditions of social movements outside of their organisational contexts.

We've also seen a debate about the future of our media landscape, with the 'Princes of Print'[2] — newspaper barons — under assault by the upstart new media. Draining off the 'rivers of gold' that once flowed from classified advertising and introducing increased competition for the advertising dollar, the internet attacks the economic base of mass-media production: the scarcity of communications that is associated with the cost of plant and equipment. At the same time, new and alternative forms of publication compete for the attention of audiences. This impacts the stable diet of most Australians' media consumption, with implications for the sustainability of high-cost content like news and investigative journalism. On the other side of the ledger, we have seen alternative experiments in new forms of journalism: non-profit publication, the crowd sourcing of stories and content, and citizen journalism have all begun to make claims for legitimacy and political significance in today's complex media landscape (Deitz, 2010). These new voices challenge established institutional loci of power to define what is newsworthy, and the interpretation of political events and issues.

On digital media

This is not a technical book. It uses the term 'digital media', however, to describe the increasingly complex and interconnected set of technologies that have been reshaping the media landscape over the last few decades. The term has been deliberately selected over other competing ones (e.g. 'new media') because of its focus on the key technical driver of change: the digitisation of media content.

---

1   'I've been told I'm not supposed to say this — however, women should avoid dressing like sluts in order not to be victimised' (cited in Pilkington, 2011).
2   A term used by former prime minister Paul Keating (1986) to describe the regulation of media ownership (Guthrie, 2011: 37).

Digitisation (the conversion of content from analog to computer-readable formats) is significant because it allows for increased communicative capacity (bandwidth), higher fidelity, and the ability to easily integrate content into computer networks (interoperability) such as the internet. This has powerful implications for the reach of information and the way information processing (data storage and analysis) is applied to 'ordinary' communication activities.

A good example of this is the remoulding of content channels into the 'social media'. Social media is defined as by Axel Bruns and Mark Bahnisch as 'technologies to provide space for in-depth social interaction, community formation, and the tackling of collaborative projects' (2009: 1). Social media is a subset of digital media that adds database capacity to communication to record and represent the social relationship between participants. In doing so, technologies like Facebook, Twitter and blogs are able to enhance communication within social groups: either through re-creating offline social networks (i.e. university mates) or generating new communities of interest (i.e. Furry fans) (Boyd and Ellison, 2007). Like 'old media' these systems allow for communication, but the addition of computerisation and networking technologies enhances the way that particular individuals and groups can be identified and brought together. Thus, these technologies enhance 'discoverability' and 'social cohesion' through automation. This changes our basic relationship with media from passive recipient to active engagement.

While the idea of 'convergence' sees a future where all digital media is contained on an internet-enabled system, to date, digitisation has produced a hybrid media system that is gradually taking previously specific-purpose technologies and turning them into devices with a wide range of applications. The most visible examples of this have been in the way computers (once glorified typewriters and calculators) are now entertainment and communication systems, and how telephones have got smart and morphed into minicomputers. Importantly, convergence is not simply a technical process, but can also be seen in the way that digital media that remain offline (not connected to an open interoperable computer network) get 'overlayed' by social media through the creation of online communities around these channels (such as the use of Twitter hashtags for particular television shows or the sharing of static content pages through SNSs). Thus, the emphasis of this book is on that part of the digital media environment that is being drawn into the networked environment of the internet, either directly through technical means, or indirectly through the social media.

Non-linear, multi-factoral implications

Each of the vignettes above is dissimilar in their scope, scale and implications. Change comes from a variety of sources (individuals, organisations, economic signals, cultural production and meaning-making). Because of the considerably diffused (or alternatively, ubiquitous) impacts that digital media have had on Australian political life, it is easy to discount the importance of digital technologies in this nation. This 'normalisation hypothesis' — that social factors and tradition bring new technological developments into alignment with existing power distributions and patterns of social action (Resnick, 1999) — is widely accepted as the dominant description of the way digital media has been diffused in Australian society. The argument rests on the premise that technologies may be catalytic for change, but this is shaped and moderated by existing power structures and norms.

Because of this, the study of new types of media within the discipline of Australian politics has not been a growth area, attracting modest levels of attention when compared with that seen in comparative nations. While the media landscape has undergone dramatic and radical successive reconfigurations over the last two decades as a result of the rise of digital technologies, a tendency in the academy has been to see the political implications of this technological reconfiguration as comparatively small. Initial 'hype' about the potential for digital media to bring about 'electronic democracy' (e-democracy) at the turn of the century did not result in a fundamental alteration in the institutional or individual political practices of Australians, and more recent moves towards 'Government 2.0' has not produced much scholarly interest by researchers in politics or public policy. Similarly, while a digital media pioneer in its early stages (through the use of digital media, but also in the development of policies aimed at increasing high-speed internet uptake in Australia), the Rudd Labor government quickly floundered in a quagmire of over-reaching reforms, with Rudd's use of microblogging-cum-instant messaging[3] service Twitter painted as symbolic of a man out of touch with ordinary Australia (Maiden, 2010).

This is unfortunate. Dramatic claims about the power of digital media technologies to revitalise political participation and practice have, largely, been unrealised in Australia. The massively expanding media environment of Australians has, and will have, however, an important impact on political practice. This viewpoint comes from the observation that citizens of developed nations are increasingly embedded in an environment that is shaped and defined by media. Changes to this environment's contours, content and actors, therefore, have impacts on the shape and nature of the political world. We take our existing expectations, beliefs, and practices with us into this new environment. Thus, there will be continuity, but continuity with change. Overall, therefore, what we see is a

---

3 I recognise the definitional ambiguity here. Following Goggin and Crawford (2010) we have to recognise that definition of new media by the technical characteristics of the specific channel/tool is problematic. The increasingly active way that users/audiences employ technologies make static definitions of questionable value. This is particularly the case where there are considerable intergenerational differences in the way media channels are used.

set of very complex and non-linear changes that have resulted from the rise of digital media (Castells, 2000: 74). Far from being technologically deterministic in nature, these changes stem from the altered social world in which we live: as active agents who use media as instrumental tools for action, but also as carriers of culture.

The nature of continuity and change in Australian digital politics is what this book explores.

Media thinking: Is anything really 'new' here?

One of the longstanding central concerns of the study of 'political communication' (the largely North American individualistic formulation focusing on political candidates) or 'media politics' (the more British and Australian transition, with emphasis on organisational power), is the impact that media has on political life (Goot, 2009: 174–75). Media in these two traditions are either seen as technologies and practices that serve as modifiers of human communication at one level of analysis, or as a set of formal social institutions with key democratic 'functions'. We have long accepted that media form an increasingly important part of political practice around the world: through the extended capacity of individuals to know about and participate in political events outside of their immediate physical environment, and as political actors in their own right. The rise of national media reflects the rise of the nation state itself, and the gradual shift to the centre, in nations like Australia, of power and authority. In addition, effective national communication systems are essential for the operation of contemporary bureaucracies, and it is possible to see political systems as not just systems for the distribution and use of power, but also as information systems: 'a collection of elements (people, hardware, software, and data) and procedures that interact to generate information needed by users in an organization' (Morley and Parker, 2009: 499).

The structure of power shapes the behaviour and responses of those who live within its sphere. An increasingly mediated politics thus requires individuals who have 'media literacies'. These literacies are what Pierre Bourdieu (1973) would call symbolic and cultural 'capital': not just skills, but also knowledge of the genre conventions and lingo of the communities in which they need to operate. This capital creates meaning in any particular area of human activity: art, sport, consumption and politics (Harker, et al., 1990: 8, 13). Without the ability to 'read' and value symbols and behaviours, there would be no cultural system that creates power relations beyond the raw exercise of individual violence. Politicians, in their special field of mediatised politics, see media as both avenues to communicate to a variety of political constituencies and organisations to be courted and controlled. Thus, the skills of the effective leader today lie in maintaining their party or organisational support base, developing effective public policy (which may or may not be 'good policy' as we'll see in Chapter 7), and being an effective media 'performer' (Louw, 2010). In addition, as politics in Australia is a quasi-competitive sport, the ability to innovate in the use of media (and particularly new forms of media), may provide competitive advantage to some individuals and organisations, encouraging the development of mediated political practices that evolve and change as the media landscape changes.

The key question we have to ask, therefore, concerns the key characteristics (technical, social and political) of digital media that observers of politics need to focus upon to make meaningful assessments of recent political behaviour in Australia, and the trajectory of political practice into the future.

Thinking about 'media': From technical to social models

Before discussing digital media, we need to think about what we mean by 'media', both as a general definition, and in comparison with current developments. Marshall McLuhan oriented us to the need to pay attention to technologies so naturalised or domesticated that we fail to fully consider their implications and effects. He chided the complacent with the observation that '... fish know exactly nothing is water, since they have no anti-environment which would enable them to perceive the element they live in' (McLuhan and Fiore, 1968). We live in a media-saturated world and, thus need to reflect on our cultural medium.

There are many ways to look at 'media'. A traditional and technical view has tended to see media as a modifier for human speech communication — something we've developed to enhance our capabilities in the same way a club expanded our capacity to kill through increasing the effective strength and reach of our arm. A good example of this is the common communication models that look at media as a transmitter of information at a distance or over time, where the optimal design is the one which reduces the likelihood of corruption or decay (through, for example, 'redundancy'), or degradation (it has 'high fidelity' (hi-fi) and introduces low levels of 'noise' to the signal) (Shannon, 1948). In these models of communication, such as the basic design of the Bell's telephone (see Illustration 1), there tends to be a focus on a very simple view of human communication: such as the conversion (encoding) of sound into electoral impulses and their reproduction (decoding) at a distance. These models have tended to dominate the views on media during most of the 20th century, with a resulting tendency to see mediated communication as a process focused on production and transportation, rather than on reception and interpretation. In addition, these models privilege speech and face-to-face communication as more 'authentic' and natural forms of communication, an assumption we'll see has implications for power and authority, as well as the methodologies employed to evaluate media power.

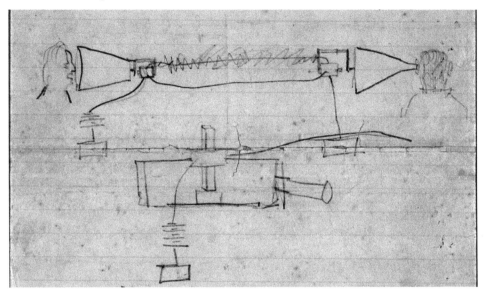

Illustration 1: Extract of Alexander Graham Bell's sketch of the telephone (1876)

Source: Library of Congress, Manuscript Division

While the idea that the communicative world we inhabited was 'naturally' dominated by face-to-face communication *may* have been true of Bell's time, since the advent of, first, widespread literacy and, then, broadcast media, Australians have been increasingly engaged in their social world through a variety of communications technology. Until the late 1990s these technologies tended to be defined by *scarcity*: either the economic scarcity of publication and mass circulation (which limited the number of newspapers, for example), or the scarcity of electromagnetic spectrum and the limited number of frequencies available for analogue radio and television broadcasting. This placed a small number of individuals — the media barons — at the apex of organisations that controlled these media organisations, a position that conveyed both status and political influence.

The advent of digital technology and computer networking (radically decentralising the production, storage and distribution of content) has had a dramatic impact on scarcity. No longer are we subject to the economics of spectrum availability as the boundaries of our media consumption; today, it's the number of waking hours that limits the time Australians spend in mediated communications of some form or other. This is illustrated in Figure

1. Demonstrating Australians' hourly consumption per week of different media forms, it shows us a number of things: first, that the type of media needed to be studied continues to expand, as the array of consumer media products and media expands.

In addition, the way that we might think about characterising media audiences — say for political segmentation purposes — also changes. This diversity makes it difficult to define media consumers with simplistic tags like 'ABC viewer' or 'talkback listener', because our array of media channels is increasingly complex and individualised. Secondly, the number of hours that Australians spend consuming media has increased over time, particularly online and digital media. Thus, while we may have once feared becoming a nation of 'couch potatoes', vacantly sucking on the 'cathode ray nipple' (Franti and Tse, 1992), Australians are increasingly supplementing — not replacing — these 'one way' media with more interactive and dynamic media forms.

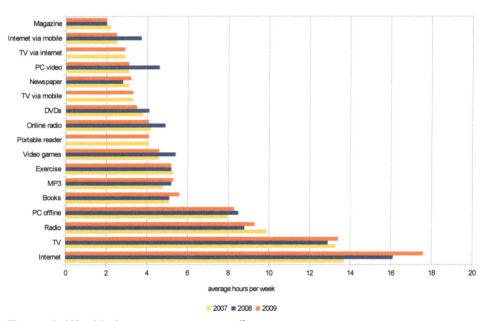

Figure 1: Weekly hours spent per media

Sources: Compiled from Nielsen, 2009, 2010

The figure shows that the nature of our world is progressively defined in terms of the media we use, for different purposes, and with different outcomes. In general there are three ways we can look at media: as a channel of communication (the 'channel effects' perspective), as a set of institutions (the 'media power' perspective), and as a set of tools that individuals can employ for different communicative purposes (our 'media environment', Krotz, 2009). Each has relevance for this book. Through either the analytical isolation of individual digital sub-media[4] of communication to look at their political use and implications (such as SNSs for 'microactivism', see SNS politics, Chapter 3); the examination of new organisations or institutional political practice; and, via a constructivist media sociology which considers how we use media to create social meaning in both deliberative and non-reflective ways. This latter perspective is critical in that it argues media so saturates our lives that it has supplanted other forms of socialisation in defining ourselves as individuals, communities or nations. This view has traditionally been a story of top-down power; an insidious process of elite media institutions 'cultivating' attitudes among a passive viewing public (Gerbner and Gross, 1976): the homogeneous group of paste-eaters formally known as 'the audience'.

Does the interactive nature of digital media change this view?

Digital media as a 'platform'

The view that mass media audiences are passive recipients of media messages is old and not without ongoing controversy. Stemming from work looking at the effectiveness of wartime propaganda, writers like Walter Lippmann (1925) saw the general public as uninformed and easily manipulated by authoritative voices. Discounting the atypical nature of war propaganda in their case selection, these authors saw the emerging mass media as highly effective in directing the biases and opinions of the 'mob', a body politic largely made up of reactionary simpletons and paste-eaters. In doing so they explained away the insanity of nations engaging in total war, not once, but twice in short order.

While later writers have shown that the public is far more engaged and selective in the way they take up and filter media messages (Lazarsfeld, et al. (1944) being the earliest influential work in this tradition), the tendency to view particular audiences as uninformed or docile remains active in our political discourse. These perspectives often contain implicit or explicit biases embedded within them about the nature of these audiences (of which there are commonly underlying narratives about the political literacy of different classes), and their impact on the wider political culture (normally negative). In Australia we see characterisations of, for example, tabloid newspaper readers and commercial

---

4   A sub-media, in this context, is a communications technology defined by a specific technical standard. Thus, within the arena of internet communication, electronic mail and World Wide Web content are sub-media, whereas blogs, webpages, and social networking services are not. These latter represent different genre conventions, channels, and/or online communities. It is recognised, however, that this classification is increasingly ambiguous as different sub-media become integrated into the web environment and the distinctions between types of online interaction are more usefully defined in terms of their social meaning. The book uses 'channel' as a meta-descriptor.

talkback radio audiences in this way. These audiences tend to be presented as followers of particular media 'lines', rather than active decision makers in their media consumption habits (see, for example, Hamilton (2006)).

While this clearly has political implications in the ongoing battle over who is 'worthy' to be represented and what defines a political middle ground in Australia (a way in which we 'prime' political discourse towards the way in which we prefer it to be interpreted), the notion of groups of individuals as passive and habitual consumers of media has to be challenged. The increasing diversity of media sources and content in Australia is also matched by increasing levels of education, and particularly intergenerationally. Studies of media effects that are based on nationalist propaganda in the first part of the 20th century are almost 100 years old in their method and assumptions, and we need to consider how technological and social changes may effect the way in which people engage in a contemporary media environment. The Power Inquiry in the United Kingdom argued that today's citizenry in developed nations are significantly different in their political concerns and capacities than when propaganda effects were first assessed. While noting a degree of disengagement with formal political institutions, they rejected arguments that the citizenry was unworthy or ignorant. They stated that '[c]hanges of the post-war era have gradually created citizens who are better educated, have a higher sense of self-esteem, enjoy and expect to make decisions for themselves, and either lack or chose their own geographic, social and institutional bonds' (2006: 103).

In addition to a shifting base of cultural capital, digital media have an important part to play in this story. First, for the more educated and informed citizenry, digital expands the number of choices available to diversified audiences. A good example of this can be seen in the proliferation of digital television channels (cable, internet and free-to-air) in recent years, which reflect the more complex composition of the Australian community post the era of White Australia (circa 1970). Second, we have to recognise that the convergence of computer technology and media magnifies the nature of change in the media landscape by altering the capacity of individuals to act within the media system. This has the effect of destabilising fixed roles like 'audience' and 'producer', and adding systemic characteristics and capacities into the media system. The embedding of information and communications technologies (ICTs) into our media systems serves to accelerate the pace of change because, instead of giving us 'channels', they provide a 'platform' for engaging in human behaviour. We no longer 'watch television', but, rather, inhabit a mixed-media environment.

The shift from 'dumb' communications technology to 'smart' digital media is important because it requires a careful re-evaluation of established thinking about media politics. The rise of the internet as a core aspect of this technological change (or more appropriately, the culmination of a variety of developments),[5] is not simply the introduction of 'a' new channel for communication. Its significance is not that it has better hi-fi than media it is displacing (in some areas, for example online video, it is popular *despite* having lower fidelity). It is significant because it is a technology that enables the expression of human creativity in novel and more effective ways. ICTs are catalytic for change because of the combination of a number of key technologies (Flew, 2008). These are:

- *Computerisation*: which accelerates the capacity for data information to be created and employed by skilled individuals and organisations. Computerisation is important because it makes information dynamic: it can be presented in a variety of forms, recalculated, and overlaid to create new information that was not envisaged by the original collectors. Increasingly data is a by-product of human activities: generated and stored whether we like it or not. SNSs represent a good example of this. They allow individuals to access social networks online, massively reducing the time cost in locating old friends or family members. These services also permit advertisers, using data-mining techniques, to identify new markets or consumption trends. The storage of personal behaviour online, and its ease of access, creates new privacy concerns that have become political debates as their social significance becomes increasingly apparent. Overall, computerisation is important because it can increase the scale of human agency through the automation of tedious or repetitive tasks (Hansen, 2010).

- *Digitisation*: which allows for low-cost reproduction of large amounts of content, as well as its manipulation and redistribution with ease. This changes the economics of content creation and distribution (creating, in some areas, a superabundance), as well as creating new tools for the production and modification of content (such as the use of low-cost personal computers to produce high-quality publications and audio-visual material). In addition, because this material can be stored with perfect fidelity,[6] it can be reused (in original or altered form) repeatedly at little or no cost.

- *Networking*: the linking together of computers and networks using technologies like the internet and mobile voice and data services. These allow complex communications systems and social groups to be formed dynamically and ad hoc, with reduced impact of, and reference to, the user's geographical location. This impacts on the way we respond to classical political problems, such as the co-ordination of individual effort and the tyranny of distance, which has resulted in considerable 'network effects'. As such, computer

---

5   The internet is a good example of how the development of media technology and practice is cumulative and draws in an array of technologies to create a more powerful system.

6   A good example of the impact of storage is to see the effect of widespread domestic refrigeration on the landscape of urban environments through alterations to commerce and distribution systems (decline of travelling vendors and local shopping) which then moved back up the production chain.

networking has remarkable generative qualities (Zittrain, 2008: 71–74), resulting in the creation of new private and public goods. Examples of these goods can be found in the creation of new public information repositories (e.g. Wikipedia or the Urban Dictionary), new virtual organisations (ephemeral, such as flashmobs (Rheingold, 2002: 174–82); or more lasting, such as the internet political site *On Line Opinion*) and new informational goods (such as the Linux Operating System or audio books online; Gensollen, 2007: 84–87).

What we do with media, what it does to us

The implication of these changes is why ICTs are more appropriately viewed as a platform for human activity that has neo-institutional characteristics. In this context, neo-institutionalism addresses the relationship between human agency (our freedom of action) with the organisational (formal institutions) and social structures (informal institutions) in which we live. Sitting firmly on the fence between an over-deterministic view of the impacts of social, technological and economic structures on human decision making (e.g. Langdon Winner's argument about the nature of technologies, such as atomic power, leading automatically to authoritarianism; 1986), and the complete free will and omniscience of radical egocentrism (Bradley, 2005: 49), a neo-institutional view of media has an analytical focus on what can be done in particular structural contexts. Thus, our structured existence (in a family, a community, a workplace or a political organisation) both facilitates and constrains our action. It does this through the provision of enablers and barriers (physical resources and constraints), as well as incentives and disincentives (social norms, rules, expectations and rewards) (Lowndes, 2010: 75–77).

This perspective recognises the ability for individuals and groups to use available tools to achieve specific objectives (such as using a religious social network to organise an advocacy political campaign), as well as the potential to be reflexive about how structures shape the 'rules of the game' in which decisions are made (Rhodes, 1997). The latter perspective also means some actors have the ability to shift action to a context more likely to advantage them (what can be called 'arena shopping'; Sabatier and Jenkins-Smith, 1999) or even reconfigure the resource and meaning structures that encourage or discourage specific forms of political behaviour (changing the rules themselves[7]). Politics plays out on these levels: using the resources and institutions available to achieve our ends in the short term, or adapting them to ensure our ends are more likely to be achieved in the future. While political resources can be physical, with an eye

---

7 For example, the incorporation of critics of government regulation of internet services in the late 1990s by giving one of the industry groups the power to create industry codes of practice (self-regulation) was a powerful mechanism by which the government shaped the nascent representative bodies of the internet industry in Australia by strongly incentivising them to join a particular body which would serve as a focal point for decision-making about the industry code.

to media politics we must also recognise the importance of information, ideas, beliefs, values and meaning and place increased emphasis on the constructivist nature of media environments to shape political culture and therein shape the temporary disposition of the formal institutions in which speech acts become law and policy.

The advantage of this type of approach for digital media lies in incorporating how active we can be in using and shaping the platform. Thus, rather than talk about internet 'audiences' we use the more active term of 'users', drawn from the computing arena. As digital media has become more prevalent and increasingly designed for the general consumer, this has considerably lowered the barriers for individuals using these platforms creatively (Lister, et al., 2003). This observation led Bruns (2008) to develop the notion of online creativity as 'produsage', the tendency for the internet and its various online communities, tools and environments to give users the capacity to be both producers and users of content simultaneously. While Wikipedia (the poster child of the 'read-write web' movement) may be the most obvious example of this, because of its high profile presence online, we see this also in a variety of situations (Benkler, 2006: 63–67). This includes the comparatively mundane activities of commenting on blogs or sharing photos, but also includes less obvious interactions like the automation of online data collection in shaping the platform itself. A good example of this more passive produsage is an online activity many people do every day: make choices from Google's list of search results, which are stored, analysed and tabulated to adjust the results for future search engine users. Whereas these online practices tend to be individualistic in nature, they aggregate into patterns of social practice (conventions and norms over time). Shirky (2008: 81), for example, has identified how the editorial conventions of media based on scarcity are becoming *inverted* with the rise of digital media. Rather than employing careful editorial processes and controls to vet material before it is published, the online convention is increasingly to publish early and then allow the 'social filtering' process of user choice, recommendation and trackbacks to determine what content has value and what does not.

We may not (yet) be cyborgs, but the digital media continues to shape us as we shape it.

New media = new politics?

As the internet, in its most popular form, the World Wide Web (WWW), reaches its 20th year, we can see how cycles of innovation and practice have evolved to develop the institutional characteristics of digital media: new structural barriers and enablers. These have arisen either through the creative destruction

of old practices (such as the decline of high-cost investigative journalism in the commercial media); through the 'remediation' of existing forms of media, their recreation in the digital environment (such as online TV as like, but unlike, the traditional broadcast media; Bolter and Grusin, 2000); and, via the development of wholly new forms of practice (i.e. Massively Multiplayer Online Games (MMOGs)).[8] These new institutional contours have developed their own social meaning and political importance.

Because of this there is no simple argument about what digital media 'does' to the practice of politics in Australia. Like any essential change to the environment in which we operate, we can make an argument that the politics we see in a digital media saturated environment will be substantially different over time to what we have seen in the past. This change, however, will not be easily predictable, and will remain in tension between the tendency for the new capabilities of these platform technologies to shift practice, while constrained by existing habits, values and political practice. In addition, the breadth and rapidity of change make prediction possible. This is an area of scholarship that is subject to rapid obsolescence.

To fully explore the implications of digital media for Australian political life, the following chapters look at a range of key political domains. Within each domain we examine available evidence regarding the way digital media has been employed, and look at the political implications these technologies and practices have had to date:

- Chapter 2 looks at the impacts on the formal practices of democratic government in Australia, with the way digital media has been employed in the electoral process. This chapter focuses on the way that parties and candidates have employed new communications channels to solicit votes and distribute political information, as well as examining new entrants into the electoral space. Considering the more active role of voters, the chapter questions the audience for political information during campaigns, and examines the way active audience members have engaged in the process of elections.

- Chapters 3 and 4 examine the discursive environment online, exploring the way new forms of participative digital media have changed the way in which Australians talk about politics. Critically employing the concept of the public sphere, this chapter considers opinion formation and debate online. This allows us to consider the active process of meaning formation among new and virtualised online communities, and we can examine what a politics

---

8   In a good example of the social shaping of technology, however, it's genuinely difficult to think of wholly new online practices. MMOGs can be traced back to freeform acting and live-action role-playing, which were popular in the 1970s and 1980s.

of 'conversation' might look like, its impact, and the new forms of agency it generates.

- Chapters 5 and 6 consider the use of digital media by political elites. Looking at an array of key political institutions, including lobby groups and the mass media, these chapters examine the way the digital age has changed their capacities. From the creation of new forms of political social movements to alterations to the political economy of existing media institutions, the reconfiguration of the fields of power that lie in the elite sphere of Australian politics needs careful consideration in a country that tends to rely on top-down mobilisation.

- The final chapter, Chapter 7, looks at the impacts of new technologies on the public sector, still the largest single-industry segment in this nation. This chapter considers not just the use of digital media tools for participation and inclusion, but also the way new technologies have shaped government services and functions. Looking at notions of e-service delivery and government 2.0, this chapter considers the implications of these developments in terms of the capacity of the state, but also in altering perceptions and expectations of the public.

Chapter 2 — Obama-o-rama?

Winning needs no explanation, losing has no alibi.

— Greg Baum

For the majority of Australians the political process is most visible during elections. In our system of government, elections serve a wide variety of perceived functions. Under the *representative* form of decision-making they have a strict *legal* role in determining who gets to form part of the assembly of legislators and cast votes in the place of members of the public. The traditional justification for this is it serves to free individuals from the onerous labour of directly legislating (Kornberg and Clarke, 1992: 176). Thinking of political systems as *information* systems, elections are also 'focusing events' (Kingdon, 1984: 98), which draw attention to policy issues and the institutional mechanisms and actors able to address them — this is an agenda-setting view. Finally we can also see them as both *ritualistic* and *symbolic*, they are public *performances* that reaffirm the participative nature of democratic government and convey political *legitimacy* on the elected government and their political manifesto. This legitimacy is important in allowing governments to achieve their policy objectives and is protected through mechanisms like independent electoral administration bodies (the Australian Electoral Commission (AEC), and its state-based cousins). Where this legitimacy is challenged (formally or rhetorically), government capacity can be undermined.

Because of the multiple functions of elections — the relative significance of which is not explicitly agreed among political elites or members of the public[1] — assessing the impact of digital media on the processes and practices of elections is complex. At the most basic level, students of digital media politics are often asked about the 'return on investment' these channels provide: does a dollar invested online 'buy' more votes than one invested in traditional media, or put into public relations, or spent on 'facetime'? As we'll see, the advent of digital media, with its undoubted ability to collect data on performance and behaviour (page views, unique visits, click through rates, dwelling times), has not yet answered this question in Australia. In addition, while votes may be the ultimate measure of electoral success for some, the position of digital media in the wider media ecosystem and the impact of this on the way political information is communicated can be seen as a more significant, but even harder

---

1   Indeed, the relative importance is one of those areas of political dialogue in Australia that Deborah Stone (1998: 137–38) would argue remains deliberately ambiguous because of the freedom of action it affords political elites. Political leaders are wont to talk about mandates when they have them, making decisions irrespective of election agendas when the need arises, and few are ever keen to discuss the dramaturgy of elections when in office (for rare examples of this, see Tanner (2011) and Latham (2005)).

impact to identify with certainty. To examine these impacts, this chapter looks at the popular debates around the use of digital media and election campaigns, the adoption and use of technology by political parties, candidates and civil society groups, and then draws together these observations to illustrate the impacts of technology on the process of elections in Australia today.

Questions for e-lections

To go beyond the descriptive, let's examine two areas of interest about the role digital media plays in election campaigns today.

Democracy +

The first questions we should ask concerns democratic impact. This focuses on how the use of digital media affects the 'playing field' of politics. In the Australian context, with the dominance of the two major party groupings, this is expressed through the ability of smaller political parties to gain representation or visibility. In this context, the features of digital media that lower the cost of content production and distribution are significant for minor parties, allowing them to employ a range of online channels to distribute their message at comparatively low cost when compared to paid advertising. Increased accessibility of information about more parties is therefore indicative of 'more' democracy, through the assumption that more players are likely to increase the competitiveness of the contest (Gibson & McAllister, 2011). Additionally, and more substantively, as the major parties have tended to move to a 'central' position in the political spectrum (Mulé, 2001: 124), this can also be seen as a proxy for the increased range of policy opinions put to voters. Thus, even if the more visible minor parties are electorally unsuccessful, their ideas and concerns may be coopted by the dominant parties, which seek to appeal to their constituencies.

These democratic questions provide us with a triumvirate of measures. At the simplest level it is possible to see how a range of existing and new smaller parties have gladly adopted digital media in Australia as a means to gain visibility. It is more difficult, however, to determine if this translates into increased electoral success given the range of variables at play. Internationally, Small's (2008b) analysis has argued that the heightened visibility of parties has not come with corresponding electoral victories. This finding is seen as a result of the inability of many digital channels to 'pull' audiences. Websites (the most commonly studied of party digital media) are visible through active search, requiring pre-existing interest. Finally, at the most difficult level, it is hard to determine if the lack of electoral success of these newly digitised minor parties comes from their comparative lack of 'push' media (e.g. advertising), or because major parties are adroit at coopting their agendas. This is by far the most difficult question to answer: requiring us to identify areas of agenda cooption, as well as assumptions of potential electoral success. Examples, like the cooption of aspects of the policy and rhetoric of Pauline Hanson's One Nation party by the then Prime Minister John Howard in the late 1990s can be identified, but it's not clear that Hanson's success was due to her party's extensive use of digital media (which they did employ with considerable success, Rutherford, 2001; Scalmer, 2002: 161), or the 'natural' recognition of an unserved section of the electorate (David Truman's notion of the 'potential interest group'; 1951: 516).

This first area of inquiry looks at the interface between macro and meso analysis: to what extent does the Australian political system produce outcomes that are democratically 'good' (a macro view) based on the interactions between formal and informal groups (meso). To join the dots further we can also ask questions about the roles of individual actors and the types of actors in the adoption and use of technology. Our neo-institutional approach to analysis, discussed in Chapter 1, looks at the interactions between individuals and their organisational structures. This recognises the coexistence of influence: *top-down* in the role of party machines on the behaviour of individual candidates; and, *bottom-up* through the aggregation of individual actions into collective 'norms'. Does the adoption of digital media arise from party organisations, or from a myriad of individual choices among political actors?

A strongly held contemporary view of electoral politics is that it has become a professional activity where entry, advancement, and success are driven through the acquisition of increasingly formalised skills drawn from international campaign practice and a range of contemporary media disciplines: corporate communications, public relations (PR), and marketing. This 'marketing model' of politics is detailed by Karen Sanders (2009: 59) as the adaptation of commercial communications and sales techniques which focus on the identification of consumer/voter desires, and serving these desires through the constant adjustment of party and candidate platforms. Rather than attempt to 'sell' a party platform to the public (convincing them of the merit of the proposals), political marketing conceptualises the voter as increasingly independent in their political allegiance and therefore more likely to engage in rational-choice decision-making. The rise of this approach to looking at the political environment as a 'marketplace' is backed up by the tendency for parties to become increasingly 'hollowed out' (where party bureaucrats give way to external professional communications and campaign consultants) and for the electorate to become more volatile (McAllister, 2011: 38–40).

A problem with the marketing model in the Australian context is the comparative inflexibility of our party system. As opposed to the United States, where the proliferation of autonomous candidates makes it easier for platforms to shift in response to fickle public demand or issues of the day, Australia presents a tension between market responsiveness and internal party processes and individual interests. While it is true that the type of sales-oriented, manifesto-focused campaign appears to have been thoroughly discredited in Australia with the defeat of John Hewson's Fightback! economic manifesto in the 1990s, Australian parties are not simply political action groups set up to support electoral campaigns, but continue to serve as vehicles for internal decision-making and debate. While the interest-mediation function of parties (the role of the party mediating between competing interests to develop party policy) has declined in recent years (Jaensch, et al., 2004: 54), the removal of Malcolm Turnbull as leader of the Liberal Party in 2009 demonstrates the power of internal policy debates over policy areas that are seen as highly sensitive to the party support base (Rodgers, 2009).

The counterargument lies in the similar (but possibly very different) removal of Kevin Rudd from the leadership of the Australian Labor Party (ALP) in 2010. While also a victim of carbon-trading policy, Rudd's departure due to poor polling is more clearly a story of his perceived 'market failure'. While considerable ink has been spilled over the 'assassination of' / 'coup against' the incumbent prime minister, what is clear is the role that the new professional skills of marketplace analysis played in his departure. Bob Hodge and Ingrid Matthews (2011), for example, examine the role of opinion polling in the removal of the prime minister, arguing that it was not public opinion that resulted in the decision to remove Rudd, but the weight given to particular interpretations of polling data by members of the parliamentary party. Thus, while Turnbull's demise stemmed from the extent to which his support for climate science separated him from his peers, Rudd's removal stemmed from faith placed in party pollsters. This reflects Eric Louw's notion of the 'PR-isation of politics' (2010: 75–80). In his view, PR-isation sees an increasingly important role of public relations professionals and consultants in stage-managing politicians-as-performers for consumption by the public, and interpreting public opinion for elites. PR becomes important in ensuring electoral success, but also in manufacturing consent from a public that is weakly attached to formal politics. In this process, argues Louw, 'low-involvement' media like television are essential tools because their one-to-many communications structure requires acquisition of the technical skills of the PR industry, and serve to focus political power on a small number of key performer-politicians.

Ruddbots and real Julias

The second question is the degree to which artifice saturates modern politics. The rise and dominance of televised politics has led to concerns that contemporary politicians emerge from 'central casting': plastic people who are unlike 'us'. This sense of alienation from elites is a unique problem of democratic government, where the expanded notion of 'we govern' implies that we share some affinity with the political elite (something not automatically assumed in authoritarian and aristocratic modes of government).[2] If this presents a problem, we need to ask if digital media are an answer to this social distancing.

Accordingly, new social media provides ways for elites to present themselves as 'real people' through a reduction in this distance. The perception of digital media as increasingly pervasive and occurring in real-time has seen an emergence of a new language of *authenticity*. Digital media allows greater interaction with, and information about, a wide range of elites (entertainment, sporting, political). It provides more substance about policies and positions, but also about elites as individuals. Social networking services (SNS) typify this: making it harder to feel distant from political elites when you can share the loss of their family dog[3] or barrack for your favourite sporting team together–apart.[4] The reduction of social distance can serve to make these individuals, once part of faceless organisations, 'ordinary people' — a characteristic that Gilpin, et al. (2010: 259–60) see as providing cues about that individual's authority, fidelity, origin, credibility, sincerity, and accuracy. In the public life, authentic politics is a place of trustworthy communication between social equals.

This approach reflects a shift towards the political ideology of populism, particularly those elements defined by Catherine Fieschi and Paul Heywood:

> … the claim to represent the 'common man', the average voter whose voice has long been lost; they claim to be able to return to a golden, more innocent age of politics during which politics and political decisions rested in the hands of those who contribute most significantly to the everyday life of the nation by their labour. (2004: 301)

Ingolfur Blühdorn (2007: 257) sees the notion of 'authentic politics' as an attempt to recapture, perhaps nostalgically, a modernist politics based on the ontological notion of an absolute and fixed reality: a politics where people mean what they say and say what they mean. This is significant in that Australia faces, if not a crisis of political trust, a tendency for it to be in consistently short supply. This is illustrated in Figure 2. Drawn from election studies undertaken by The Australian National University, we can see that, while Australians' have an increasing level of satisfaction with our democratic system of political

---

2   Walter Benjamin (1936) would argue that this leads to a more ready and easy criticism of political elites: 'The audience's identification with the actor is really an identification with the camera'.
3   Malcolm Turnbull; http://twitter.com/#!/TurnbullMalcolm/status/148633314268422144
4   Anthony Albanese; http://twitter.com/#!/AlboMP/status/102604447611494400

organisation, they are far less enamoured with the individuals who actually work within it (logarithmic trendline). Trust and authenticity, therefore, may help to close this gap.

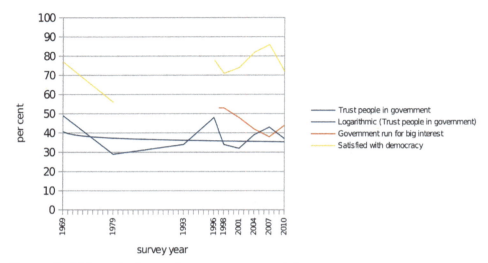

Figure 2: Citizens' views of government and democracy

Source: McAllister, 2011: 74–76, 82 (annotated and rescaled)

While distrust of politicians is not new, the increased mediatisation of politics facilitates the rise of professional inauthenticity (Newman, 1997: 155). The concern about trust picks up on the notion of the development of the virtualised world as articulated by Jean Baudrillard. Looking at the development of media, technology, and society, Baudrillard examines a technological process by which the ability to (re)produce a representation of the world (say an image) moves from the capture of the real world, through to hyper-real representations of it: from enhanced or modified versions (the airbrushed model), through to purely artificial representations that claim a basis in reality. While Baudrillard sees this historical process embedded in the economic and social world,[5] the separation of the real from signs masquerading as the real has led to an inversion of reality: the imagined representation precedes the real and shapes it (Baudrillard, 1988: 169–72). In this way, he argues that '[e]verything is metamorphosed into its inverse in order to be perpetuated in its purged form' (177). This allows us to see how the PR-ised 'Julia' can be denounced to produce the 'real Julia':[6] a more authentic, human, and electable politician.

---

5   The estrangement of workers from the value and meaning of the goods they produce, and the separation of individuals from the natural environment.

6   This is drawn from a campaign speech by the Prime Minister Julia Gillard where, in response to criticism of her campaign, she announced that she would 'make sure that the real Julia is well and truly on display' (Hudson, 2010).

There is a tension here. Politicians want to be approachable and likeable, but run the risk of diluting that which makes them special and provides authority. From a non-political perspective, Sue-Ellen Case observes the power of the virtual 'as alternative to the ubiquitous, pedestrian realm. Acting within that space requires particular codes of behavior, traditions of costuming, and training in specialized gestures or functions' (2007: 2). These are apparent in the political world where politicians have their own recognisable argot, staging, and mode of dress. These conventions can be recognised and commented upon, such as in the popular blog *Tony Abbott Looking at Things* (Illustration 2) that illustrates the specific dress of politicians, regardless of its appropriateness. In this way, Case argues that virtuality is not simply a technical process of the representation of this specialised social environment, but that virtualisation conveys the performance space as 'special' and 'specialised'. Overall, this questions whether adopting social media serves as a response to decreasing levels of trust that have emerged from the era of televisual politics. In so doing, however, do political performers run the risk of breaking the suspension of disbelief that gives them symbolic authority and influence?

Illustration 2: *Tony Abbott Looking at Things* Tumblr blog

Source: http://tonyabbottlookingatthings.tumblr.com/

'10 in 10': The evolution of online campaigning

The long primary and presidential campaign that led to the election of Barack Obama in 2008 is cited as a catalyst for renewed interest in digital media campaigning around the world. Obama represented a new form of politics for a range of reasons, both ideological and social and learned (and not so learned) books have been published exploring all facets of the campaign: the use of slick websites, campaign blogs and blogger conference calls, of social networking and micro-fundraising (Williamson, 2010: 15). Campaign staff and strategists, like Blue State Digital,[7] were quick to tout their media strategies as key to this dramatic electoral event.

In the lead-up to the 2010 federal election, Google Australia hosted a series of events for political insiders to advise them of the services the company offered for election campaigning. Far from being simply a search engine, the multinational IT giant offers a range of products, from advertising to webmetrics, and the company was keen for Australian campaign professionals to consider the most effective/extensive way to use those products in the campaign. The core of the pitch, however, was a simple '10 in 10': spend 10 per cent of your advertising budget online (personal correspondence: Stewart Jackson, 16 July 2010).

This anecdote is revealing about digital electioneering in Australia today. Over the past 20 years, parties and candidates have gradually expanded their engagement with these technologies: first tentatively, then tangentially and, now, as an essential part of their media and communications strategy. What has not happened, however, is the radical displacement of traditional methods and channels of communication. In the 2010 campaign, political parties continued to use mass media channels to distribute undifferentiated messages, and candidates employed direct mail and local signage as their most cost-effective campaigning tools. Given the high cost of TV advertising in Australia (Maher, 2010), only large institutional actors are able to take advantage of mass advertising. In addition, compulsory voting encourages campaigning that targets the undecided and the weakly committed (Taft & Walker, 1958: 162): a market that favours the use of intrusive advertising on high rotation. Google's pitch to the parties, however, demonstrates the way in which online campaigning has moved from the realm of the amateur to that of the professional. The company advised party officials on the most effective ways to use online advertising, the need to set levels of expenditure, the nature of 'always on' campaigning, and — critically — the

---

7   Strongly associated with the campaign's voter outreach and fundraising strategies, the company was formed by staff who worked on the innovative Howard Dean campaign. Dean was a presidential candidate in the 2004 Democratic primaries in the United States. Generally regarded as an unlikely nominee, his use of digital media was highlighted as a strength of his campaign.

need to integrate online and offline campaign management (Google Australia, 2010: 2). What remains unclear is if a 10 per cent spend offers good or bad value for money.

This section examines the contemporary electoral digital landscape in three parts: first, we examine the way parties have engaged with digital media to win elections; second, the role of individual candidates in the online space — do low barriers to entry serve to unshackle these individuals from their parties?; and, finally, we assess online campaigning against the marketing and PR-isation hypotheses presented above.

Vote for us

The core of the Australian electoral process rests on parties. This is due to a range of factors, including the Westminster system of legislative management (Wlezien, 2010: 102), historical tensions between organised labour and the anti-Labor parties (Marsh, 1995: 17–19), the entrenched notion of the two-party preferred voting system (Sharman, 1994: 135), and the comparative homogeneity of Australian society that has remained stable over long periods of time. This party-centric model is not a universal way of organising political competition. As structure develops to reinforce culture, a range of laws and institutional behaviours have developed to entrench parties as the primary way in which Australians are encouraged to think about electoral politics: from how-to-vote cards (employed by half of voters to direct their vote based on party recommendations; Farrell & McAllister, 2005: 89) to the structure of the Senate voting system which assumes party-level competition for quotas.

In the Australian context this is important in the way public and private resources disproportionately favour, not just parties, but established parties who alternate in government. This is achieved through the disproportionate amount of donations these parties-of-government receive from corporate and union donors (Tham, 2010), but also in parties' increasing use of public resources to support campaigning directly (public election funding) and indirectly (use of government advertising and parliamentary allowances; see Information subsidies and the growth of PR, Chapter 6). Overall, this is anti-democratic in the way it captures public resources to reinforce the dominance of a small, closed group of 'insider' parties. This 'cartel hypothesis', originally proposed by Richard Katz and Peter Mair (1994), argues that parties who share government become entrenched in power, become 'insiders' and move away from a genuine connection to the public, and increasingly limit the competitiveness of the political system by adjusting electoral laws and processes (a good example of this being the alteration of the number of seats in the Tasmanian parliament to prevent the election of candidates from the Australian Greens; Crowley,

1999: 186). Under this hypothesis, Labor and the Coalition can be seen as a cosy club who limit competition to alternation between these parties. However fierce their language, Australia is increasingly a 'managed democracy' guided by entrenched political elites.

Regardless of the rights and wrongs of the party-centric system of electoral competition (a question to which we will return), it is appropriate to begin the examination of digital media in electoral campaigns by a look at these most significant of actors.

Learning to love digital media

Political parties' use of internet-based communications emerged slowly over the last two decades. While parties established their first websites in the mid 1990s, the new millennium saw online campaigning increasingly rise to prominence as an active area of study and media attention. Interestingly, this initially emerged in Australia at the level of state government: marked by contested use of a political campaign website by the Liberal Party's Jeff Kennett in the 1999 election (Martin, 2000). This website — part of a personalised campaign — set the tone for online elections in Australia for some time: particularly in the use of specific, time-limited sites for the election campaign, as well as a focus on the figure of the leader. Sites largely remained static, information-based repositories (Chen, Gibson & Geiselhart, 2006: 35), serving as electronic brochures aimed at wide audiences.

The longevity of this model is interesting given that this early iteration of the campaign website was quickly parodied by online pranksters (Illustration 3)[8] who demonstrated just how low the barriers to entry to online publication are. Ridiculing the 'cult of Jeff', which had emerged around the flamboyant premier, parodies and more substantively critical websites received considerable publicity during the election.[9] This highlighted the risks parties faced in the open access and anarchic medium of the internet. Where parties' near monopoly on TV advertising allowed control of message and timing, the internet allowed participation from a wide range of individuals and groups who could use guerrilla-marketing techniques and steal visibility from the party ('brand hijacking'; Levinson & Gibson, 2010: 162).

---

8 Source: http://yoyo.cc.monash.edu.au/~vik/realjeff/message/ (site archive; accessed: 23 January 2012).
9 A good example would be Stephen Mayne's *jeffed.com* website which was critical of the policies and management approach of the government. In some ways the success of *jeffed.com* led to the development of the alternative media site *Crikey!*

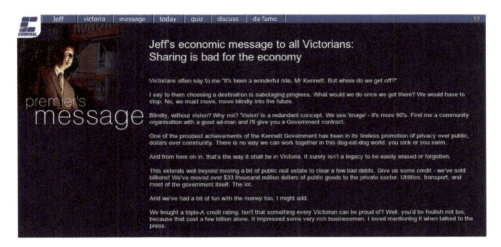

Illustration 3: The *Real Jeff* parody website

Source: http://yoyo.cc.monash.edu.au/~vik/realjeff/message/

These lessons shaped party engagement with digital media in a number of ways. First, an emphasis on control developed: digital media was a risky proposition that parties did not understand well and should be treated with caution. Unsurprisingly this led to a tendency for established Australian parties to limit their exposure to the web, particularly interactive content. Second, where innovation did emerge, this focused on negative campaigning that could not be hijacked. A good example was the *Political Big Brother* (*PBB*) site that was accessible during the 2001 election. Based on the reality television program *Big Brother*, the site encouraged subscribers to 'vote out of the house' key members of the government through an interactive set of voting rounds staged over the weeks leading up to the election: with the prime minister being the last person to be 'voted out' (Chen, 2001). *PBB* had a range of innovative and engaging elements: a focus on younger voters (Kerr, 2001), provision of information about the performance of the government as part of the voting system,[10] and the collection of democratic user data as part of participation. Reflecting the emphasis on control, however, the site's voting system was carefully managed to prevent subversion: Howard was always going to be voted out online just before polling day, if not in reality.

Barriers to adoption

Structural dynamics of the Australian political system have played a role in restraining innovation in the use of digital media. Compulsory voting limits the

---

10   Thus, like the argument made in favour of negative campaigning in general, there was substantive content delivered via this channel.

role of digital media in selective 'get out the vote' strategies that can be critical in most other nations (Green & Gerber, 2008). Similarly, the limited number of political parties with entrenched parliamentary representation has reduced completive pressure towards innovation and adaptation, making Australia very different to the pattern of political competition seen in countries like the United States, where local campaigns fuel a diversity of behaviours for adoption and replication. Additionally, federalism is relevant in the evolution of campaign management in Australia, acting as a counterweight to the natural tendencies towards centralisation that exist due to the dominance of the party system. The Australian Greens, for example, ran their first national campaign in 2007 (although elements of strong parochialism remain within the party), allowing resources to be centralised and a standard presentation of online content to emerge in the 2007–10 elections (personal correspondence: Peter Davis, The Greens, 19 December 2007).

Over time these factors have become less significant and, in 2007, Australia saw a shift in the role of digital media from a peripheral element of the overall campaign, towards a more central role in the planning and execution of the campaign strategy. The 'Kevin 07' campaign moved back into the risky terrain of jeff.com: a personalised campaign portal, removed from the ALP's main online properties, that emphasised the new leadership (of the party and the country) of Kevin Rudd (personal interview: Simon Banks, ALP, 18 February 2008). Again the federal dimension was important, with the leader-centric website model having been previously employed by Peter Beattie in campaigns for the premiership of Queensland. This election saw a range of digital media innovations take centre stage: use of social media strategies, heavy investment in online video, and leader branding through association with digital media.[11]

The 'internet election': Drawing it all together

The ALP's 2007 campaign drew considerably from the campaign strategies of Howard Dean and Barack Obama, but the lessons were not restricted to the Labor party. The Coalition were active in incorporating online fundraising into their campaign strategy (personal correspondence: Brad Henderson, The Nationals, 10 December 2007), while the Greens appropriated the value of open-source software (OSS) in building a low-cost national campaign platform.[12] In the 2010 election this accelerated pace of international learning was also visible. Illustration 4 provides examples of more recent idea transfer: the adoption of a parody website from the United Kingdom to Australia allowing for the

---

11 This was supported by a set of policy positions emphasising a break with the Coalition government of John Howard: technology in schools, broadband expansion, climate change, an apology to the Stolen Generations (Indigenous Australians who were forcibly removed from their parents under colonial and neo-colonial policies aimed at accelerating racial and cultural integration).

12 The Dean campaign employed a modified version of the OSS CMS Drupal to manage its campaign.

customisation of online billboards (transfer from a third party to the ALP), and the use of supporter image uploads to populate web content (transferred from the NZ Greens to the Australian Greens).

Illustration 4: Examples of learning and transfer among political parties

Sources (clockwise): http://mydavidcameron.com (Von Pip/Susie Wilkins), http://tonyabbottisright.com (ALP), Australian Greens, Green Party of Aotearoa New Zealand

The second example of 'cross-ditch' transfer was also facilitated by the movement of Greens campaign personnel between Australia and New Zealand (personal correspondence: Peter Davis, New Zealand Greens, 19 December 2007). Additionally, the ideational exchange is undertaken by the major parties who are more systematic in their use of fact-finding missions to other jurisdictions for the purpose of learning new campaign techniques, as well as the recruitment of international consultancies to provide input into, and management of campaigns. In this case Australia may not be a thought-leader, but the major parties do appear more reflexive in their adoption of ideas and strategies from overseas, with the ALP rejecting the majority of the strategic recommendations made by their American contractors in the 2007 campaign (Hatcher, 2011).

Picking the right targets

While these aspects of the campaign demonstrate experiments in 'viral' media strategies (electronic word of mouth promotion), the role of websites is largely employed to support party strategies in contemporary media. Party strategists use the websites to customise content for a range of key target audiences, making websites 'landing pages' rather than 'destinations'. Landing pages are specific pages, 'mini-sites', or sections of a site customised for particular readers (Ash, 2008: 28–30). They may or may not be generally accessible through the main page of the website depending on their purpose and the desirability for access by a wider audience. The most common example is the provision of press releases, photographs, and video clips on party sites that are then 'pushed' directly to journalists and other media workers through text messages and may be of limited interest to the wider public.

Other audiences, like party members, donors, supporters, or interest group representatives, may be provided with specific landing pages to collect donations, provide specific policy information, refute claims, spread disinformation, or redirect a web search through targeted advertising against a competitor's name. The advantages of these strategies are for messages to be customised to specific audiences, but also for the response to particular messages to be measured through tools like 'conversion rates' (the number of potential donors who respond) and 'click through rates' (the number of advertisement viewers to click on a link). These measures allow campaigns to develop, test, and adjust their messages rapidly throughout the election (King, 2008: 85). To date the scope of this activity has been comparatively modest, but the major political parties have resources in place that will be able to make greater use of these methods over time. Thus, in addition to their financial and structural resource advantage, the major parties have extensive electoral databases built up over many years which provide them an advantage in the development and distribution of customised communication with the electorate (van Onselen and Errington, 2004). So far, these databases have been significantly underused when compared with data-driven campaigns in the United States (Kreiss and Howard, 2010), possibly because of the somewhat disorganised nature of these systems (such as their inclusion of large amounts of information in comparatively unstructured free-text formats; Millar and McKenzie, 2010).[13]

As their websites are not channels aimed at mass publics, parties have increasingly used a variety of strategies to attract audiences, including the extensive use of online advertising and the creation of issue-specific websites and social

---

13   The parties try to keep the nature and content of these systems out of the public eye and, accordingly, have exempted these systems from privacy legislation. In 2011 a police investigation was launched into a story reported in the *Age* newspaper under the auspices of illegal access to the party computer system (Murphy, P, 2011).

networking service (SNS) pages and groups to draw attention to the party's messages and values, and to build customised mailing lists for direct messaging (personal interview: Peter Davis, Australian Greens, 20 December 2007). With a combination of fundraising and public financing of campaigns, major parties have a virtual monopoly on television advertising, and considerable advantages in the purchase of print and radio. Given their focus on uncommitted voters, who they perceive as largely disinterested in politics, mass media form the majority of campaign advertising. Figure 3, is a representation of party web traffic in the period preceding the 2010 federal election. While the election produces a spike in traffic at the very end of the campaign, the overall growth in interest in these sites is modest. This is supported by AEC survey data in Table 1, which shows the comparatively limited direct engagement that voters have with party sites, but also how parties with lower mass-media resources (Australian Greens in this instance) fair better in drawing voters to their websites.

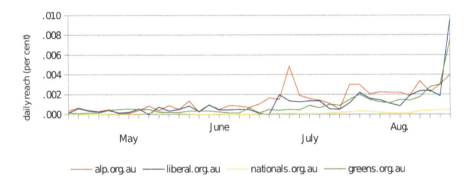

Figure 3: Traffic to party websites, May–August 2010

Source: Alexa (smoothed)

	Party identification of respondent			
	ALP	Liberal	National	Greens
Read/accessed official sites	10	6.5	8	20.5
Signed up as supporter/for e-news	2.2	1.8	2	7.7
Used online tools to campaign/promote parties	2.4	2	5.9	3.4
Total engagement with official party campaign	11	8.1	13.7	22.2
n	628	596	50	117

Table 1: Australians' use of digital media in the 2010 election

Source: Gibson and Cantijoch, 2011: 13 (extract)

Winning the higher ground

Further to this argument for the comparatively static impact of digital media, we can see modest evidence for an association with democratisation. Figure 3 shows that the Australian Greens gain a disproportionately high increase in web traffic to their site during the election campaign. It is likely that this is due to the party's demographic base of urban, educated voters who are more inclined to access the internet regularly (Jackson, 2011: 77). This interpretation is supported by evidence of the modest level of traffic to the Nationals, which has an older, rural support base. This is recognised by the Greens' campaign managers, who place a higher value on online channels than their major party competitors (Gibson & Cantijoch, 2011: 9). Even so, this level of interest does not carry over to other important online campaigning channels. Had the democratisation hypothesis held up, we would see considerably higher interest in the Greens online video content (making up for their funding deficit and lower levels of television advertising) during the most recent federal election (Table 2), and greater levels of support among their key Facebook and Twitter profiles (Figure 4 and Figure 5).

		ALP	Liberal	Greens
	Views	256,279	290,444	84,290
2010	Videos	59	22	19
	Average views	4344	13,202	4436
	Views	160,896	150,719	36,686
2007	Videos	14	25	14
	Average views	11,493	6029	2620

Table 2: YouTube videos posted within 50 days of the 2010 federal election date

Source: Author's research

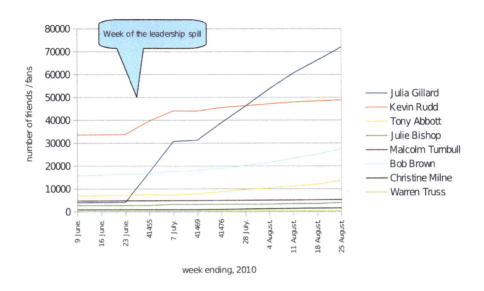

Figure 4: Politicians' Facebook friends/fans in the 2010 federal election

Source: Compiled from Facebook

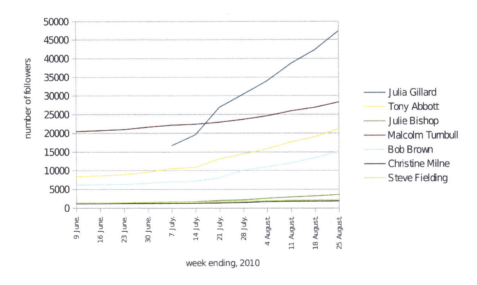

Figure 5: Politicians' Twitter followers in the 2010 federal election

Source: Compiled from Twitter

What is not evident in these last two figures is an automatic linear relationship between SNS performance and the position of the major parties in Australia. If technology is subsumed under pre-existing political power relations in this country — that is, if the powerful institutional actors employ their human, economic, and structural resources to become dominant in digital media in the way they are in old media — then we would see higher levels of performance of the opposition leader in both Figure 4 and Figure 5. What this demonstrates is a space for individuals to employ SNS to great effect, irrespective of the tendency for parties to control media strategies and focus attention on the leader. Certainly, the rapid rise of SNS popularity of Julia Gillard demonstrates the focusing power of the party PR machine, but the position of the two disposed leaders of the major parties is problematic for this style of communication management. Figure 5 is significant in this regard as, to demonstrate the relative growth of Gillard and her performance compared with Tony Abbott, the figure has had to be adjusted to exclude the followers of deposed leader Kevin Rudd, which sat at over 900,000 during this period. Leadership figures may be largely pre-packaged ham, but the results of the ALP's use of SNS to build demonstrable support in the community runs counter to the centralising tendency of party machines.

The significance may be overstated. During the leadership spill in 2010, Rudd's Facebook follower numbers increased as members of the public came out in support of the incumbent prime minister. This, however, had little bearing on the outcome of the spill. Overall, the tendency has been for the development of more and more sophisticated mediatised election campaigning techniques with a corresponding increase in the power of centralised campaign managers over root and branch party structures. This cuts both ways: when the management team is competent and experienced, the ability to coordinate a national campaign out of the party headquarters can be effective, but, when that team is inexperienced or lacks a local understanding, it can produce a systematically terrible result (Hatcher, 2011). Australia lacks the continual campaigning seen in the United States, where individual candidates across three levels of government support a huge permanent industry of campaign professionals. Because of this, it is more difficult to sustain expertise, both technical and experiential, even among the two major parties.

The tendency for this system to deliver variable electoral outcomes raises the question of whether this centralisation is inevitable and a feature of the media landscape. Looking at the emerging political forces in Australia we see two propensities. First, the rise of independents in recent years (as well as their longer history at the state level) might point to a break away from the power of undifferentiated national campaigns (Costar & Curtin, 2004). Should independents be a more permanent part of the landscape, it will be necessary to examine their relationship with select media and, particularly, social media. Alternatively, the centralising tendency appears evident in emerging party politics in recent years. Thus, in his analysis of the evolution of the Australian Greens from a social-movement-based political party to an electoral-professional party, Stewart Jackson argues that digital media have served to further strengthen a centralising tendency within the party organisation. Placing this within the context of electoral success, which provides greater resources to members of parliament, Jackson notes that digital media allows the party to '… reach the bulk of the electorate without the need for mass organisations, so tended to centralise their operations using professional campaigners to do the work once done by staff or volunteers on the ground' (2011: 25–26). What this highlights is the way resources drive power towards campaign managers, a shift that draws in the very professionals who will advocate for a PR-ised approach to election campaigning.

Vote for me

The observation that leaders and parties are the pre-eminent focus of election campaigning in Australia does not prevent the possibility that a more candidate-centric model *could* emerge. We can posit drivers for an inversion of the status quo. One is social. The shift towards celebrity culture places increased power in the hands of individuals with personal branding. Darrell West and John Orman see the rise of televisual culture as encouraging the expansion of everyday celebrity and the blending of different, once-distinct realms of social and professional life (2003: 14). Pop stars can become 'soda-pop stars' (e.g. Michael Jackson), musicians can be ministers of the Crown (e.g. Peter Garrett), journalists can be transformed into politicians and vice versa (e.g. Maxine McKew, Peter Collins, Aden Ridgeway), and politicians can perform as reality-TV stars (e.g. Pauline Hanson). In political terms, the rise of celebrity culture can serve to provide individuals with the valuable assets of personal constituencies and ready access to mainstream media.

Another reason behind an expanded electoral role for candidates is structural. Recent experiments in US-style primaries for candidate selection increases the power of candidates over the selection panels of political parties.[14] While the Australian party system has traditionally encouraged loyalty to the system that promoted the individual into office (branch, faction or party), the introduction of primaries weakens this system of patronage (the extent remains unclear at this time). Finally, there may be specific reasons for extending the electoral role of candidates, who can build personal constituencies directly through existing

---

14   In recent years Labor and the Nationals have experimented in primaries in an attempt to increase public interest in party politics (Mark, 2011).

or new social and professional networks. While commonly portrayed in a negative way, concerns about 'branch stacking' reflect the ability of individuals to use personal networks to become candidates. While this has been a result of the decline in party membership over the last 50 years (Zappala, 1998), an expanded capacity of social networking can increase the ability for individuals to consolidate their influence at the local level.

Engines of creation and control

On the surface these tendencies are unrelated to digital media. What is interesting is how media has an effect on the factors that enable or prevent political candidates from having a greater role in the electoral process. While the previous section argued that online channels of communication are increasingly expensive to employ effectively in national election campaigns, this does not preclude the effective use of digital media for local electoral success. Digital media is seen to be associated with innovation because it allows for sophisticated experimentation at low cost, be this in terms of personal branding, local campaigning, or building and maintaining online networks. The ability for individuals and small political organisations to develop sophisticated websites and social media strategies has increased in recent years, particularly through the advent low-cost and free content management systems (CMSs)[15] (Myers, 2011), but also as these skills become readily available within the community. Digital media, therefore, serves as an interesting place to look for a new autonomy of individual candidates in Australia.

This, of course, is not necessarily a given. In considering the nature of innovation in digital media, Christian Sandvig observes that the characteristics associated with challenging accepted practices lie not just in the availability of technology, but the presence of a 'subculture of innovation' (2008: 89). In the context of political innovation, this runs counter to the notion of the cartel party discussed in the preceding section: cartels' response to innovation is suppression (external entrants) and discouragement (internal agitators). The message of the party system in Australia is join or die. What Sandvig would argue, however, is the existence of innovative subcultures allows for change even in industries that have entrenched monopolies. The disruptive role of companies like Google in the information technology industry is a good example, taking an innovative idea and rising to the challenge presented by the monopoly of long-established firms across a range of industry segments.

The extent to which Australian politicians have embraced digital media is an interesting story of experimentation and attempts at control by parties. While

---

15   A website management system that allows for the publication of content online without programming or knowledge of HTML.

candidates are far less likely than their American counterparts to employ digital media, candidates' use of digital media in elections is increasingly common. In addition, technology adoption by political candidates is not strictly linear over time. As we will see, this is partially a result of control by party machines, but also a function of the highly fluid nature of the digital media ecosystem.

Brochureware

If we first look at what is commonly called 'web 1.0' technologies (generally speaking, these are the type of online channels that were popular in the first decade of the World Wide Web (WWW): such as email and hard-coded websites that did not use CMSs).[16] Figure 6 and Figure 7 provide a useful overview of the uptake of channels and channel elements (e.g. website functions) over time by candidates.[17] In Figure 6 we can see the majority of candidates represented online, and this level of adoption has been increasing slowly. The majority of online representation, however, comes through the use of email and campaign mini-sites. Mini-sites, small websites which are generally part of the party website and located at a subdomain (normally in the format http://electorate. party.org.au) tend to be provided (and commonly 'populated'[18]) as a template by the candidates' party. Only a minority of candidates in Australia establish a personal campaign website and, given the comparative importance of party list tickets over direct campaigning, senators are less likely to employ campaign sites (Chen, 2005a). Overall, the degree of sophistication of these sites is modest and more focused on the provision of static information than interaction with electors. In recent years, particularly following the proven success of small unit online fundraising in the United States, more sites include 'take action' functions that generally focus on donations, but even these redirect the visitor back to the main party site rather than to local-level fundraising[19] or volunteering options.[20]

---

16 Francisco Valverde and Oscar Pastor (2009: 131) provide this useful, but not perfect, definition: 'From the social perspective, in "Web 1.0" websites, the end-user was a passive consumer of information that had been identified by the webmaster'.

17 The data presented in these figures comes from a series of content-analysis projects that were undertaken during successive Australian federal elections. Data was collected by searching for candidates, sampled by electorate.

18 Filled with content. This term commonly relates to the notion of 'populating fields' — filling pre-determined database structures with information. These sites are therefore highly generic and similar in look and function.

19 The inclusion of e-commerce options on the candidate site would be indicative of a higher level of technical sophistication.

20 Individual volunteers, however, tend to be directed to the candidate's campaign.

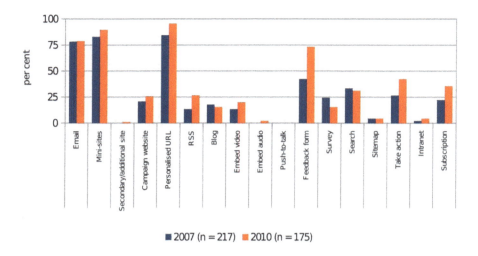

Figure 6: Candidates' website functionality in the 2010 federal election

Source: Author's research

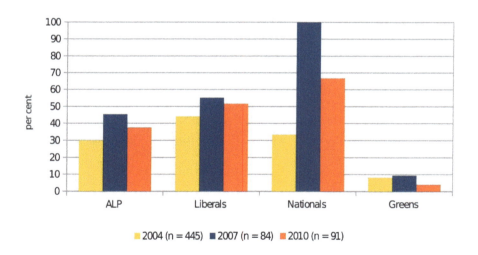

Figure 7: Candidates' use of websites, federal elections 2004, 2007, and 2010

Source: Author's research

What is worth noting in Figure 7 is that the uptake of personal campaign websites by candidates from parties who are most likely to have electoral success has plateaued and even declined in the 2010 federal election. Overall, this reflects a degree of scepticism on the part of candidates about the value of these channels. We can see this by looking at survey responses from candidates in the 2007 election in Figure 8. This figure shows candidates' views of the value of a selection of campaign communication channels based on a four-point Likert scale. While websites were not the lowest-ranked communication channel, candidates substantially preferred more established forms of communication. This survey also indicated that candidates consistently feel that their resources are insufficient to meet their campaign needs and that access to more resources would result in their investment in channels of communication they feel are more effective.

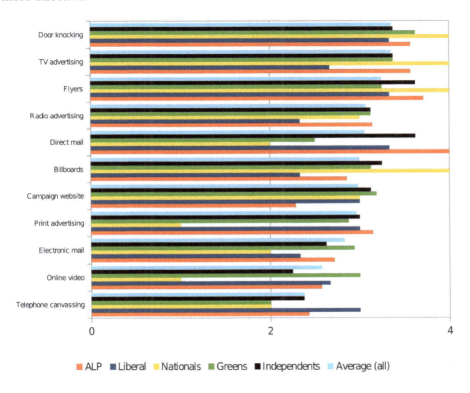

Figure 8: Candidates' perceptions of channel value in electioneering 2007 (n = 55)

Source: Author's research

This argument is admittedly at odds with both the notion of the web as 'naturally' becoming more important in politics, as well as the empirical findings of Jim Macnamara and Gail Kenning's (2011: 5) comparison of *incumbents'* use of websites between 2007 and 2010 which saw a 14.6 per cent increase in the use of personal campaign websites. This points to the benefit of being in office, where parliamentarians (opposed to other candidates) (a) employ parliamentary entitlements to employ and sustain online communication, (b) have greater resources overall and can be less ruthless in their use of channels, and (c) be able to maintain websites over time. This has important implications as incumbents are generally more likely to field legacy websites that are built on older platforms.[21] This explains, to a large degree, the slow level of uptake of newer website features seen in Figure 6 and is reinforced by Macnamara and Kenning's observation of a considerable decline in parliamentarians' use of interactive website functions like e-surveys and e-petitions.

Points of presence and visibility

This observation, to some extent, explains why parties with parliamentary representation are better online performers. Looking beyond websites we can construct a measure of the 'visibility' of candidates online by mapping two factors:

- The total different 'points of presence' they employ to campaign (including, not just websites and mini-sites, but also the range of SNS profiles and other methods of distributing election content and interacting with electors); and,

- The amount of content and information they populate these points with.

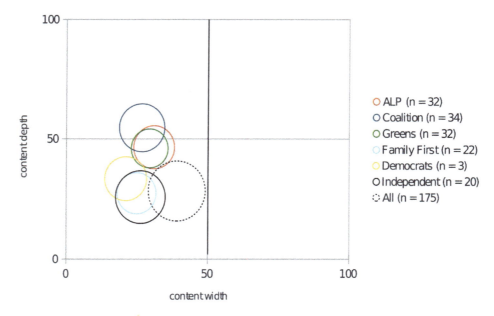

Figure 9: Candidates' 'points of presence' online in the 2010 federal election

Source: Author's research

---

21   A good example of this can be found in the low use of RSS feeds in Figure 6. These simple tools to increase visits are standard parts of modern CMSs.

Figure 9 is based on a competitive comparison between parties' candidates.[22] The figure clusters party candidates together in this competitive space to show the average performance of candidates based on their use of all digital media. As is clear, with the exclusion of the Nationals (more likely to represent rural and regional electorates with lower levels of internet connectivity and take-up on average) and Family First (an anomalous senator whose election resulted from the vagaries of Senate preferencing), Australian candidates from parties with parliamentary representation are better performers in terms of the amount of content they produce online. They are less likely, however, to have a wide range of points of presence online. This makes sense as these candidates, as representatives of parties with higher levels of visibility, need not compete for attention as they already have higher levels of 'discoverability'.

You voter. Me friend.

In the production of the analysis presented in Figure 9, we see it is necessary to look beyond websites as the focus of digital electioneering. In the 2007–10 period candidates rapidly adopted SNS into their communications portfolio. The advantages of these services are clear: simple to use and set-up, they are timely and immediate, provide measures of performance out-of-the-box, can be maintained easily by telephone on the road,[23] and they can be used to direct internet traffic to party or personal-website landing pages, and switching between and syndicating across services is comparatively easy. For campaign managers, the value of SNS is their appeal to electors who may have lower levels of political knowledge and, therefore, are unlikely to head towards party homepages (personal interview: Simon Banks, ALP, 18 February 2008). Figure 10 demonstrates this trend, showing a doubling of use by candidates of SNSs from 2007 to 2010. Candidates also appear able to discern and respond to trends in the popularity of different services, rapidly abandoning Myspace over Facebook in the more recent period as the latter rapidly supplanted the former in the Australian marketplace (Moses, 2009a). Interesting, and contrary to the notion of a drag on innovation that comes from being within the cartel system, Macnamara and Kenning (2011: 5) identify the growth of Facebook at 1725 per cent among parliamentarians in this period — a higher rate than candidates.

---

22   The axes are based on the individual candidate in the data set with the highest performance.
23   Not just with high-end smart-phones, but also with simpler technology and slower services, including email-to-web and SMS-to-web publishing.

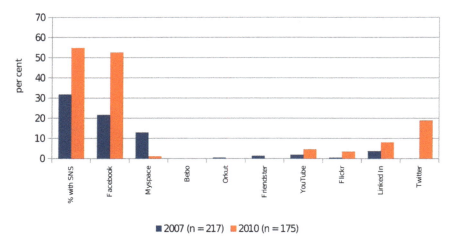

Figure 10: Candidates' use of SNSs, elections 2007 and 2010

Source: Author's research

In many ways politicians appear to be taking SNS very seriously. For some, they serve as their primary point-of-presence, with less emphasis being paid to populating websites (see Figure 11). As we can see in the figure above, however, there is a tendency for candidates to employ only one SNS in their campaign, rather than using multiple services to cover a range of different constituencies and therefore target their messages (Bebo, for example, remains popular among Indigenous Australians, and LinkedIn is popular among professionals). Overall, the more free-flowing nature of SNS has an impact on the way candidates approach online interactions. Macnamara and Kenning (2011: 11) observe that, while heavy moderation of posts to candidates SNS pages was de rigour in 2007 (deleting and vetting negative comments), this intervention lessened to some degree by 2010. Similarly, parties relaxed their moderation of comments posted on party sites and mini-sites (Chen, 2011a).

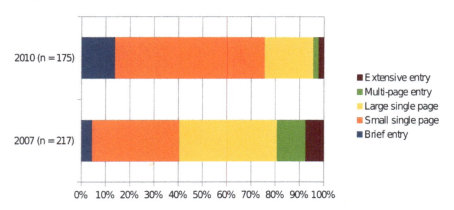

Figure 11: Depth of content in campaign mini-sites in the 2010 federal election

Source: Author's research

Patterns of adoption

The adoption and use of digital media shows a mixed pattern defined by experimentation within constraints. The use of digital media remains a lower priority than conventional advertising and interpersonal interactions with members of the public, but candidates are interested in tools that provide a quick, visible presence online and with low cost. Were the financing of elections to change (either through anti-cartel provisions that shifted money to the level of candidates, or as a result of the expansion of primaries that encouraged investment at this level of electioneering) candidates have considerable under-utilised capacity to expand the use of digital media. For candidates from non-mainstream parties, there is evidence they are utilising digital media channels more expansively than the entrenched parties: demonstrating a democratising effect to some degree (at least in terms of visibility or potential visibility of alternative political figures to members of the public), but there is also evidence that the amount of detail being provided online is decreasing through a focus on social media over websites.

From the central party perspective, campaign managements are uneasy about the use of digital media by candidates. In response to this concern, they continue to exert control over candidate communications through a variety of strategies. This includes: the provision of candidate training, direct provision of websites and online services, discouraging some activities online for fear of going 'off message' or producing material of poor quality[24] (personal interview: Peter Davis, Australian Greens, 20 December 2007), and through the use of online systems to exert discipline over local campaigns. In this latter area Ainslie van Onselen and Peter van Onselen (2008) have discussed how parties have employed secure websites (intranets) to create virtual campaign teams and regulate the behaviour of local candidates through the distribution of approved campaign materials and key message strategies ('talking points'). The importance of these systems should not be understated, particularly as they can be used not only to pump prime local candidates, but can also serve to regulate them through the collection of performance indicators (such as fundraising levels).

Examples of 'blow ups' from social media are common enough to justify some concerns. Some candidates unthinkingly have linked official campaign sites to personal pages that contain photos and posts including criticisms of party leadership, expletives, and inappropriate images (Rolfe, 2010). Family First, for example, has come under considerable negative attention in successive elections: in 2007 a candidate's naked photos were distributed online (Murphy, 2007) and, in 2010, a tweet equating gay marriage with child abuse became a major embarrassment to the party's lead senate candidate for Queensland

---

24   Particularly video.

(Grubb, 2010). In the 2012 Queensland state election, Labor lost a minor candidate following the discovery of homophobic comments made online when he was still under the age of 18 (Wordsworth et al., 2012). Even the normally invisible behaviour of political workers have come under scrutiny; in 2011 a member of Sophie Mirabella MP's staff was the focus of attention after they were outed bragging on Facebook about running up a $1000 taxi fare (Bunn, 2011). While these problems have been highlighted through the tendency for social networking services to hold and make available personal histories, it is questionable if these problems are ones of digital media, or are more reflective of the limited ability of some parties to effectively recruit and vet quality candidates given their decreased membership levels. What this does show, however, is how the long memory of SNS can feed into the shallow end of political reporting and 'gotcha journalism'.

A 'Marketing democracy'?

What is the impact of this on Australian political culture? Certainly the use of a wider array of communications technologies by parties represents the longer trend towards professionalisation and mediatisation. In addition, the adoption of personalised campaigning and negative messaging has been associated with the influence of the type of campaign styles developed over many years in the United States. While the idea of 'Americanisation' of politics is a common concern across the world (see, for example, Negrine and Papathanassopoulos; 1996), with underlying assumptions about cultural colonisation through the importation of media techniques, it is not clear that this is strongly the case in our experience. Australians appear more selective in their appropriation of techniques and campaign styles, pointing more to a 'shopping model' of selective adoption from a wider range of English-speaking jurisdictions, than a hybridisation or standardisation approach which sees American techniques and messages adopted systematically (Plasser and Plasser, 2000).[25] What is apparent is that Australia selects from both American and British experiences in adapting campaigning technologies to local conditions. In recent elections the growth of the 'marketing model' of campaigning has been very apparent, reflecting both the professionalistion of political campaigns, and an inherent weakness in the Australian party system.

This change allows political communication to be read — as Steven Dann and Andrew Hughes (2008) do in Australia — through a purely marketing lens, which focuses on aspects of the campaign in terms of an increasingly familiar set

---

25   A multi-stage colonisation can, however, be seen. For example, in their 2008 campaign, the New Zealand Greens borrowed heavily from the web-design approach taken by Barack Obama's camapaign (personal interview: Gary Reese, Green Party of Aotearoa New Zealand, 14 January 2009). This, in turn, informed the Australian Greens site design.

of elements: longer campaign, audience selectivity, heavy use of market research, simple messages repeated often, clear coordination and planning, and external expertise (Gould, 1998: 55–56). Margaret Scammell (1988: 251–75) has observed that, while professionalisation of campaign management is not a particularly recent trend, technological specialisation has led to the displacement of amateur campaign organisation focused on large amounts of labour mobilisation in exchange for a smaller set of campaign professionals. This process has displaced internal party strategists for external professionals, while reducing the role of parties in the political socialisation of non-professional volunteers.

Hollow bells ring

The marketing model has a range of implications. One is that it increases the speed and variety of sources from which contemporary campaigns can draw their expertise. The 2007 election campaign saw a considerable role for advertising professionals (such as the advertising firm Lawrence Creative) in developing and delivering the Kevin 07 campaign from design to execution (similarly for the Union movements' Your Rights At Work campaign, discussed in Chapter 5). In 2010, this was expanded with the ALP employing a multinational firm to develop the core messages of their campaign (Greenberg Quinlan Rosner), while the Liberal Party employed specialist advisors in female marketing to address candidate deficiencies (Splash Consulting; Cowie, 2010). Another implication, stemming from the undermining of the reason for party members to remain active in their branches, is the loss of local knowledge. There is also a tendency for attenuated relationships between party and campaign structures in these professionalised campaign structures, where considerable numbers of temporary staff and volunteers move between corporate and political environments (Farrell, et al., 2001). While this brings skills into the political process — particularly commercial public relations and advertising — it also reduces the longevity of the connection between the campaign team and the policy team, except to the extent that volunteers from the corporate sector often return in their professional capacity to act as lobbyists to the governments they helped elect.

In the last decade in Australia this trend has become increasingly acute and it has led to problems of governance. The Kevin 07 election campaign is a good example of this. On the one hand, the party employed key strategic and creative leadership from the mainstream Australian advertising industry, imported to deliver an innovative and creative media strategy based around online properties (particularly the integrated www.kevin07.com website and use of SNSs). On the other, three years later, the party was barely able to redevelop and launch a new social networking system. This shows how the absence of social media professionals in the intervening period failed to capitalise on the work undertaken for the 2007 election. This contrasts with the United States where the movement of key campaign staff into government following the Obama election saw the social networking memberships reactivated in government to support the new president's legislative campaigns, such as his heath-care initiative.

Overall, there remains a misfit. In Australia, research has identified that the two major parties are more likely to invest in their electoral-roll database systems and therefore build on the intelligence infrastructure of previous elections to extend their incumbent positions (Chen, 2005a). This does not, however, appear to have transferred into the area of digital-media campaigning, as the majority of the key planning and execution lies outside of the party proper. The NSW state election of 2011 is a good example of this, where local members had previously employed polling of their electorates to determine the allocation of community development funding. The ALP did not go on to employ the rich data this provided about preferences to 'push' information to members of these databases (Chen, 2012: 266–67).

Two steps forward ...

It appears that campaign management in Australia remains in an intermediate phase between Pippa Norris's (2000) notion of the 'modern' mass-media-focused national campaign model, and that of the 'postmodern' campaign approach which employs greater narrowcasting and localisation within a national structure (or narrative). This is illustrated in the way the Obama campaign managed a tight, centralised campaign, but also empowered local campaigning through face-to-face meet-ups and localised campaign teams. Elements of postmodern campaigning in the 2010 Australian election was seen in the use of differentiated advertising by the Liberal Party in Western Australia (Liberal Party of Western Australia, 2010). There was also internal criticisms within the ALP that this approach was not adopted as national campaign themes had less tractability in that state.[26] The implications of this are important, however, with evidence that the 'stratified electioneering' approach undertaken in the United Kingdom by New Labour contributed to voter disengagement, and considerable reconfiguring of the relationship between citizen and the state in terms of direct service provision in an increasingly narrow range of policy domains (Wring, 2005). Paradoxically, this may not lead to greater levels of voter satisfaction, but 'professionally sanctioned cynicism' (179). That this approach may present similar problems in Australia has been proposed in the aftermath of the 2010 election, where the narrow focus of both marketing-based campaigns failed to engage voters.

---

26   In addition, the emphasis on a limited set of concerns associated — correctly or incorrectly with western Sydney — were used by the ALP as national campaign issues, possibly at the expense of support on the left wing of the party that has been eroding towards the Greens.

While these developments are evidence of the increasing seriousness with which parties are regarding digital media in electoral campaigning, the impact of these developments in Australia is less clear. One key question about the role of digital media has been its impact on the nature and conduct of the democratic system: the extent to which democratic practice — a practice traditionally seen as informational in character — can be enriched by new information technologies. This tends to take a number of forms including the range of 'voices' (individuals and organisations) that can find expression within the public sphere, and new methods of engagement between elites and electors.

... two steps back?

In this regard we see mixed evidence. On one hand, the relatively low cost of online publishing has seen the ability for a wide range of minor party, individual activist, and alternative media organisations to emerge in Australia during the last 20 years. This has increased the range of information options available to electors. While Rachel Gibson and Stephen Ward (2002) observe that the uptake of digital media by parties (particularly websites) was strong in the mid-to-late 1990s, they also observe, however, that smaller parties were not systematically more likely to take advantage of these channels of communication compared with established parties with considerable resource and access advantages in the conventional media space. While minor parties were more likely to see these channels as more valuable than their larger competitors, they note that the ALP and Greens were more active in the late 1990s with regard to establishing their online presence. This appears to reflect a number of tendencies: first, that these two parties were in substantial opposition to the government of the day; and, second, a different nature to their demographic base of support (younger and urban).[27]

More mixed evidence comes when we consider that the expectation of a gradual and natural increase in the amount of content published online by candidates and parties has not been realised. The shift by candidates towards the use of mini-sites (discussed in You voter. Me friend, this chapter) shows that technology adoption is not linear among this group of political actors, and parties are increasingly providing campaigning tools under a hosting model.[28] This is interesting for two reasons: first, these emphasise the party over the local area and serve to tie candidates more closely to the centralised resource base of the party machine. Second, while SNSs are more personal (although these are also often set up as a service by the central campaign team; personal interview: Simon Banks, ALP, 18 February 2008), the immediacy and linear presentation of

---

27 Additionally, it is important to consider the social movement origins and residual connections of the Labor Party in Australia, which is associated with the adoption of networking technology.

28 Or 'software as a service', where the tools and storage are provided as a service offering with varying levels of support and functionality, rather than a singular product.

content in these feeds emphasise the flow of events and issues more commonly associated with the wider campaign narrative, again something that ties the candidate more closely back to the party.

Expanding on this observation about the relationship between candidate online campaign strategies and their relationship with centralising tendencies, Figure 6 (this chapter) showed that, while the functionality of candidate websites is more limited than international comparisons, we can see that these sites have developed in the last two Australian electoral cycles in terms of the interactivity they offer (see also Macnamara, 2008), both in 'thin' forms of democratic interaction that do not engage citizens very strongly (Barber, 1999) like donations, but also 'thicker' informational aspects, such as subscription options and feedback form provision. Similarly, while the use of web 2.0 technologies,[29] such as social networking, was actively discouraged by some parties as recently as 2007 because of perceptions that these channels introduced risks of subversion and attack that the central party were unable to control (personal correspondence: Brad Henderson, The Nationals, 10 December 2007), this has also begun to change as candidates become more experienced through use of the technologies in their personal and professional lives.

The 'thickening' of online interaction can be seen — albeit gradually — at the party level also. In 2002 Gibson and Ward observed that party sites were largely information repositories, rather than more interactive channels between parties and voters, a tendency that dominated the 2000s. In anticipation of the 2010 campaign, however, both the Labor and Liberal parties produced revised party websites with public discussion boards and social networking components, while the Greens used a Formspring (question and answer service) account for interactivity with members of the public. While these services attracted low levels of participation in the election, when compared with the SNS profiles of leaders and candidates (as illustrated in Table 3), their use demonstrates a willingness of the parties to engage in more dialogue online.

---

29   For a detailed discussion of the concept of web 2.0, see Rewiring the state: Gov 2.0, Chapter 7.

Party	Indicator	Week ending					
		21 July	28 July	4 Aug	11 Aug	18 Aug	25 Aug
ALP	Members	963	1325	1723	2073	2323	2608
	Groups	30	35	39	47	47	47
	Issues	2	2	2	2	2	2
	Ideas	60	101	162	238	267	287
	Comments	63	115	161	220	264	288
Liberal	Ideas	23	26	47	54	55	55
	Comments	209	400	550	737	804	854
Greens	Questions	0	20	1	0	3	5

Table 3: Voter engagement by party website in the 2010 federal election

Source: Compiled from www.alp.org.au; www.liberal.org.au; www.formspring.me/GreensMPs

Experiments in online electoral democracy

If, as the cartel party model would indicate, innovation is unlikely to come from the established party system, we should also be alert to attempts at change from outsiders. This drive towards innovation need not be associated with elections (see Chapter 5), but, as elections offer an attractive 'focusing event' whereby members of the community may be primed to receive political information, challenging the dominance of parties is most likely to be found during the electoral process. Possibly the most high-profile example of this in recent years would be the role of GetUp! in overturning electoral laws in 2010 that brought forward the cut-off date for new enrolments (see GetUp!, Chapter 5). Similarly, but less successfully, the organisation attempted to increase the ability of electors to choose candidates (rather than parties) that suited their policy preferences through the use of an online candidate matcher in the 2007 election. This system, which could have enabled a more candidate-centric electoral process, failed because of one obvious flaw: since the 1970s, the mainstream parties have forbidden their candidates to complete surveys distributed by lobby groups and non-governement organisations following the disastrous outcome of a survey of candidates by the then nascent Women's Electoral Lobby that revealed the archaic views of gender held by many MPs (Sawer, 2009). Without data on candidate's policy preferences, a matching system is worthless.

To consider active experiments by insurgent democrats in the Australian electoral process, we will therefore explore two different innovations: one radical and one incremental.

Senator Online

One of the more interesting democratic experiments in recent years is the online political party Senator Online (SOL). Established three months before the 2007 federal election by Berge Der Sarkissian, their objective is the introduction of a form of direct democracy using a combination of online polling and the existing electoral system. The party promises that issues and bills will be put before the public through the SOL website with explanatory material (SOL, nd), and Australian voters will be able directly determine the issues on which the SOL senators will vote in the upper house. Rather than attempting to introduce this within established institutions or parties through constitutional or institutional change (see An electronic constituency surgery, Chapter 3), the pitch of SOL is simple: elect our candidates to the Australian Senate and they will act as delegates of the Australian people. This approach picks up on an age-old ambiguity in representative democratic practice: should elected officials act as *delegates* (agents of the people) or *trustees* (agents for the people). When keeping promises, politicians are inclined to point to the former — they claim their legitimacy comes from being elected. When exercising their discretion or breaking commitments, they are more likely to call for their performance to be judged at the next election as trustees of the public good.

Traditionally the problem with the effectiveness and legitimacy of the delegate model has been the need for the representatives to both act as a delegate and also have the capacity of accessing the views and preferences of their constituency (McCrone & Kuklinski, 1979: 278). In many cases, even if the former is met, the practical difficulty of the latter is problematic. Proponents of the representative trustee model have deemed movement of legislative debate to be too rapid, the public too disorganised, and the questions too complex for direct democracy. In the information age, however, this is challenged by the ability to reduce information costs and transaction costs. SOL sees the implementation of online information and polling systems to be feasible in the context of the technologies to hand: that parliament already generates considerable information about legislative initiatives under consideration, and two decades of experience in online transactions would allow for the automation of the Australian electoral roll.

SOL represents an interesting initiative in that it does not come from within the established political system, but from an individual who had limited previous political engagement and no experience within the Australian party system (personal interview: Berge Der Sarkissian, 10 January 2012). As we'll see later in this book, this represents a minor trend where people who perceive the Australian political system to be deficient see the new communications and information technologies as means (and inspiration) to take direct action to address their concerns.

Often this involves active experimentation to determine what works and what doesn't.[30] In the context of SOL, Der Sarkissian is realistic about the long-term nature of the enterprise, recognising the considerable cost of developing a viable political party[31] and the slow nature of change, and the difficulty in communicating the core concept to the Australian public. He sees, however, the influence of distributed, collective models of decision-making as an inevitable development in the way politics is undertaken around the world. There are examples of approaches that have similar elements to the model, including the proposal for citizen-initiated legislation in the United Kingdom (Hannan, 2010), and similar referenda processes in parts of the United States, New Zealand, and Switzerland. These approaches are varied (some are legislative, some non-legislative; some binding, others not), but they are all analogue in their administration and require the arduous and time-consuming collection of signatures as the basis for action (Maer, 2008: 9–13).

Ready for direct democracy?

The challenges in communicating its message and converting the public to direct democracy are clear in the small impact that SOL party has had. Even with strong media interest in its first outing (largely due to novelty; Karvelas, 2007) SOL received 8048 first preference group votes in 2007 (0.06 per cemt of the total vote) and 17,441 in 2010 (0.14 per cent) (AEC). The party has also had to overcome scepticism about the ability to undertake the type of polling system it promises in the timeframe in which the Senate considers legislation (Moses, 2007), a process that can be unpredictable. Government is commonly thought to have only two speeds: very, very slow and very, very fast. Because of this, the party has introduced changes to its constitution to allow for proxy voting, a move away from its direct model and demonstrative of the problems of scaling direct participation that leads to representative democracy in the first instance. To ensure the party has the ability to respond to volatile legislative agendas, it will find itself having to proactively poll its members on large numbers of issues and interpret these findings against issues of the day at short notice. This will present the party with difficulties maintaining a perception of trustworthy neutrality when in office: interpretation remains a political act, and the party is likely to be forced into positions where it must choose between abstention and interpretation.

---

30   The party, for example, experimented with an online primary system to select candidates for the 2010 election, with nominees using Facebook to raise money and votes. This novel approach was problematic because low levels of participation lengthened the polling process, and it was eventually abandoned because of the issue of the writ.

31   By 2012 he had personally expended approximately $100,000 on the venture.

Below the line

Another, but less dramatic, attempt to increase the democratic character of the Senate has been the introduction of a number of 'below-the-line' voting websites (www.belowtheline.org.au and www.blowtheline.cc). These free services were established by individuals with the objective of assisting voters, using intuitive drag-and-drop interfaces, to prepare in advance their preference allocations for below-the-line voting on the Senate ticket. The use of the single vote for Senate list tickets was introduced in the 1980s. As nearly 95 per cent of Australians vote above the line, this system provides parties with considerable influence in determining the way preferences are allocated and — while reducing the tendency for invalid votes to be cast through error — can produce strange outcomes. Examples of this include the failure of Peter Garrett to win a seat for the Nuclear Disarmament Party in the 1980s with 10 per cent of the primary vote (Sawer, 2006) and the election of Steve Fielding in the 2004 election with only 0.08 per cent (Walsh, 2008).

Inspired by outcomes like the Fielding election (Rice, 2010), these systems assist voters in making a more informed and accurate allocation, demonstrating the power of new online programming techniques to deliver services of benefit, at low cost, even by individual members of civil society (Bellamy, et al., 2011: 20). Compared to the modest performance of SOL, which needs to get a quota to have a direct impact on the senate, these two sites together attracted approximately 100,000 unique visitors during the 2010 federal election, which produced approximately 50,000 customised how-to-vote cards (personal correspondence: Benno Rice, 22 August 2010; Cameron McCormack, 22 August 2010). At 0.378 per cent of the number of votes cast, this is a direct challenge to the control parties have in the negotiation of preference flows, if only a small one. The promotion of this type of service by the Australian Electoral Commission (AEC) (something that is likely to be resisted by parties) would serve to increase their visibility and uptake. Practically, however, it is difficult to determine the impact of the service on below-the-line voting. Certainly the number of people who voted below the line increased from 4.22 per cent in 2007 to 4.88 per cent in 2010 (AEC, 2011: 70), however, this does not imply causation. What is important to note is that those jurisdictions with shorter ballot papers have higher levels of below the line voting, most likely due to the ease of completion.

What do voters *do* online?

Given their supposed centrality to the democratic system, it's important to say something about the role of the public in electoral politics. In conventional interpretations of mediated politics this was a shallow role: voters, if they were active beyond simply turning up at the polls on the right day, were likely to engage in comparatively low levels of information gathering from mass media. The market for high-quality and detailed political information is seen to be small, and tends towards those with higher levels of income and education (Young, 2011: 59). This state of affairs is generally seen as problematic as the quality of electoral outcomes is regarded as a function of public awareness of policy issues (being able to proactively determine which parties and candidates offer policies most suited to their preferences) and the behaviour of incumbents (being able to hold government to account for its performance). More specifically, in Australia, as compulsory voting sees higher levels of participation from the less-involved voter, the general level of political knowledge is of more direct relevance to political outcomes than in the majority of nations that lack this compulsion. Summatively, the willingness and ability of citizens to access relevant information marks the difference between a democracy that is of high quality because of good process (effective and corruption-free management of the machinery of elections) and those that are high quality because of good citizenship.

In the pre-digital-media age, two questions were asked of political audiences: First, were they good citizens — active consumers of information upon which they could make informed decisions (Lupia, 1992: 390)? Second, what was the quality of the political information available to citizens seeking to be informed? While these questions remain valid (for a consideration of media quality see Stories of decline, Chapter 6), we need to add to the discussion of information seeking with that of information production by citizens (see also the two-step flow model discussed in Social media as a deliberative space, Chapter 3). Picking up on the notion of the user-producer we discussed in Chapter 1, therefore, the digital era requires a more focused consideration not simply of audience attention, and top-down information provision from parties and professional media, but also bottom-up and horizontal information distribution from active citizens-as-producers who may be active constructivists through the receipt, transformation, and redistribution of information about the political world.

Grist for the mill: Information seeking

The conventional story of citizen information access during elections is spelled out in the two figures below. Contrary to the perception often presented that citizens in the developed world are generally increasingly political apathetic, disengaged, and/or alienated (McAllister, 2011: 95), research drawn from successive Australian Electoral Studies (AES) of voter's beliefs and behaviours tends to point to a mostly static level of importance placed on elections over an extended period of time. In this way Figure 12,[32] tells more of a story about the relative importance of individual elections (fluctuation), than any shift in the way Australian's generally see the electoral process overall. This supports the argument that elections still serve as important 'focusing events', as well as the findings about the resilience of Australian's views about the quality of our democracy, of which elections are generally one of the most visible aspects (see Figure 2: Citizens' views of government and democracy, Chapter 2).

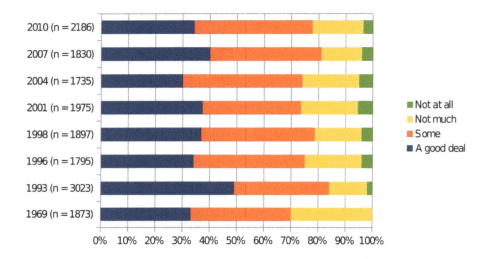

Figure 12: Australians' interest in election campaigns

Sources: Sally Young, 2011a: 25; McAllister, et al., 2012: 34

This resiliency of political interest aside, we should look at the level of information consumption relevant to our notion of good citizenship. To this end, Figure 13 illustrates the extent to which voters actively follow Australian elections across a range of media forms. While this figure is based on relative, rather than absolute measures of consumption (e.g. hours), it points to declining use of media to engage with elections. This is interesting because it is specific to the contemporary media landscape, rather than a more general aspect of declining engagement. Thus, for example, this decline is not matched when measuring the propensity of Australians to attend political events or donate money (consistently low over the last 40 years; McAllister, 2011: 100). Internationally these findings have been explained by a variety of factors, including disengagement and apathy, a decrease in citizens supporting each other's participation through social surveillance, the impact of individualism and material wealth on collective institutions (making politics less important for

---

32   Note that 'not at all' was not collected in 1969.

social mobility), and socio-technical factors like changes in the media landscape. This latter cause has been championed by writers like Robert Putnam (1995) who argued for a correlation between social inclusion and participation, and rates of television consumption. In short, TV rots your political brain.

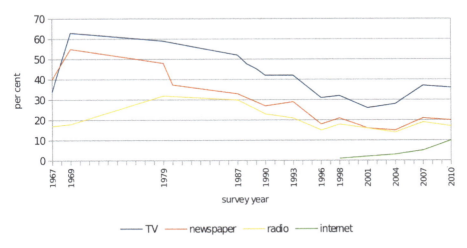

Figure 13: AES media research 'Followed the election in the mass media'

Source: McAllister & Pietsch, 2011: 8 (rescaled)

The difficulty with studies like the AES (aside from known concerns about respondents' bias towards being more politically interested overall; Young, Sally, 2011: 24) is their inherent relativism. In striving to produce valuable longitudinal datasets, there is an assumption that the questions and concepts evaluated remain largely static. While this may be generally true (depending on the degree to which you subscribe to a constructivist point of view), it is not a universal. Take, for example, concepts like 'the environment'. In the 1960s, if surveyed on this idea, Australians would have likely had very little, if any, interest in the subject. If they did have an interest, the majority would have seen 'the environment' in the policy terms common to the era: principally nature conservation for the purposes of human recreation and non-destructive exploitation. Ideas about sustainability, let alone the importance of carbon, were yet to have an impact on public consciousness. Similarly, it is possible to argue that the notion of 'following' an event has considerably changed in the way people view and use media. If we look at the media landscape of the 1980s, the perception of 'following' an event would entail an individual being attentive to that event in the heavily programmed and linear presentation of news found in free-to-air broadcasting, and the selection of relevant stories in newspapers where the order of importance were heavily signalled through the editorial process of placement, headline writing, and image selection. There was once a time when the only thing on television at 6pm was the news.

Today, 'following' an issue conveys a different idea: the fragmentation of communication channels, but also in the more conventional media environment (e.g. through pay-TV, digital multi-channelling, and time-shifting), places greater emphasis on audiences' agency in actively following an election. In short, it is not possible to argue that following an election in a variety of media means the same thing over time, nor is comparative across media types. This is particularly the case with online media. To unpack the extent to which audiences are accessing politically relevant information online, it is better to employ methods that record their actual behaviour over time, rather than self-reported perceptions. To do this, it is useful to examine a study of Australian voters undertaken during the 2010 federal election. This research captured and analysed all the webpages visited by a panel group in two time periods: one before and one during the formal election period.[33] The aim of the research was to identify the nature of the participants' web browsing behaviour and the extent to which the pages identified could be classed as having political content.[34]

Contrary to the perception given in survey research of low levels of online gathering of political information, this project found that the panel group was exposed to political content of some kind in nearly one third of their pages visited. This includes political content that was manifest (such as political party websites or news articles specifically about politics or policy), but also 'mixed' pages that only included more minor political references (such as newspaper homepages that included a mix of headlines of a political and non-political nature). Figure 14 illustrates the sources of the political content visited by the panel. Overall, visited political content is largely from media organisations online. This reinforces the findings that party websites do not appear to be significant destinations for the general community during elections (see Figure 3: Traffic to party websites, April–August 2010). What elections do produce, however, is a shift in the consumption of mixed political content (which has correspondingly

---

33   The research employed a two-wave panel design, with the inter-wave period lasting 26 days. Data was collected from 56 participants recruited from an existing online research panel of approximately 10,000 individuals. Following induction, participants completed a survey to collect demographic, voter intention, party support, and issue identification data and were provided with a customised version of Google's Chrome web browser for installation on their primary computer. This software allowed each website visited to be recorded against a unique identifier assigned to each individual participant. In total 93,743 URLs were collected for coding and analysis.

34   For the purpose of this study, 'political content' was defined at content 'explicitly pertaining to: Electoral politics; Organisations established for the contest of political office (parties); Organisations established for the advocacy of policy (political interest groups); Activities pertaining to electoral politics or policy advocacy by individuals or groups. Excludes implicit content and private politics'.

less detailed information relevant to the electoral decision-making process) to more specific political information (e.g. from homepage browsing to greater reading of stories specifically about the election and election issues).

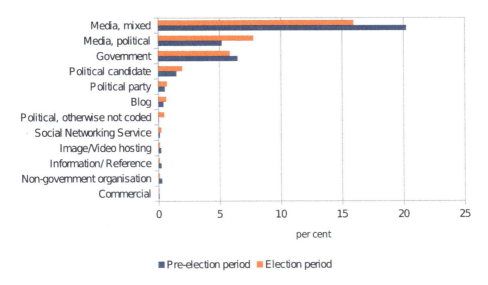

Figure 14: Source of web browsing of political content

Source: Author's research, with Ariadne Vromen

We should recognise that, when compared with the AES, this research is based on a considerably smaller sample size, and is more likely to be biased towards the politically interested participant. The nature and source of political information, the tendency for elections to be relevant focusing events, and the smaller role of political campaigns as direct sources of information are, however, important observations. This stresses the enduring role of intermediating institutions, like media firms and journalists, in shaping the presentation of political information to the public (see Chapter 6 for more discussion).

Additionally, to address some of the limitations of this method, we can develop these findings using some of the more detailed AES survey data regarding the range of activities that voters engage in. Looking at Table 4 it is evident that a considerable portion of the respondents access online news where political information is likely to feature during the election. The extent to which this is engaged with in an active manner is lower. Active engagement by audiences — where audiences take ownership over the channel and are more involved in constructing the media environment — produces a higher level of intellectual and emotional response to the material being consumed, partially because attention is focused more directly on the content under active manipulation (Wicks, 2001: 100–02).

		Party identification of respondent			
		ALP	Liberal	National	Greens
Low-activity	Read/accessed mainstream news sites	31.7	33.1	15.7	42.7
	Viewed/accessed non-official online video	6.8	4.2	5.9	7.7
High-activity	Joined/started political group on a SNS	0	0	0	0
	Posted political comments to blog/SNS	7	6	5.9	13.7
	Forwarded non-official content (jokes, news)	8.3	3	5.9	2.6
	Embedded/reposted non-official content	2.7	0.8	0	2.6
Total non-official campaign engagement		33.9	35.7	24	53
n		628	596	50	117

Table 4: Election activity

Source: Gibson & Cantijoch, 2011: 13; annotated extract

Voters as participants in electoral discourse

The greater source and channel selectivity of digital media may be fundamental to its users' changing agency towards political information. As we saw above, however, this interactivity remains low when compared with more passive information handling. The ability of once-passive audiences to become active content creators provides new avenues for political expression, as well as the potential for the movement of information horizontally (within the 'audience'). In the bandwidth-rich, but attention-poor digital environment, the provision of interactivity tools ('email this story', discussion boards, reposting tools for SNS) has become a way that content producers have attempted to make their sites and services 'sticky': increasing the time individual users spend on their properties (Woll and Raccah, 2010: 318). But this has had other impacts, including the ability of audiences to 'talk amongst themselves' and be more critical of the media they consume. Active engagement therefore comes from the top-down (from digital publishers through making once-static digital services into content creation and sharing 'platforms') and bottom-up (from individuals' desires to be expressive and participative).

In the electoral context this is significant in that it serves to further undermine the 'cartel' of parties, large media organisations, and professional communications practices and norms. Participation becomes enabled through technology, but is also increasingly visible to other users. This has a feedback effect, the social surveillance aspect stimulates the production of 'user-generated' content.

Internationally, we see this clearly through the uptake of blogging. During the first half of the decade, the number of blogs grew at an incredible rate (the vast majority — 60 per cent — of whom are individual hobbyists; Technorati, 2011), at one stage doubling every six months over a period of 42 months (Sifry, 2006). Because of this, it is important to see elections as both simulating the interest of Australians into accessing political information online, but also the interest of Australians into (re)producing political information online.

Voters as an active audience

The study of this area of digital media remains formative, partially as we shift gears into thinking about audiences as producers, due to the natural lag between social behaviours and research data, but also because of the rapid changes that have occurred in how this productivity is expressed. If we look at that 'first-generation' of blogs with user-generated content, we can see that Australians do take an active role in elections, generating content about the electoral debates of the day. This is illustrated in Figure 15, which demonstrates a spike in references to key party leaders during the election period.

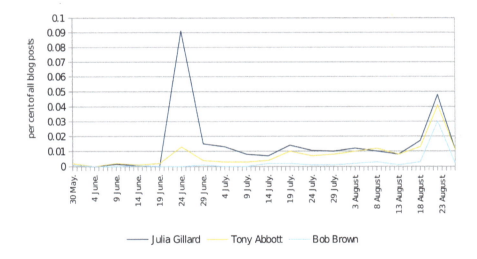

Figure 15: Mentions of party leaders in blog posts, May–August 2010

Source: BlogPulse (smoothed)

This is also reflected (Figure 16) in similar references on Twitter, one of the recent digital media channels that was the subject of considerable interest in the 2010 election campaign. Introduced in 2006, this channel has had considerable growth through the uptake and use by a range of political and entertainment figures in the 2007–10 period. Twitter has been the focus of research because of its emphasis on real-time and continual short posts (as opposed to longer, less frequent ones on that are common to blogs) and the comparative ease with which posts can be located on the Twitter service (in one location, as opposed to blogs which are spread across services and individuals' websites; generally all public, as opposed to Facebook) and aggregated together through the user convention of inserting hashtags (folksonomy[35] classifications) in posts.

In their extended analysis of the use of Twitter in the 2010 election, Axel Bruns and Jean Burgess (2011: 44–49) identify a very active discursive community around the '#ausvotes' hashtag. Their analysis of this community is interesting in that, while it contains political and media elites as core members of the social network of tweet exchanges (measured in terms of @username responses), the substantive content of users' tweets does not map perfectly onto mass-media news agendas. The implications of this research is that this community of user-generated political information is not simply an extension of media topics (something we might assume by only looking at the data on passive information gathering only), but has its own interests and concerns that are more reflective of the political and policy interests of this specific community.[36]

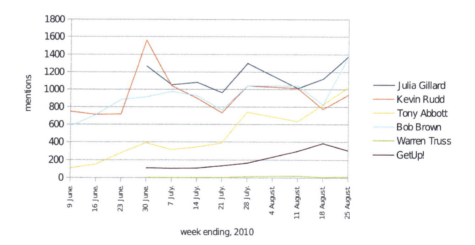

Figure 16: Mentions of party leaders in tweets, July–August 2010

Source: Compiled from tweetVolume

---

35 Informal classifications undertaken in a distributed manner by users, rather than pre-determined taxonomies that are regulated by a central body, professional standards, or other hierarchical system (Gruber, 2007: 1).

36 In this case, given these individuals are generally 'early adopters' and high-intensity users of digital media one of the key interests was the National Broadband Network (NBN). The NBN is of interest to this community because it will have a considerable impact on the cost and performance of digital media over a long timeframe.

Biting the hand that seeds

While this demonstrates media consumers can be independent, they can also be active critics of the media. Thus, these channels have been a useful place to locate criticism of media coverage of election campaigns in general, but also the staging of media events by campaign teams. This is important, particularly where the co-production of campaign news by journalists and campaigners can be too cosy and lack transparency regarding the artifice behind news making. Some good examples of this would be: The 'July 12 incident' in the 2007 election, where media coverage of polling data led to disputes by political bloggers over the statistical validity of poll reading within the *Australian* newspaper (Flew, 2008).[37] This dispute, which was at times personal (Bahnisch, 2008: 10), did lead to increased sensitivity on the part of newsrooms to the way polling data was produced. More recently, in 2010, the conduct of Sky News's televised 'town hall' debates was placed under scrutiny by Twitter users, who identified the son of a Liberal MP in an audience of supposedly 'undecided' voters (Kwek, 2010). This led to exposure on how media organisations 'stage' and 'frame' these events, led to questions about the quality of work done by Galaxy Research, and served to 'de-naturalise' (make visible) the artificial nature of these pseudo-events (artificially constructed events designed specifically for media coverage that do not exist 'outside' of media representations of them; Boorstin, 1992: 7–12). These, admittedly rare, interventions in dominant media narratives demonstrate how systemic barriers to journalistic discretion can be attacked by outsiders who do not operate on the media logics of access and competition (Semetko, et al., 1991).[38]

More commonly, however, the ability of these bottom-up media to break into the highly scripted and performed media events is limited. The tweets regarding audience selection in the 2010 election was heavily reported by broadsheet newspapers, which used the initial Twitter reports as colour for their stories and pursuit of the issue. As we see in Illustration 5,[39] a still from the public affairs panel show *Q&A*, the use of Twitter posts selected by ABC production staff to comment on the program's content is less an intervention in the highly controlled process of media production as much as extension of the audiences' shared perception of their passivity. Taking the type of references normally growled or shouted at the screen and broadcasting them may provide the sense of instant edification, as much as it remediates the viewership as a national

37 A good example of where the new media and mainstream media came into direct conflict due to a challenge to the self-conception of journalists as having a special insider insight into the political process (Louw, 2010: 71).

38 Semetko, et al. identify a range of systemic limitations on journalistic discretion, including: strength of the party system, degree of media competition, and campaign professionalism.

39 Source: ABC (2010) *Q&A*, 16 August (broadcast date), accessible: www.abc.net.au/tv/qanda/txt/s2978032.htm accessed: 3 September 2010.

'lounge room' conversation discussing and dissecting the performance of the participants, but it does not necessarily 'break though' into the programming. This does, however, grow a community of discussants around the show's advertised hashtag ('#qanda').

Illustration 5: Opposition leader Tony Abbott responding to the audience on *Q&A*

Source: ABC (2010) *Q&A*, 16 August (broadcast date), accessible: www.abc.net.au/tv/qanda/txt/s2978032. htm, accessed: 3 September 2010; used with permission, *Q&A*, ABC TV

Stockholm syndrome

Overall, there is a strange and symbiotic relationship between established mass media and the online community of political conversationalists. On the one level, the online community depends on news reporting as catalysts for discussions. On the other, there is a wariness about the content and methodologies behind corporate news. Mapping analysis of blog content during the 2007 election prompted the argument that '... political debate in the blogosphere does not operate independently from mainstream journalism, but ... it continues to derive substantial impulses from the opinion columns published by major news organisations' (Kirchhoff, et al., 2009: 12). Combined with a crossover of membership between journalism, academia, and amateur writers, this explains, to some degree, why many bloggers and Twitter users have adopted the limited set of 'neutral' conventions of mainstream media when writing about politics.

These stylistic conventions are identified by David Swanson and Paolo Mancini (1996) and represent what we would call the 'horserace' focus of journalistic election coverage: an emphasis on campaign blunders and strategies over policy substance, and the 'disdaining style' of narrative voice (a tendency towards third person writing). Good examples of this include campaign commentary that discusses strategies and tactics and is synchronised with the flow of campaign (pseudo-)events, emphasis on reporting polling data and overemphasis on the importance of this data, and the focus on minor personal observations about candidates and leaders. The example of this par excellence was Twitter users' fascination with the prime minister's large earlobes during the televised leaders' debate in the 2010 election campaign (becoming a significant subset of online discussion during the debate as a trending topic on Twitter; ninemsm, 2010).

Implications for Australian electioneering

It is clear that the non-linear nature of change, identified in Chapter 1, is borne out in the evaluation of the way digital media have impacted on, and been employed within, Australian elections. While the number of new communications channels being employed in electioneering has been increasing, this is not a simple case of incremental adoption. Different channels and approaches to online communication have come in and out of fashion, and successive elections have not automatically seen the work of previous campaigns built upon over time. This has a lot to do with the complex nature of the electoral process, but also the way new technologies have enabled different actors to participate in online campaigning. That digital media is going to have an increasingly important presence in electoral campaigning in Australia in the future is clear, but this may be more likely to be found in increased areas of niche messaging and 'behind the scenes' use of internal party intranets, targeted advertising, and the use of electoral databases.

To make a more circumspect summation of the impacts of the technology on electioneering, however, we can consider two related questions: does the adoption of these tools 'win votes' and how does the use of the technology — particularly by political parties — affect the way elections behave as mediated events.

Winning votes

The impact of digital media on the distribution of votes cast is a key question for practitioners and scholars. Unfortunately, it is a difficult question to answer. Based on successive comparisons of digital media performance and electoral outcomes, Gibson and McAllister (2011: 238–40) have been able to demonstrate a significant correlation between the use of more interactive online services (blogs, SNS and online video) and higher primary votes, controlling for other factors (including incumbency and resources). This advantage, however, is small

— in the order of one per cent increased vote per interactive channel used. Further, the finding is not generalisable, as it is only attributable to the success of Australian Greens candidates, rather than the major parties.

Significantly, this finding is demonstrative of a decline in the value of political websites in Australia, as these authors (2007: 256) had previously seen an electoral advantage of two per cent in use of candidate websites in the 2004 election. This makes the evidence on the under-investment in candidate websites, identified in Figure 7, a rational choice by practitioners. In general terms, these findings point, not to channel effects, but to a combination of audience characteristics and novelty as the core drivers of the value of these campaign tools. Overall, this makes sense. The notion that we could quantifiably ascribe electoral success to the adoption of channels is ludicrous. It would be like asking the per cent of increased vote received by using radio, rather than talking both about the extent of use and the nature of use.

A limitation of this type of research stems in its use of candidates and electorate-level vote as the data for its modelling. While Jackman has identified that individual electorate factors and candidate quality are not irrelevant in shaping electoral outcomes (2005: 340–47), we need to recognise that the majority of votes remain largely informed by decisions about parties over candidates in Australia. This area of competition is not amenable to the type of regression analysis undertaken by Gibson and McAllister and simple measures (such as traffic data) don't serve to explain variations in vote given the complex way that parties employ their digital media assets in elections. Certainly the electoral success of the Australian Greens has seen a lockstep increase in their use of, and sophistication with, new forms of media, but it is not possible to determine causality here. While the Greens have more than doubled their primary vote between 2001–10 (Bennett, 2008), a wide range of other factors have to be taken into consideration including increased membership, fundraising and the decline of the Australian Democrats. Particularly their overall visibility in the wider media landscape and the way this presents them as a viable alternative to the other parties. This is a topic we should turn to.

Winning media. Winning hearts?

This leads us back to the argument that the impact of digital media, particularly in the context of election campaigns, is most significantly felt in the way they shape the wider media ecosystem. Rather than looking at a specific direct impact on voter behaviour, the use of digital media by parties, candidates, advocacy groups, and the public have a role in shaping the amount and focus of political information that is produced and consumed. For parties this is very indirect: as they already 'own' direct communications with electors through mass media, the value of select media lies in shaping the content of newspapers and television, and directing the discussion of policies and candidates in the community through setting news and commentary agendas towards issues that benefit them, and framing the way in which discussion is undertaken.

This is relevant to comparatively conventional strategies regarding the media. First is the provision of repackaged content to media organisations. This takes a variety of forms, including press releases, reports and data, events and stunts, quotes and access to interviewees, audio and video 'packages' for broadcast. Their value is that they lower the cost of news production, particularly when provided in a timely manner and a format most convenient to their particular channel of communication (VanSlyke Turk, 1985). This can lead to an inherent bias where those parts of the political economy with the greatest ability to generate and distribute information subsidies have the greatest ability to shape debates (see Garbage in, garbage out, Chapter 6). With the advent of blogs and other forms of user-generated content, this process can operate via traditional distribution models (source-media-audience) as well as a more direct manner (source-producer).

Information subsidies are invaluable to political organisations, as they allow their messages to be repeated, not just in paid advertising, but also in 'neutral' news settings. This is common where framing comes into play. Framing is defined by Robert Entman as an:

> ... omnipresent process in politics and policy analysis. It involves selecting a few aspects of a perceived reality and connecting them together in a narrative that promotes a particular interpretation. Frames can perform up to four functions: define problems, specify causes, convey moral assessments, and endorse remedies. (2010: 391)

Framing can stem from a variety of sources (professional norms, channel effects, cultural prejudice, audience expectation, timing and sequencing), but the provision of information subsidies also serve as a mechanism to shape news and commentary through the transmission of preferred frames. In the context of the 2007 federal campaign, Ward (2008: 11–14) has argued that the use of SNS and online video were useful in framing the representations of Rudd as a progressive figure more in touch with the interests of younger voters. Rudd, through a combination of channel selection and messages about technology policy (medium and message), was effective in creative a narrative of 'newness' and change.

Digital media assists parties simply in conducting their election strategies, old and new. Parties have been able to, without giving away conventional revenue streams from donors and public funding, introduce new ways to raise funds online through e-commerce systems that make small unit donations more cost effective. Targeted advertising and the ability to test ads against online audiences provide for more effective use of resources in conventional advertising. Similarly, digital media allows for the lower-cost (for parties) production and distribution of subsidised content to mainstream media organisations, as well as increasing the scope for timely delivery of material (by pushing information directly at journalists as they work up stories). This has been significantly aided by the crisis in publishing, which weakens journalists' resistance to 'spin' (see Chapter 6). When undertaken effectively and in a strategic manner, digital campaign tools allow for the more sophisticated management of media agendas. The argument, however, that direct framing impacts have moved to the user-generated social media is less clear and, while there are tendencies for mass-media agendas and frames to be emulated online, there is also evidence of independence from the conventional narrative of elections.

Democratic?

In democratic terms, it would appear that the implications for electoral democracy in Australia is modest at best: while minor parties are more visible online, it is not clear whether this provides them a significant benefit. There is limited evidence that minor parties and independents can actually 'level the playing field' through digital media. The proliferation of channels and strategic integration with offline marketing strategies and other media means digital electioneering is no longer a cheap option. There are good structural reasons why parties who are traditionally likely to win government are advantaged in the era of digital media, even if their entrenched position in power may limit the competitive pressure to innovate and adopt the most cutting-edge forms of campaigning. The primary reason is clearly the resource advantage that parties of government hold. In addition, the likelihood of holding government after the election (or within a conceivable timeframe) means these parties are also more likely to raise private funds, particularly from organisational interests (unions, business interests and established pressure groups). Overall, while the major parties clearly made modest investments in online campaigning until the mid 2000s, once they became more convinced of the value of digital media, these resources allow parties to buy in expertise in online campaigning rapidly from an expanding international market of campaign providers.

The ALP's 2007 election campaign is an excellent example of this, demonstrating how quickly the major parties could colonise the online space when they wanted. In this way the 'Obama-effect' can be seen as somewhat self-reinforcing: the association between Obama's digital media campaign encouraged parties around the world to look again at digital campaigning techniques, and tended to recruit US-based campaign professionals to assist in emulating this effort. To date, the minor parties' key advantages remain in the area of social networking, where the construction of online discursive communities appear to buck the trend of normalisation towards message dominance by major parties. The question we need to examine is about whether this is because these online communities naturally counterbalance dominant political agendas, or if members of the particular minor party of the milieu, the Greens, are more likely to be discursively active — making this a phenomena of this particular minor party, rather than minor party members in general. To examine these questions and others, look at the rise of new public spheres in Chapter 3.

Chapter 3 — Social media

Twitter: Where 140 characters is more than enough to get you into trouble, but not nearly enough to get you out of it.

— Angela Byron (@webchick)

Elections play to a mechanistic model of politics. Rule-driven and highly structured events, they allocate power to political parties based on a specific formula: populations separated into electorates, Senate quotas, and 50 per cent +1 vote to win a lower house seat. Elections provide access to the institutions of government and legislative design, but they take place within temporal, economic and social contexts. The most significant of these is the cultural and symbolic. While classic institutionalists would explain electoral systems and constitutional design as determining political behaviour by elites (in terms of the impact on elite behaviour due to channelling preferences through rules and procedures; Lowndes, 2010: 62–63), constructivists see these formal political behaviours more likely to be responsive to cultural norms and values that are plastic. This can explain problems that elected governments have in pushing through their agendas, as was the case when the Labor government under Kevin Rudd attempted to institute the Carbon Pollution Reduction Scheme and the Resource Super Profits Tax. These were not failures of institutional politics as much as problems with the ability of the government of the day to seek and receive support from the community and add the resources of popular legitimacy to that of the institutional.

This chapter explores this subject and, through it, the creation of the valuable political resource of *legitimacy*. To do this, we examine the notion of 'the public sphere', a metaphor for the sum total of public dialogue: the articulation of individuals' opinions and beliefs, and the aggregation of these into 'public opinion'. This opinion informs elites about the scope and boundaries of their authority, and in so doing directs public-policy making. It also reflects the way the community(/-ies) see politics and issues, revealing how our understanding of the political world is composed. To explore this topic we will first discuss how political theorists have conceptualised the public sphere, before examining 'sites' of opinion formation in the Australian digital environment. In doing so we need to ask how these conversational spaces work in channelling opinion, what opinions they most effectively promote, as well as who is left out of this new conversation.

'The' public sphere and public opinion

Popular legitimacy exists as a substance we call 'public opinion' in a vague place we call the 'public sphere'. The significance of public opinion is clear: governments rise and fall based on it, and policies are statements of pure reason or ridiculous follies depending on their correlation with it. What 'it' is, however, is ambiguous and contested, and subject to change over time. As Senator Cory Bernardi sends his weekly 'dose of common sense' email to supporters, he makes a claim to represent the 'sensible centre' of public opinion — the reasonableness of the average person with their practical concerns and 'real life' experience (Pearson & Patching, 2008: 7). When John Howard used the inclusive 'we decide' to talk about immigration restriction measures in his 2001 re-election speech, he too made the claim that his policies represented wider public opinion and, by extension, encompassed the public's view of who was excluded from the 'us' of Australianness (van Onselen and Errington, 2007: 225). Julia Gillard's proposal to establish a 'citizens' assembly' in the 2010 election to determine a policy for carbon pricing presupposed a process by which it could be determined.

These claims are the bread and butter of politics, and politicians who are 'out of touch' with 'the public' are punished. This logic has entered the popular vernacular of political discourse, privileging those psychic politicians who have an innate understanding of the 'mood' of the electorate. Thus, it is generally an accepted pejorative to describe a government as 'poll driven' or dependent on 'focus groups' (Clune, 2012: 310). Why? We know that elections are a terrible way to determine the policy preferences of the public beyond a very few top-line issues, particularly in a majoritarian political system such as Australia's, which distorts voter intention and focuses it on a few major parties (Hobolt & Klemmemsen, 2005). The use of opinion polling or other deliberative processes could, in a different view of politics, be seen as a positive way in which governments can be responsive and listen to the electorate, and balance out the lopsided access of 'monied' lobbyists (Lindblom, 1977).

Regardless of what could or should be, the relationship between politics and this idea of an aggregate measure of the political and policy views of the nation have become interlinked. Indeed, we can argue that the concept of an assessable view of a unitary public has become *naturalised* in political discourse in this country. Naturalisation refers to Hall's notion whereby the representation of something (in this case aggregate opinion) is presented as an objective truth beyond the capacity of the viewer to verify (1982). This is a powerful process in that it conceals the way information is constructed, in so doing stripping doubt and methodology. The reality, however, is far more complex. Like Gibson's notion of computer networks as 'cyberspace' (1984: 51), the public sphere is also a 'consensual hallucination'. We know we can't actually go into a specific place called the public sphere, but, through a variety of mechanisms, we can interact with it and others 'within it'. The public sphere is a construct where political ideas are debated and considered. The product of the public sphere is snapshots of public opinion: highly abstracted representations of the collective will commonly materialised by news organisations as opinion polls in a regularised manner that suits news production demands.

The public sphere

The problem presented by the notion of the public sphere is its tendency to be used without due regard to the scope and limitations of the concept. Popularised following the translation of Jürgen Habermas's *The Structural Transformation of the Bourgeois Public Sphere* (1991), the idea is historically specific. Habermas argues that the rise of the educated bourgeoisie sees the development of a culture of public engagement and debate supported by emerging journalism (journals and newspapers facilitating an expanding information society). This process rests on enlightenment rationalism: the idea that truth (vis-à-vis Mill, 2009) is not the preserve of specific institutions or traditions (such as Christian churches or beliefs), but can be determined through active participation in reason and debate.

The educated and time-rich bourgeois class, according to Habermas, was able to gather and reflect on issues of public concern in salons and coffee houses to determine their shared interest. This social change also required the end of monarchical rule — with its arbitrary exercise of power — and an emerging consensus on the separation of the 'private sphere', the public sphere, and the sphere of government. Thus, the public sphere is not simply synonymous with 'public opinion'. The public sphere is *performed*. It only comes into its own when these publics mobilise their views and opinions into the governmental realm. Thus, public spheres come in and out of existence, rather than transcending their production and being reified as public opinion. Public opinion, as we see it today, is a static attribute of the public that can be measured. The public sphere is an active process of political expression.

Bursting the bubble

In unpacking this idea we can see its limitations are numerous, both in the historical context proposed by Habermas, and also as an analogy for practices of forming public opinion today. Nancy Fraser was one early observer to attack the concept for failing to recognise both diversity and alternative spaces for the formation of 'counterpublics' to the dominant gender and class composition of Enlightenment-era public spheres (1990). Using the example of women, but this might also apply to other (formally or informally) disenfranchised groups (such as, at that time, labour), these criticisms note the contested nature of rationalism as being constructed of those views and opinions formed by a small and elite group of men. The public spheres of Habermas's historical review were exclusive clubs, and their ability to form a relatively cohesive set of opinions about what government should do was based on a comparatively narrow definition of the public interest. For a small, emerging class of professionals and business people, the development of a minimal state that ensured the provision of key infrastructure for the preservation of the public good, a system of laws and rules to allow citizens to interact and engage in trade in an effective way (contract law), and national defence. It is not surprising that this period of time sees the emergence of contemporary capitalism as a meta ideology which influences views of what is good and right in both public and private life (Salvatore, 2007: 216).

For Habermas, it is the expansion of the scope of the state (ironically in response to increasingly active participation by excluded groups and 'lower' classes) that drives the decline of this public sphere: the welfare state places 'spoils' into the public arena for groups to compete to be able to access them (Gómez-Ibáñez, 2003: 46). This shifts the public sphere from a place of rational debate to one where the mobilisation of large parts of the electorate can win greater access to public goods. Hannah Arendt diagnosed this as the 'rise of the social': the tendency for private production to come out of the home and into the public realm (1958: 38–49). Thus, where people were once free in the public realm because they had escaped the day-to-day concerns of 'economy', the development of industrial capitalism tends to force the process of identity formation and political articulation into the private realm. For Arendt this leads to the public sphere becoming dominated by the 'grubby' tasks of material debate, rather than the pursuit of higher-order values.

This argument is well developed through the insights of public choice theory and analysis of the conditions that favour rent seeking (concentrated benefits and diffused costs; Farber & Frickey, 1991: 24). Under the historical diagnosis of the public sphere, it is not the decline of the 'space' for civic participation that sees the end of the bourgeois-rational public sphere, but the changing nature of the state and expectations we hold of it. Australia, 'born modern' with strong state provision of welfare and the material conditions for private production (Simms, 1981: 83), has never experienced Habermas's classic public sphere. To reconstruct a society that was predicated on such fanciful public spheres, therefore, would be to adopt a radical liberalism that has not been seen globally for hundreds of years (if ever) and was never part of the pattern of state settlement in this nation.

The upshot of this is that while we rhetorically favour 'classic' Habbermassian public spheres with their implied warm cosiness, public opinion today is seen in stark methodological terms: defined by positivist social science's development of the survey instrument, forced-choice decision-making (to increase response rates), and statistical inference that blurs correlation and causation. This means that, in practice, we tend towards a model of political decision-making more commonly associated with the 'marketplace of ideas' which sees participants as bringing preferences into the political realm fully formed and working to aggregate them together into simple majorities (Erikson, et al., 1991). This is the antithesis of the classic concept. As Cass Sunstein observes '[a]ggregate or marketplace notions disregard the extent to which political outcomes are supposed to depend on discussion and debate, or a commitment to political equality, and on the reasons offered for or against alternatives'(1993). In mass society, this technocratic mechanism for opinion formation clearly solidifies views that may not be firmly held (Bourdieu, 1979), but also speaks to a conception of society underpinned by individualism (Herbst, 1991).

Plug in your USB coffee warmers

Does the era of individualism preclude the return of policy debates based on rational discourse? In recent years, appeals for enlightenment-values have re-emerged in public life: in diffused appeals to govern in the 'public interest', or through more explicit programmatic attempts to incorporate 'evidence-based' policy-design processes in government (see An evidence-based Australian politics?, Chapter 7) (Marston & Watts, 2003). Here, Habermas and Arendt would differ. The waning of sectarian politics in Australia — most visible in the decline of unionism and the decreasing strength of party identification (McAllister, 2011: 41, 159) — would be seen by Habermas as reducing the factors that drive the seeking of 'spoils' through block mobilisation. Alternatively, Arendt would point to a shift in values away from the material towards the expressive (e.g. the rise of 'post-materialist' citizens; Charnock & Ellis, 2004; Hamilton & Denniss, 2005: 153–77) as a way in which more human values of self-expression and solidarity may be rediscovered in public dialogue. Both, however, would warn of the risk of ideational dominance from our key 'democratic' institutions: the mass media and government (see Chapter 6). This is because of their ability to mobilise propaganda to overwhelm a burgeoning new public sphere culture.

It is important to understand how the public spheres of mass society depend on media to constitute their discursive spaces. While Habermas's bourgeois public sphere talks of media *of* the public sphere (providing information for the subject of rumination and debate), mass society sees media *as also constituting* the public sphere. This has implications for the three key elements of public opinion formation: the type of interactions facilitated, the quality of interactions, and the legitimising role of media over particular types of opinions or issues (Crespi, 1997: 1). This raises the possibility that our digital media environment will facilitate the creation of new public spheres that are: (a) more directly interactive and conversational than, say, the letters page of the newspaper, and (b) more likely to be outside of the control of mass-media gatekeepers.

Thus, the advent of the internet as a new and better means for public opinion formation has been the go-to argument of deliberative democrats since before its emergence as a popular medium. Early computer networks were used as discursive political spaces by Polish unions in the 1980s (Jacobs, 2005: 68–69) and low-cost computers and dial-up modems were employed for local political debate and information exchange (McCullough, 1991: 17). Scott London was an early proponent of ICT-driven discursive democratic practice under the term 'teledemocracy' (democratic talk at a distance) (1995). More recently Lincoln Dahlberg, for example, talked about e-democracy initiatives (see 'the opinion makers', this chapter) in the United States as promising examples of new places for the formation of public opinion (2001).

Social media has more recently been identified as emergent sites for civic discourse and opinion formation that allow for spontaneous discussions. This type of fluid discussion reduces the ability of technology and service providers to control the nature of public discourse. Using the example of the comments sections of the video-sharing site YouTube, Kasun Ubayasiri (2006) argues that these places provide an array of spaces for political socialisation and interaction because of the high degree of control users have over conversational topics.[1] More recently, Andrew Murray has argued the contemporary internet is a place '... where political discourse may more freely be exchanged between the proletariat and the bourgeois, and one where thanks to the pseudonymity offered speech is less susceptible to [suppression and censorship by social, economic and government institutions]. This attractive prospect has encouraged many academics to discuss the 'virtual public sphere' as an extension of Habermas's original public sphere' (2010: 523).

Social media as a deliberative space

In recent years the term 'social media' has become a popular way to describe a collection of online systems that allow for the production, storage and distribution of user-generated content (UGC). Social media allows for the creation of a virtual social space where groups of users can come together in synchronous and asynchronous interactions. These interactions can be structured (such as threaded responses to blog posts that are moderated), semi-structured (e.g. the discussion amongst groups of friends within extended Facebook social

---

1   This is not to say these views are universal; as early as 1995 Poster argued that the analogy between the public sphere and the internet was a poor one.

networks), or unstructured in nature (such as in Twitter, where topics are not 'owned' but tied together through the ad hoc application of hashtags that can be used to locate and link together posts by a variety of different users).

Because of this comparatively diverse set of technologies and social conventions at play, Heidi Cohen (2011) points out that definitional ambiguity reduces our ability to make concrete statements about social media. Common definitions include allusions to the comparative ease of participation in social media, and its emphasis on multiple and simultaneous user participation in production of conversational elements (communication initiation, response and comment, social filtering/quality control). For our purposes an expansive definition is best. Andreas Kaplan and Michaeil Haenlein provide a useful typology that highlights variability, particularly in the extent to which these channels provide interactivity and self-disclosure (Table 4). This demonstrates the diversity of digital media channels in this category, and the way different combinations of social presence and interactivity come together to fill different user needs.

		Social presence/media richness/interactivity		
		Low	Medium	High
Self-presentation/ self-disclosure	High (nonymous)	Blogs (inc. Twitter)	Social networking services (e.g. Facebook)	Virtual social worlds (e.g. Second Life)
	Low (anonymous)	Collaborative projects (e.g. Wikipedia)	Content communities (e.g. Youtube)	Virtual game worlds (e.g. World of Warcraft)

Table 5: Social media typology

Source: Kaplan & Haenlein, 2010: 62 (extracted and annotated)

The political importance of social media is not simply that it provides alternative channels for institutional political actors' communication in structured election periods (as discussed in Chapter 2). Increasingly, the social media is seen as a place in which public opinion is formed, and where interventions in public opinion are possible by an increasing array of institutions and individuals. As Cohen points out, marketers and publicrelations professionals have been at the forefront of interest in this new environment due to perceptions that non-elite influencers who participate in social-media conversations are increasingly important in shaping public opinion (see, for example, Hot House Interactive, 2010) (2011). If this sounds familiar, it is. The notion of a 'two-step flow' of information and opinion from institutional sources to key influencers and then into their social network was introduced in the 1950s as media scholars attempted to understand the cognitive and social aspects of media consumption in real-world (social) settings. Recognising that media did not have simple, immediate and direct effects on behaviour, field research identified that individuals in existing social groups (family, work, recreational), who were identified as having expertise on particular topics, were consulted by their peers to provide their opinion on information presented by mass media (Katz & Lazarsfeld, 1955). This is a good example of heuristic-based decision making, where information can be assessed by reference to choices made by those deemed to be more informed than oneself.

This raises the question: is there something *really* new here? On the one hand, media has always been 'social', human communication, even of the barest facts, rarely exists outside of a social context, and commonly incorporates some notion of feedback (even if it is the most bare of responses, such as the 'market sensing' of media organisations that use sales or readership figures as proxy indicators of communicative success). The notion that mainstream or mass communications would be subject to 'social filtering' is not new, and the two-step flow model and its various descendants showed this. Alternatively, proponents of the power of social media as a new significant factor in public opinion formation point to a range of elements that make it significant for study: social media significantly increases the scale of social interactions because of the magnifying effect of the internet and computerisation. These media, therefore, provide a possible example of 'collective intelligence', the 'genuine capacity of a group to think, learn and create collectively' (Moral & Abbott 2009). Social-media conversational trends are visible and provide strong signals to mass media and elites about public opinion (Rana, 2009: 261).

To date we have seen some notable uses of collective intelligence by political elites in policy debate. Roxanne Missingham, for example, cites the use of Twitter by the opposition treasurer, Joe Hockey, to solicit feedback on carbon trading during parliamentary debate over the emissions trading scheme (2010: 11). Thus, the nature of social media provides the possibility for manipulation and the construction of public opinion (Long, 2011). If these practices have an effect politically, it is likely to be evident in Australia: Neilsen (2010a) has identified Australians as some of the heaviest users of social media, both in terms of overall rates of adoption (72 per cent) and time spent browsing these services (7 hours and 20 minutes per month in 2010).

Kids today ...

This argument is not without critics. These focus on a disconnect between social media's expressive politics and 'realpolitik' (Ma, 2009), the shallowness of these users' political interests and commitment (Jack the Insider, 2012), and a view that effort engaged in online politics may salve the conscience, but 'expends' political energy without effect. This latter view is neatly summarised in the notion of 'slacktivism':

> ... feel-good online activism that has zero political or social impact. It gives those who participate ... an illusion of having a meaningful impact on the world without demanding anything more than joining a Facebook group. Remember that online petition that you signed and forwarded to your entire contacts list? That was probably an act of slacktivism. (Morozov, 2009)

Evgeny Morozov's criticism is the most damning, describing this kind of engagement as a mix of narcissism and political masturbation. This is not simply a slap-down of slacktivists, it has currency within media theories of a range of 'gratifications' that audiences derive from their choice of media (Blumler & Katz, 1974). In addition, shallowness is commonly associated with the misplaced political energy of youth (Morris, 2011). This, of course, raises the question of what counts as 'real' politics. As with our constructivist reading of media effects, Alan McKee is clear that we have to be expansive in looking at the cultural dimension of political action: 'what changes in culture makes political change possible' (2005: 192–93, 210). For him, arguments about slacktivist politics are important because of the explicit invalidation of particular forms of creative industry. This type of cultural pessimism is a coded way of endorsing the status quo, both about who can and should 'speak' (creating meaningful political content) and in terms of the policy arrangements of the day.

Using Australian survey data from four different social media: blog, Twitter and Facebook users, and the conservative online community CANdo (discussed in detail in The anti-GetUp!s, Chapter 5), we can scrutinise these questions. One of the easiest questions to examine, however, is that of demography differences and misconceptions. Figure 17 provides a demographic breakdown of the political users of these social media compared with the current Australian population (N). As this figure shows, the majority of these channels *under*-represent youth, with the sole exception of Facebook. The notion that social media represents a youth counterpublic (a 'safe' constituent space for non-mainstream discursive activity; Warner, 2002: 57) is not, therefore, wholly accurate.

Similarly, Morozov's views about slacktivism have encouraged interest in determining the relationship between digital media use and 'real' political participation (assuming, for one moment, that online political activity is wasted). Examining this 'displacement' theory we can identify research that contradicts this. Henrik Christensen (2011), for example, points out the existence of a positive correlation between internet use and political engagement in the population overall. Looking specifically at youth in the US context, a large survey found that offline participation by younger voters was *positively* associated with the use of that most egocentric of digital media, Facebook (Vitak, et al., 2011). Looking at Australian evidence, Figure 18 compares the political activities of social-media users on average with those aged under 30. This figure shows that there are clear behavioural differences between youth and the population average. These differences do not, however, indicate a greater likelihood of political non-participation as much as different opportunities for participation: greater investment in activities that require a commitment of personal time (protests and meetings) over financial resources (consumer activism), lower levels of participation in industrial action (unsurprisingly, as younger people are more likely to be unemployed or work in non-unionised workplaces; Jenkins, 2012), and a greater likelihood to indicate positive intentions to participate in the future, rather than reminiscences of the past.

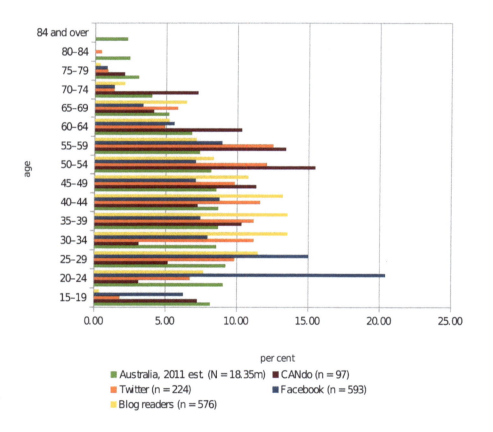

Figure 17: Age distribution of social-media survey respondents, compared to N

Source: Author's research

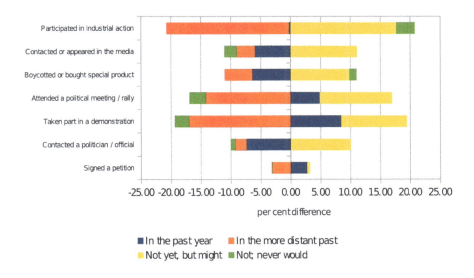

Figure 18: Difference between the political engagement of users of social media (n = 1393)

Source: Author's research

This appears to square with the US study which showed a tendency of younger people to engage more in low-resource-intensive activities (such as information acquisition, which is connected to political socialisation). Interesting, concerning the relationship between the amount of time spent on social media and political engagement, the US study found a non-linear, tapering-off shaped relationship: at some point the level of use of social media begins to reduce the tendency for political activity (Vitak, et al., 2011). While this finding is not supported by the Australian data (Table 6, showing average level of political activity on a four-point likert scale against self-reported internet use), it is logical under the uses and gratifications model (which sees rational media consumption choices as competing against other sources of personal gratification) that, at the extreme end of internet use, other activities would be squeezed out.[2] This illustrates the existence of a more subtle set of drivers than simply equating digital media use with the increased potential for political socialisation and mobilisation.

---

2   Here the use of time categories, as opposed to estimated minutes spent, may be a too imprecise tool to see this in the Australian dataset, rather than ruling out this hypothesis.

Access Internet ...	n	Political activity
Continuously throughout the day	311	3.04
Several times a day	124	2.98
About once a day	6	2.81
Less often	6	2.88
All	447	3.02

Table 6: Time spent on the internet and political activity, under 30s

Source: Author's research

The evidence for Australia is clear. Rather than talking about 'slacktivism', it is more useful to adopt Saayan Chattopadhyay's 'surrogate activism': political activity and the shaping and creation of meaning that leads to action (2011: 64–65). Chattopadhyay see this as a *process* 'where gradual legitimization and the solidification of the politics of belonging occur prior to the deployment of the movement in realpolitik'. In this view we need to recognise that classic definitions of media as 'speech modifiers' *privilege* speech as more authentic and real than other forms of communication. In the political realm, the privileging of any one form of communication should be a red flag to us that something significant is going on, because it demonstrates a gradient in the distribution of power within, or attributed to, particular forms of communication.

A bourgeois public sphere?

Before we examine the nature of these new public spheres, it is relevant to ask: are they bourgeois? That is, following Habermas's concern with the emergence of a new trade-focused middle class, to what extent do these deliberative spaces represent a narrow segment of Australian society? This is a harder question to answer than would appear at first glance. It has been observed that the notion of 'class' is subjective, particularly in a country like Australia where a shorter European history has led to less entrenched views of what constitutes social classes based on cultural capital (Hamilton, et al., 2007: 9). Indeed, there is evidence that most Australians identify themselves as 'middle class', reflecting a mix of social aspiration and avoidance of being a 'tall poppy' (Hamilton, et al., 2007).

Nevertheless, the question is relevant: if social media is an important emerging public sphere that may have real impacts on policy making, to what extent does it represent a narrow and privileged segment of the population? This concern plagued digital-media scholars in the early years of digital media, through recognition that 'early adopters' where more likely to come, if not from the educated and financial elite of society, then from those for whom the status quo was serving them nicely (Margolis & Resnick, 2000: 110). This represented a bottom-up view of the normalisation-hypothesis discussed in Chapter 2, that the privileged in society would use these new channels to ensure their favoured access to the sphere of government would remain unchallenged.

Times have changed, however, and the cost of accessing digital media has fallen considerably in the decade since Michael Margolis and David Resnick's work.[3] We need to explore to what extent privilege is still inscribed in this space. This is aided through figures 19 and 20, drawn from our surveys of users of political social media. The first figure shows that the distribution of respondents closely matches the distribution of incomes in Australia: a pyramid that rests on a small base (ABS, 2011). Between the social media we can see differences that largely reflect age composition of their user base (as demonstrated in Figure 17 above): the higher proportion of retirees in the CANdo group and students in the Facebook group skew their incomes lower than the average for the group. What is interesting is the educational attainment levels reported in Figure 20, which disproportionately includes Australians with university degrees, particularly higher degrees. These findings replicate similar research undertaken in the United States, which associates higher levels of education with political interest, rather than economic position (Kaye, et al., 2012: 9).

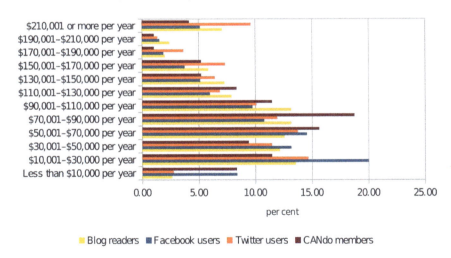

Figure 19: Gross household income, users of political social media (n = 1392)

Source: Author's research

---

3   In addition, positive access programs have been undertaken by governments in response to this 'digital divide' through community-based access programs (e.g. internet services provided in libraries) and the direct subsidy of access technologies (e.g. laptops in schools and the provision of digital set-top boxes for people on low incomes).

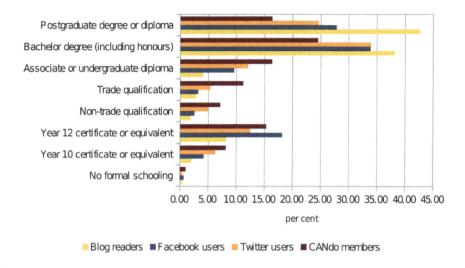

Figure 20: Highest level of education achieved, users of political social media (n = 1415)

Source: Author's research

These similarities and differences with the general public lead to the obvious question: is this important? This depends largely on the way the public sphere is viewed: if the public sphere is primarily a *deliberative space* for the exchange of information and formation of public preferences for policy makers (aka, the development of 'good ideas' and innovation), then broad economic representation combined with education might be seen as beneficial. In discussing the notion of collective intelligence in digital communities, Douglas Schuler sees the importance of having analytical skills and capacities to achieve new solutions to social problems (2004: 275, 7–8). Alternatively, if the public sphere is about *consensus building* then the disproportionate representation of certain types of people (those with the inclination or resources to undertake formal education) might only serve to drive a wedge between parts of society. This marks a considerable difference between the ideational and legitimising aspects of the notion of the public sphere.

Social media by the numbers

The long-form opinionistas: The Australian 'blogosphere'

Blogging represents one of the earliest forms of social media. Part genre (through the use of the chronological presentation of regular posts with a tendency towards informality), part technology platform (allowing authors to post material and enable comments to be attached to specific posts), blogs once represented *the* way for those outside of the media industry to court the attention of potentially large audiences. During the first decade of the new century these channels were regarded as one of those places where we were most likely to see the ambiguity between professional and amateur.[4] This interactive space led to conflicts at the time (as discussed in Chapter 2), but also encouraged creative engagement with the medium and experimentation in styles of public engagement and writing (Quiggin, 2006).

One of the most prominent early political blogs in Australia, Margo Kingston's *webdiary* resulted from the journalist being slowly pushed out of the Fairfax organisation and looking for an alternative channel for her views and opinions, eventually becoming independent of the company in 2005 through the use of readers' donations and contributions (Kingston, 2006). In this way, writers like Margaret Simons (2007) has identified blogging as part of the 'gift economy' — a cultural paradigm closely associated with the notions of the 'commons' (a shared space and public resource; Sievers, 2010: 3) and reciprocal altruism (a gratifications basis for participation).

While this is largely true — in that a self-supporting economic model for independent blogging has not presented itself in Australia (Ward and Cahill, 2007: 12) — there are a wide range of motivations behind blogging that include their use by academics (e.g. John Quiggin) and think tanks (e.g. The Interpreter, Catallaxy Files) to promote particular intellectual positions and ideas. From a more 'thermostatic' or functionalist perspective (see Media in an age of 'attention' economics, Chapter 6) there are prominent arguments that blogs have the potential to 'balance' the range of voices in the wider public sphere. Where a topic may not be well covered by commercial media (either because of media bias or due to market failure), low-cost digital publishing represents a perfect vehicle for counterpublic discourse. Examples range from blogs representing the view of the extreme left to right, but also those servicing specialist communities (for example, vegans or goths; Hodkinson, 2006: 187) and as embedded reservoirs of culture for extant social movements (see Digital media and movement (re)mobilisation, Chapter 5).

In the Australian context Axel Bruns and Debra Adams (2009: 90) have argued that the predominance of more left-leaning political blogs was a direct response to the perceived right-wing bias of the major media organisations.[5] A similar,

---

4   Whereas, by the end of the decade, the majority of political bloggers are journalists (Solly, et al., 2007: 121).
5   A view contested by some bloggers who reject the focus on situating blogs on a political continuum precisely because of their interactive and community-building nature (Garden, 2010: 20). Thus, the 'nominal' orientation of authors may not necessarily indicate that of their audience/commentators.

but alternative perspective is put forward by Frances Shaw's (2011) arguments that the Australian feminist blogosphere represents a 'crisis response' by feminists who use blogging as a form of counter-hegemonic discourse in direct reaction to dissonance with mainstream representations of women and their social movement. This latter view is less about the projection of an argument in the face of a dominant media ideology as much as active defence against an imposed subjectivity.

During the era of John Howards Coalition government, prominent right-wing blogs were based either in mainstream media organisations (such as Andrew Bolt's popular blog; http://blogs.news.com.au/heraldsun/andrewbolt) or have associations with commercial media. A good example of the latter would be the early prominent blogger of the right, Tim Blair, whose blog eventually became part of the Murdoch press (Goggin, 2010: 436). This absence has also been noted within the political community of the centre-right, who formed the Menzies House (www.menzieshouse.com.au) conservative community in 2010. Founded by a staff member of Cory Bernardi and Tim Andrews (see the discussion of the Australian Taxpayers Alliance, Chapter 5), the purpose of the site is to act as a platform to host content from this perspective and grow the number of authors from the right. In this respect, Menzies House has been only partially successful, with Andrews seeing the Australian party system's strong pressure against expressing deviant opinions as a barrier to the recruitment of politically active writers in this community (Personal interview: Tim Andrews, 22 May 2012).

This 'competitive' view focuses on the nature of public discourse as an elite activity that leads to a 'protracted competition for cultural hegemony' (George, 2009: 7). In the context of recent Australian politics, this is called the 'history wars' (or 'culture wars', drawing from similar arguments in the United States). The limitation of this view is that it focuses on political competition as zero-sum activity between binary positions.[6] This is at odds with the notion of the public sphere as a site for meaning creation (as opposed to the establishment of ideational dominance), while also ignoring the existence of centrist voices in the Australian blogosphere (for example, *Club Troppo* (clubtroppo.com.au) or Press Gallery Citizen Journalist (http://parliamenthouse.wordpress.com)).[7] What does support this 'elite-driven' view of blog influence is the level of educational attainment of blog users (as discussed in A *bourgeois* public sphere, this chapter),

---

6   Here, I would argue that the post-modern movement towards the deconstruction of binary oppositions is, in fact, reifying differences that may not exist.

7   Greg Jericho (2012: 48) identified 24 per cent of Australian political blogs as centrist, 49 per cent left-leaning and 27 per cent right leaning (n = 324).

combined with the disproportionate representation of public servants in the user base of political blogs when compared with the population overall (Figure 21, compared with approximately 16.56 per cent of the population as at June 2011).[8]

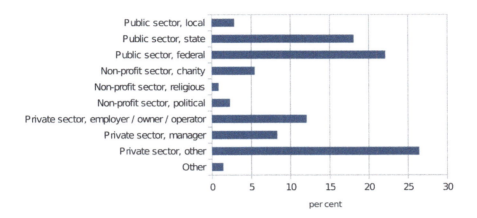

Figure 21: Political blog users, employment characteristics (n = 348)

Source: Author's research

The composition of blog users is significant in identifying the relationship between the discourse on these channels and connections to the sphere of government (in the 'conveyor belt' view of the public sphere moving ideas between spheres). At the civic level, political-blog users are active in political discourse, both online and off. This is demonstrated in Figure 22. Political-blog users, when compared with their non-political peers, are more likely to engage in interpersonal political dialogue, with a small, but significant group participating in persuasive political speech ('who to vote for'). This illustrates how issues developed in specific public sphere spaces 'break out' into the wider civic conversation about policy and politics in Australia. Other examples involve the identification of unique information contained in the discursive communities around blogs by journalists and other mainstream organisations that use these non-elite contacts as sources of specialist information.[9]

---

8   The blog-user research was undertaken in the first half of February 2012. Participation requests were published by a number of participating blogs. These blogs were divided into two groups: explicitly political blogs (*An Onymous Lefty*: Andrew Catsaras: Andrew Norton: *Commentary from Carlton*: *Hoyden About Town*; and, *Larvatus Prodeo*) and not-explicitly political blogs (*kootoyoo*, and *Library Clips*). Because of the nature of the request (a public post), this was also reprinted by additional political blogs (*Club Troppo, Poll Bludger* and *The Intepreter*).

9   An example being the 'slackbastard' anarchist blog maintained by Andy Fleming (a *nom de guerre*) (http://slackbastard.anarchobase.com), who has increasingly been used by mainstream media as an expert on the far right in Australia (Fleming, 2012).

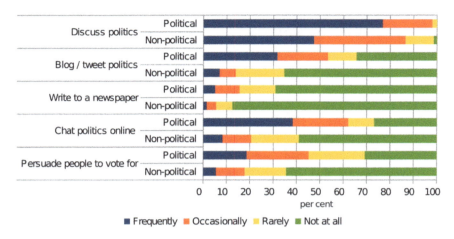

Figure 22: Discursive transfer: Political-blog users compared with general users (n = 580)

Source: Author's research

A more moderate notion of this thermostatic view is the idea that blogs can serve as non-exclusive checks on powerful institutions, particularly where existing sites of social oversight are ineffective (for example, in the cartel-party mode introduced in Chapter 2, or through a 'propaganda model' of capitalist media interests, discussed in Chapter 6). This represents an example of the use of these information sources by the 'monitorial citizen'. This notion of citizenship, proposed by Michael Schudson, talks about a type of individual who scans their political and media environment for issues that affect their personal and general interests and are willing and able to take action when these interests are placed at risk (1998). This idea expands upon the classical republican ideal for citizenship as focused on civic education for the participation in electoral politics, recognising the expanded range of political opportunities that are manifest following the 'rights revolution' of the 1960s (the increased capacity for direct litigation and other forms of administrative justice that stem from increased recognition of civil liberties), as well as new forms of political action (Kivisto, 2010: 262).

Examples of new forms of activism include political consumerism, stakeholder activism, and the increasingly common use of media campaigns attacking corporate brands to influence the policies of large commercial organisations. Two recent examples have been the advertiser boycotts aimed at the *Kyle and Jackie O Show* (Today FM) and the *Alan Jones Breakfast Show* (2GB) organised in response the male presenters' attitudes towards women (AAP, 2011). The latter example — still underway at the time of writing — is significant in its more partisan political implications, pertaining to Jones's statements that women in leadership roles are 'destroying the joint' (Farr, 2012) and an distasteful attack on the Prime Minister Gillard related to the death of her father (Aston, 2012a). The power of social-media users to mobilise a distributed campaign of letter writing aimed at advertisers led to Alan Jones's show losing a majority of major sponsors (Gardiner, 2012). This in turn emboldened the prime minister to attack sexist language in politics in the most vigorous manner of her premiership (ABC, 2012).

Looking at our survey data of blog users we can see that, while the readers are generally politically active overall, they are likely to have engaged in consumer activism, with over 80 per cent of users having 'Boycotted or bought special products for a political reason' at some time, over 60 per cent in the last year. In response to this, companies have become more active in monitoring social media for negative comments about their brands, increasing the value of political action to elicit a quick response from these organisations (Cox, et al, 2008: 6). This highlights the observation that the emphasis on explicitly 'political' blogs may be less important than the broader political impact of social-media participation on the political expressiveness of these citizens more generally (Bruns, et al, 2011).[10] Overall, Figure 23 demonstrates that blog users are willing to be politically expressive through a range of media (petition, direct interactions with elites, and through mass media).

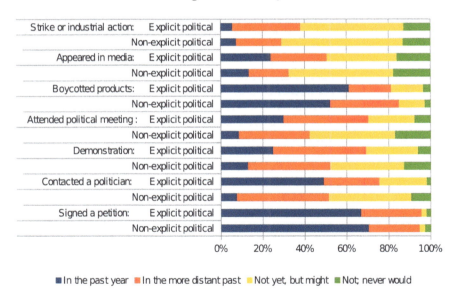

Figure 23: Political behaviour of blog users, comparative (n = 580)

Source: Author's research

---

10   Political parties have begun to court non-political bloggers in Australia to influence their discussion of government policy. An example would be the 2012 morning tea for 'mommy bloggers', hosted by the prime minister (Poole, 2012).

With specific regard to the history wars and the reporting of politics and public policy, this idea is important in explaining the way in which bloggers have 'taken on' the mainstream media organisations that provide the bread and butter coverage that regularly drives blog content. The notion of blogs as providing citizen oversight of institutionalised media in the same way that commercial media established itself through the political claim of a legitimate watchdog on the powerful (Palser, 2002) remains, however, contestable. During the 2010 federal election, then anonymous blogger Grog's Gamut became the focus of attention when his negative comments about the conduct of political journalism during the campaign were cited by the ABC's managing director.[11] This led to a News Corporation journalist 'outing' Grog's identity and employment as a senior public servant.

The extent to which this positively (as opposed to the reactionary model of the monitorial citizen) shapes public policy in Australia is uncertain. While the public sphere would argue that the formation of opinion and its transmission to the political elite represents the most powerful part of the public sphere's role in shaping policy, this is often hard to identify. From a more conventional media paradigm Matthew Marks (2007) argues that the failure of Australian bloggers to 'break news' means their impact on politics in this nation remains comparatively limited. The comparison here is with prominent bloggers in the United States, such as Matt Drudge (who was prominent in highlighting the Monica Lewinsky scandal) and Andrew Breitbart (influential in a number of scandals, particularly the publication of undercover videos showing staff of a community organisation network engaging in illegal activities). To date only a limited number of Australian bloggers have moved into more formal 'journalistic' activities, but these tend to be either time-limited (see I'm figgering on biggering, Chapter 6) or minor interventions into ongoing stories. An example of the latter would be the use of *Freedom of Information Act* requests by climate change sceptic Simon Turnill (*Australian Climate Madness* blog; www.australianclimatemadness.com) regarding reporting of email threats against scientists working at The Australian National University (Readfearn, 2012).

Alternatively, Bruns argues that while news-breaking might be largely beyond the resources of most bloggers, blogs can serve a valuable function in the media landscape through presenting a new editorial role: 'gatewatching' (2006: 15–16). Gatewatching is a form of online curatorship over information where relevant and interesting material is identified and drawn together for the blog audience. As information overload is a real problem online, these forms of

---

11   '... the voices of the public being heard more than ever before ... through blogs and the Twitter traffic. Half way through the campaign, the ABC Executive met on a Monday morning and discussed the weekend blog by the Canberra public servant, writing under the tag Grog's Gamut. It was a lacerating critique of the journalists following the candidates, their obsession with transient matters, the political scandal of the day. He met a chorus of praise and support, triggering a barrage of criticism of campaign coverage' (Scott, 2010: 4).

new editorial activities can provide a considerable service for individuals with specific interests, but who lack the time or specialist attention to cull important information from the wide range of sources available. An example of specialist aggregation service would be *Open and Shut* (http://foi-privacy.blogspot.com) maintained by Peter Timmins. Open and Shut aggregates together media articles, government reports and other news about freedom of information and privacy legislation issues in Australia. These content communities are important, not only in addressing market failures in specialist information provision, but in drawing together communities of interest, which has the potential to lead toward mobilisation into more direct political action.

#shortform

For those with a too limited attention span for blogs, Twitter is a popular way to jump into the social-media public sphere without the onerous task of establishing a blog or becoming a commentator in a blog community. While primarily a textual medium, Twitter is not necessarily a 'readers channel'.[12] Its constant flow of updates and interleaved responses makes it impossible to engage in a holistic understanding of any particular conversational thread. Instead it is ideal for downtime 'grazing' and hit-and-run participation with an opinion, counterpoint or non sequitur (Cross, 2011: 3–5). The flexibility of the medium comes from its use of social-networking tools to identify and follow other users, with the incorporation of hashtags that allow the formation of spontaneous discussion topics on the fly and without the need for a central organiser. Presently the exact number of Twitter accounts held by Australians is unknown, with estimates ranging from a low 550,000[13] to a high of 2.5 million.[14]

Interestingly, while often attacked as a trivial medium because of the default content limit of 140 characters (Hartwich, 2010), the high proportion of politicians, journalists and celebrities who have embraced the form in recent years have seen it receive considerable attention in mainstream media (for a detailed discussion of this, see Who's following whom, Chapter 6). There are also practical reasons for this level of visibility. Malcolm Farnsworth (2010) argues that the medium's inherent focus on the immediate makes those who use it seem responsive to their publics and 'in touch'. Twitter has also been one of the most visible of the 'convergent media',[15] being used to provide instant feedback

---

12   Though it does serve an important gate-watching function through the use of embedded links as positive referrals by posters.

13   An underestimate, based on those accounts that include Australia in the location (Bruns, 2011).

14   A second-hand report based on now unverifiable research by BinaryPlex/Tribalyistc (Sperti, 2010).

15   'Convergence' remains a contested term in the study of new media. Henry Jenkins (2004: 34) observes that 'Media convergence is more than simply a technological shift. Convergence alters the relationship between existing technologies, industries, markets, genres and audiences'. The importance here is that the technical is just one part of a wider *process* of change.

on television broadcasts through the selection of tweets marked with a show's hashtags. That Twitter is increasingly being taken seriously by established elites is also evident in the number of high-profile lawsuits it has generated in recent years,[16] as well as strong advocacy by civil society groups to encourage public figures to adopt the channel as an indicator of increased transparency. The website *TweetMP* (http://tweetmp.org.au), for example, not only provides a list of Federal Members of Parliament Twitter accounts, but facilitates users to send messages to their MP encouraging them to use the service as a way of being more democratically accountable.

This immediacy clearly responds to perceptions of social distance between citizens and elites that are associated with forces such as globalisation and the decline of locally based political party structures in Australia. Jim Macnamara (2010a: 155–57) sees this also as part of a 're-voicing' of the public: providing a means by which individuals achieve a sense of political efficacy through the ability to express their views in the public sphere *in a visible manner*. He would see this as a positive salve for the perceived 'democratic malaise' (see An electronic constituency surgery, this chapter) associated with the decline in participation in traditional political structures. From a cultural studies perspective, Jason Wilson (2011: 458) has highlighted the use of fake/parody profiles as a convergence of 'fan' and news-junkie cultures that allows 'average' users to break into the mediated political world that was once reserved for those with access to institutional power. The genre convergence here is reflective of the wider move towards 'soft news' — the use of comedy and satire within the context of news content and commentary highlighted by the popularity of television shows like *The Project* (Channel 10) (Duck, 2012).

Like most trade-offs, however, this is not a simple case of rebalancing the net level of political participation in society. The nature of the channel shapes the focus of political discussion and debate in the new public spheres it facilitates. In the case of Twitter, the machine-gun rapidity of the channel aligns itself (and accelerates) with the accelerating news-cycle (Turnbull, 2012: 60) and the emphasis of a lot of political communication (practitioner and journalistic) in focusing on only the most immediate issue or political event (Parmelee & Bichard, 2012). This is not a unique observation; other forms of communication have been long recognised for the ability to adjust the flow of events. Photography, for example, has particular implications for shaping meaning through its ability to 'freeze time' and highlight or capture a specific aspect of an event (Humphreys, 2008: 58). The implications of Twitter's effect on political temporality are mixed. For the average user, Twitter allows them to be 'in the action', part of the

16 For example, the threat of litigation against Canberra-based academic Julie Posetti by the editor of the *Australian* (see Chapter 6); Lynton Crosby and Mark Textor suing Labor MP Mike Kelly over a tweet questioning their polling methodology in 2012; Berkovic, 2012.

evolving narrative-making of public events. For elites it provides the ability for high visibility and responsiveness, but — gaffes aside[17] — at the cost of agenda control. Twitter, and the 'rapid-response' political communication model in general, have reduced the agenda-setting power of political elites today.

This is not to say that Twitter presents an anarchic medium of disconnected individuals 'shouting into the void' (Green, 2011). In their analysis of the semantic content of discussion around the #WikiLeaks hashtag, Simon Lindgren and Ragnar Lundström (2011: 1015) demonstrate the relationship of each tweet within a shared community of discourse (see Online anarchists and the democratisation of hacking, Chapter 5). Through the use of a set of communicative tools (slogans and frames) within and through the Twitter feed (links to external sources and media coverage of the issue), this community develops and sustains a shared frame of reference, set of discursive conventions, and flow of dialogue about the political issues of concern to them. This type of research demonstrates the power of these fluid media to demonstrate how simple structural characteristics of a technology can assist in the development of emergent communities and patterns of social interaction (Fuchs, 2008: 134–35).

It is therefore 'natural' (or demonstrates a degree of automaticity) that this medium would develop concentrations around political issues and debates which, over time, exhibit enough ideational stability to be seen as genuine discursive public spheres, rather than simply places for pure self-gratification. In political discourse on Twitter this is clearly demonstrated as topics move towards more specific areas of discussion. This is depicted in Illustration 6, which compares snapshots of two Australian political topics, one general and one specific. This means that this medium has more 'value' (in the classic Habermassian sense of practical consensus formation in the public sphere) in the specific over the general, a finding which reinforces the view presented in Chapter 2 about the comparatively frivolous nature of some political discussion online associated with general observation-making about politics and politicians.

Turning to survey data collected from Australian Twitter users[18] we can see that this channel attracts a similar user base to that of political blogs: generally well educated and engaged in politics online and offline. Again, survey data demonstrates that Twitter participation does not substitute for other, more

---

17 Such as the example of then leader of the opposition Barry O'Farrell's accidental public tweeting of a private exchange where he called the prime minister a 'ranga' (redhead) (Jackson, 2010).

18 The research used two twitter profiles with embedded requests to complete the survey instrument. One profile contacted active twitter users posting using relevant hashtags (#auspol, #qldpol, #nswpol, #actpol, #vicpol (excluding policing references), #taspol, #sapol (excluding Philippines references), #wapol, #ntpol), who used the words 'Gillard' and 'Abbott' in posts and users with 'Australian politics', including in their bios (through the search engine tweepz.com). The second profile contacted a geographically disbursed group of Australians using the tweepz.com search tool to identify Australian Twitter users based on location. The survey research was undertaken between 14 December 2011 and 12 January 2012.

traditional forms of participation in either Twitter users who employ the medium for political or non-political purposes. While political Twitter users are more likely to be members of parties, online and offline advocacy groups and local citizens groups than their peers from the non-political sample, they are not more or less likely to be 'joiners' overall.[19]

Illustration 6: Twitter conversations: #auspol and #nbn (29 March 2012) (user tags obscured)

Source: Twitter

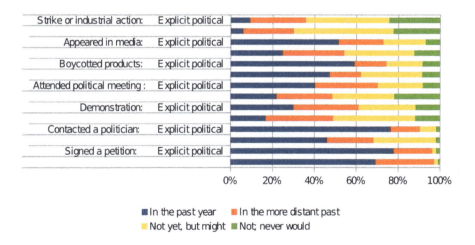

Figure 24: Political behaviour of Twitter users, comparative (n = 312)

Source: Author's research

---

19 Non-political twitter users have greater representation in social groups, sporting organisations, and — interestingly — unions.

This flows through to the level of political activity undertaken by Twitter users (Figure 24), which, like that of blog users, is high. Political Twitter users, however, are more likely to have 'contacted or appeared in the media' for political purposes as well as 'contacted a politician, government official'. This is not surprising given the high proportion of politicians and media professionals who use the channel. One additional observation is that difference between political and non-political Twitter users' political activities is more considerable than that for blog users (Figure 23, this chapter). This is likely to be explained by the higher level of education of blog users (4.10 per cent are more likely to have a bachelors degree or equivalent and 15.21 per cent are more likely to have a postgraduate degree or equivalent). The implications of this are complex. While Twitter use appears to be strongly correlated with political mobilisation, this is moderated by educational differences between these channels.

All things being equal, it would appear that Twitter use is a stronger predictor of an individual being involved in other political activities. Non-participation appears not to be explained by either slacktivist arguments about expended political energy, nor does it appear that the channel promotes political cynicism. The combative tone of a high proportion of the discussion seen on Twitter does not significantly weaken the political trust of political Twitter users. Across four of the five measures of trust in government,[20] this group were less cynical of the capacity and motivations of government than the control group of non-political users. The one exception to this, interestingly, was in response to the proposition 'The government doesn't care what people like me think'. Thus, while overall more positive towards the government than the average Twitter user, political Twitter users see a deficit in the effectiveness of the political system to identify their demands. Twitter, as a public medium, therefore, appears a rational solution to this deficit through the broadcasting of their interests and concerns into the public sphere. As Twitter content (both substantive and in terms of aggregate trends — 'trending topics') is increasingly being picked up and reported by the media (see Chapter 6), this is a useful channel to amplify one's opinions and concerns.

Social networking services and politics

Over the past decade in Australia, interest in the political role of social networking services (SNS) (initially focused on MySpace and presently on the market leader, Facebook) has developed. There are a number of sources for this. First, profile-based SNS services have rapidly come to rival email as one of the most popular online applications (Vascellaro, 2009). As at January 2011,

---

20   Most of the time we can trust people in government to do what is right; federal politicians know what ordinary people think; people in government usually look after themselves; and, government is mostly run for big interests.

Facebook contained 9.3 million profiles for Australian residents,[21] over half of the adult population (Cowling, 2011b). Aside from membership, two-thirds of Australian internet users view content on the site (Nielsen, 2010a). Second, SNSs have been the focus of two recent high-profile election campaigns: the 2007–08 presidential race in the United States and the 2007 Australian federal election (Small, 2008a). In these races, the role of younger voters has been identified as playing a significant role. For Obama, younger voter turnout was important in the non-compulsory electoral setting of that country.

In the Australian context, Ben Eltham has talked about a 'young voters theory' (2007) putting emphasis on a range of policy debates (particularly industrial relations) that are of concern to younger voters. These voters are less likely to have a strong party alignment, and are subject to increased social mobility. Thus, the role of social media and SNSs in shaping their political decision-making is increasingly important. Valdis Krebs talks about the context of political decision-making for this group as best characterised as 'social voting': 'the social networks, voters are embedded in, exert powerful influences on [electoral] behavior' (2005). As discussed in Figure 17, these SNS are employed more by younger voters, serving as an ideal match for this constituency (Ward, 2008: 13; Howell & Da Silva, 2010), particularly as stable patterns of mass-media consumption (television viewing) break down.

Facebook users who demonstrate a political interest[22] are like other social-media users (particularly Twitter) in their level of political participation (Figure 25). Where this group differs from other social-media users is in their higher level of memberships. As we can see in Figure 26, Facebook users with political interests are active in a range of political and non-political groups. Most relevant for this discussion is their high level of party membership, and extremely high level of participation in political action groups that work predominantly online. This should not be surprising, as the nature of Facebook's social networking system reinforces and supports existing relationships, as well as providing access to new wholly virtual ones. In this way we can depart from Negroponte's notion of the digital environment as 'place without space' (1996: 165–66), but one that overlays the real and the simulated world in mundane, as well as interesting, ways (Dean, 2010: 36).

---

21 Source: http://facebook.com; 4 January 2012.
22 The research on political Facebook users was undertaken between 9 August 2011 and 23 January 2012. Two recruitment methods were employed. First, requests for participation were posted to political group walls. Second, targeted advertisements were delivered to Facebook users resident in Australia, over the age of 18, who included an interest in politics in their biographies ($N = 22,360$).

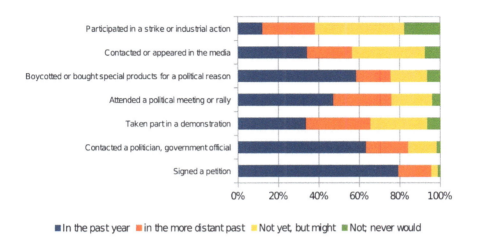

Figure 25: Political behaviour of Facebook users (n = 543)

Source: Author's research

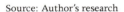
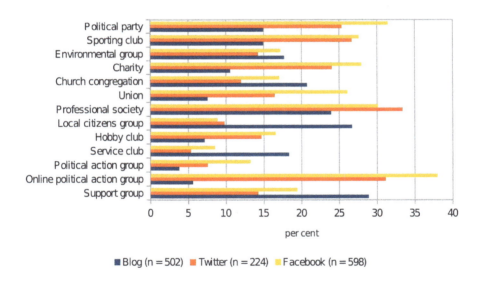

Figure 26: Propensity to group membership among social media users

Source: Author's research

The immediate impact of this may not be great. Kim Bale observes that the majority of these political groups and online causes have comparatively limited success in converting their popularity into more tangible political resources (particularly money) (2010). While the idea of political organisation via Facebook is viewed as a simple and low-cost method of converting passive support into politically useful resources, the reality is that these channels require considerable organisational effort in cultivating supporters, maintaining interest, and demonstrating legitimacy and tangibility. The predominant use of SNSs for personal news may undermine its channel credibility when topics shift from the personal to the societal. There is some evidence that more established channels (email and print) are still preferred sources for donation appeals, even by younger donors (Engelhardt, 2011: 64). This has implications for the cost-benefit calculus in adopting these tools. Converting 'likes' into resources through active strategies to mobilise and motivate their supporter base is a creative and time-intensive activity (such as preparing content for re-posting, Illustration 7). The upshot of this is that, just as it has become easier to connect with supporters, the number of requests of them increases, keeping the 'conversion' costs — costs spent on supporters relative to their returns — comparative over time (Hart & Greenwell, 2009).

GO YOU GOOD THING!!

Revolution - Block Aid Action against Woodside - Save the Kimberley
www.youtube.com

http://www.savethekimberley.com/ Honorable Tony Burke MP, Minister for Sustainability, Environment, Water, Population and Communities, PO Box 6022, House of ...

 13 July at 22:34 · Share

Illustration 7: Referral to advocacy website (user tags obscured)

Source: Facebook

Proponents of SNS-based non-profit marketing see these criticisms as over-focusing on immediate financial benefits, cultivation of one-off 'transactional' donations, and the low unit donation rate largely seen to date (Chen, Te Fu, 2011). What these channels do allow is ongoing low levels of interaction between organisations and supporters, allowing for progressive reporting on fundraising activities to provide donors and potential donors with the social proof that their contribution has been matched by others (Margetts, et al., 2009), reassurance that 'paltry' levels of support are not wasted (relating to the building of personal efficacy; Shearman & Yoo, 2007), and fast turnarounds on information about the impact of contributions. Over time these interactions build shared identity with causes, and allow non-profit organisations to cultivate long-term donors through their lifecycle (e.g. picking up younger supporters who may be low-unit donors, but retain their support as they move into paid employment). Alternatively, the provision of applications to support political causes (i.e. Causes, Pledgie, Petitions on Facebook) that provide rapid access to social networks, online world-of-mouth advertising, and cause infrastructure[23] can allow for effective promotion of 'flash-causes' (Watson, 2009). These causes, like the Kony 2012 campaign,[24] are often aligned with wider media coverage or specific events, and this level of attention can be capitalised on through the use of cause applications to capture and stabilise a community of interest.

Like my cause: Microactivism

When thinking about quasi-virtual political organisations it is important to consider the impacts that they have on the political activity of members (mobilisation from membership to action), and the way these associations impact on the wider communicative landscape. Following the slacktivist argument, some have questioned if participation in these types of 'microactivism' results in extended and enduring membership in social-media causes (Scholz, 2010: 27). This may put the cart before the horse: virtual organisation membership is often an extension of political life. As Jodi Dean argues, this fits with the nature of social-media practice that focuses on the personal connection with actual experience, the shared lifeworld (common understandings) (2010: 48–49). In a similar vein, José Marichal argues that microactivism enables self-identity creation and the development of 'activist identities'. Through the provision of an anonymous space/'front stage', individuals can experiment with political causes and activist personas in a public, but relatively safe place (2010: 6,15).

Here we can examine the value of political behaviour from the top-down as well as bottom-up. Reflecting the tendency of concept proliferation that still exists in this area of scholarship, Trebor Scholz uses the term 'nano-activism' to describe this form of behaviour (this will be picked up in Chapter 5). This is seen to have a different orientation: rather than focusing on the individual's engagement with the campaign (as in the above usage), the prospective campaign organiser might look at microactivism as a way in which activism can be purposively disaggregated into smaller and smaller component parts. This allows participation at lower levels of commitment (again picking up on Sachiyo Shearman's and Jina Yoo's research into 'paltry donation'; 2007). Just like the new-found value of micro-payments, micro-/nano-activism can be effectively co-ordinated through digital media at a lower transaction cost. This increases the number of low-level contacts and interactions that individuals may have with campaigns, without undermining the value of either each small act of participation to the cause, nor in identity-building. Research that finds a comparatively low level

---

23   Such as petition systems, email gateways and e-commerce (payment) systems.
24   An online campaign developed by the charity Invisible Children aimed to highlight that Lord's Resistance Army commander Joseph Kony who remained at large in central Africa.

of direct translation from this type of activism, therefore, does not understate the potential of these spaces to develop political awareness and commitment. Indeed, concerns that low conversion rates indicate a weakening of political commitment may be unfounded. The low-cost of establishing a new online political group will invariably lead to both a proliferation of groups, as well as increased awareness of groups and cases that fail to effectively mobilise participation beyond the confines of social media. Clearly we run the risk of visibility bias towards online groups.

One way of examining in greater detail the political visibility and use of Facebook across the Australian population, therefore, is through interrogating the political content of material posted to this service.[25] This allows us to delineate between static 'affiliation' (liking a cause and having this part of the user's profile) and the generation and re-posting of political content. In addition to the extent of political material posted, this method also allows the content's character to be evaluated.

In the most general analysis, Table 7 demonstrates that the vast majority of content posted to users' Facebook walls is not political in nature (less than half of one per cent of posts made concerned institutional or issue-based politics).[26] This said, almost one in 10 users studied *did* post at least one political post to their wall during the study period of approximately one month's worth of wall posts. This tends to reiterate the general observation that Australians are not generally publicly politically expressive individuals. While it is difficult to determine in this context what contributes a large or small amount of political content, it would appear that Facebook is not a site for widespread political expression online by Australians. Even so, making political posts is not a social turn-off, as there is no correlation between a user's number of friends and their propensity to post political content on their wall (−0.015).

What is interesting about the Australian public's use of social networking services to exchange political information is the considerable *difference* that exists between the source of political content on SNSs compared with other environments. If we compare the Facebook research results with the political web-browsing behaviour discussed in What do voters *do* online (Chapter 2), we see in Figure 27 that users are far more likely to self-generate political content

---

25   This analysis was based on a 2011 study of the content of 600 Australian residents' Facebook wall posts. Using a new Facebook user profile with no friendship ties, quota sampling was employed to randomly select user profiles with walls that were visible to the researcher (public). Quota categories were geographic, attempting to get a representative sample of Australians based on their location of residence (by state or territory and by rural or urban location). In addition, an equal number of men and women were sought. Users were excluded on the basis of: newness (too little content), predominant use of non-English (due to translation issues), or non-individual profiles (largely commercial profiles).

26   This study employed the same definition of 'political' as employed in the 2010 voter panel study, see footnote 37, Chapter 2.

on SNSs rather than simply repost material prepared by political organisations. This is illustrated by the figure's low numbers of 'institutional' content having been posted.

		All	Men	Women	Capital	Urban (non capital)	Rural
Posts (entries)	n	29,660	15,201	14,459	19,028	9524	1108
	Political (n)	136	68	68	110	22	4
	Political (%)	0.45	0.44	0.47	0.57	0.23	0.36
Posters (people)	n	600	309	291	382	193	25
	Political (n)	55	22	33	37	16	2
	Political (%)	9.16	7.11	11.34	9.68	8.29	8

Table 7: Political use of Facebook

Source: Author's research

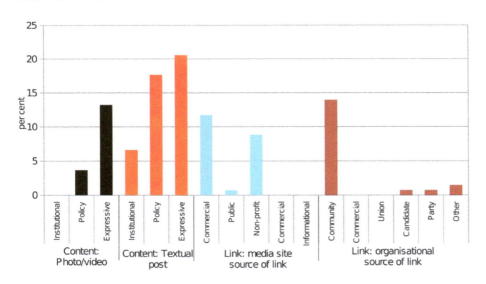

Figure 27: Political content on Facebook wallposts, by type

Source: Author's research

In alignment with Marichal's identify formation argument, we do see that text and media posts tend to be more expressive than substantive: 'I support' statements rather than policy detail. An example of this is seen in Illustration 8, a pro-trucking wall post made in the period following the release of the

Commonwealth's carbon pricing policy that does not lead into a political or policy-oriented discussion, but one about shared identity (as car aficionados in this case).

Illustration 8: Pro-trucking Facebook post, ascii cut and paste (user tags obscured)

Source: Facebook

While some of this material does come from third parties, the sources are interesting. Unlike the previous study looking at browsing habits, links to political news sources only marginally favour mainstream commercial media, with a high level of representation of non-profit (non-public) media being distributed through Facebook. Similarly, outbound political links largely ignore established political organisations (parties and candidates), and favour non-profit community organisations. This, to some extent, demonstrates the influence of applications like Causes (www.causes.com) in assisting these organisations to gain a degree of visibility, even if their financial benefit remains in question.

Two-step flow, 2.0

The discussion of the political content and practices of social-media users is relevant to an aspect of the notion of the public sphere: that of political discourse within these new sites for opinion formation, as well as the mobilisation of these individuals within the realm of conventional politics. Following our discussion of the two-step flow model (Social media as a deliberative space, this chapter), we can also explore the question of whether these individuals are not simply politically expressive, but are active as opinion leaders outside of social media.

This is significant for two reasons. First, if, as we have identified, those engaging in these new public spheres are in the minority, we need to question if their deliberation and ideational exchange 'spills over' into wider political discourse. This is similar to the way commercial publications measure both their sales figures and secondary (or 'pass-along') readers to measure their real impact (Lee & Johnson, 1999: 192). If political social-media participants are engaged in political discussion outside the social-media space, ideas move between these on and offline communities. Second, and with relevance to the slacktivist arguments, it is also important to determine if participation in online political discussion extinguishes or expends levels of political engagement outside of these fora.

To this end we can construct Figure 28. This shows the willingness of social-media users who are interested in politics to engage in political dialogue outside of that setting. The figure is drawn from the survey data discussed above, with specific responses to a scenario where the respondent has the opportunity to have a conversation with a person who holds an opposing political view during a long journey in a confined space: the 'stranger on a train scenario'.[27] The purpose of this question is to determine the individual's comfort in engaging in political dialogue outside of a socially safe space. By nature, the train is public, but has a degree of intimacy, and the timing of the scenario means it would be difficult for the respondent to disengage from the conversation easily.

Figure 28 demonstrates that the users of political social media self-report as being willing to engage in this form of speech. Interestingly, we can also see that there is a tendency for increased willingness to talk to this stranger based on the degree to which participation in the medium in question is a 'performative' act. Blog users, for example, can be active or passive in their engagement with the blog and its content, whereas membership of Twitter and Facebook political communities tends to be defined more by participation. Similarly, the 'walled

---

27   For example, the CANdo respondents were asked this question: 'You are taking a five-hour train trip and there is a person in sitting in your compartment who thinks that government regulation of business should be expanded to better protect the rights of workers. Would you talk to this person to get to know their point of view better, or wouldn't you think that worth your while?'

garden' nature of the channel employed appears to be correlated to a willingness to talk. Facebook and CANdo provide the opportunity for communities to self-select towards homogeneity through explicit membership requirements (CANdo's rules of membership, enforced by the site's management) or social pressure against 'trolling' political groups[28] that demonstrates the inclusiveness of members 'inside' this group.

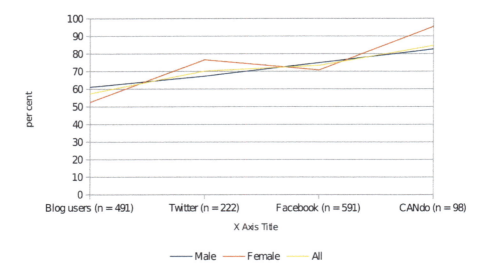

Figure 28: Stranger on a train scenario, willingness to talk

Source: Author's research

This confirms research undertaken in the United States that participation in social media and SNSs can encourage active political participation through cultivating individual's *capacity* for political speech (Fernandes, et al., 2010). This is a key methodological point, as it orients us to the distinction between action and agency, behaviour and capacity. The capacities approach focuses on the resources individuals have which permit the achievement of their objectives and desires (Qizilbash, 2008). We can see that the 'front stage' of social media both serves as a place to develop identity, but also communicative skills in areas of one's political interest. This varies between the different social media, which reiterates the demographic differences between the groups identified above. This is illustrated in Figure 29, but demonstrates a close tracking between these

---

28   Claire Hardaker (2010: 237) defines a troll as a 'user who constructs the identity of sincerely wishing to be part of the group in question, including professing, or conveying pseudo-sincere intentions, but whose real intention(s) is/are to cause disruption and/or to trigger or exacerbate conflict for the purposes of their own amusement'. This definition captures the hostility aspect of trolling (as opposed to playful disruption) that fits well with the 'stranger on a train' scenario.

interests and the degree to which these issues get covered in the mainstream media (this is discussed in Chapter 6's consideration of mass media and agenda setting). It is interesting in that, if interest is shaped by the conventional media agenda, the finding illustrated in Figure 24 regarding the selection of outbound links for posting to SNS walls points to the translation of commercial media agendas through social media: annotation rather than reiteration.

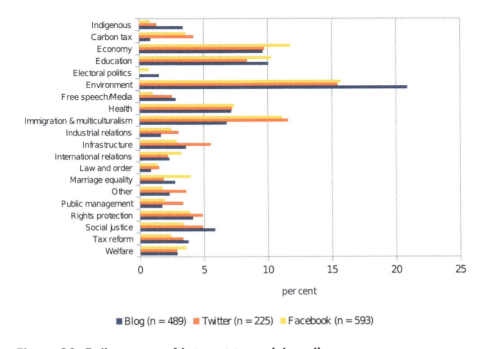

Figure 29: Policy areas of interest to social media users

Source: Author's research

Channel bias: Social media is 'leftist'

At this point it is worth exploring an essentialist proposition about social media and politics: that they tend to be more aligned with the politics of 'the left'. This argument stems from a number of sources. Empirically, in the United States, Lee Rainie and Aaron Smith's survey work has identified 'liberals' as more likely to join SNSs than conservatives (2012: 4). Generally, left-wing political ideology is commonly associated with underlying communitarian principles (Browne & Kubasek, 1999) that, in effect, point to greater participation in social commons. In this observation we can also see how the focus of research into new social movements in the 1960s and 1970s (for more detail, see Chapter 5) also tends to focus attention on existing organisations in support of social movements of the left and see how they have used a variety of digital media to create a virtual presence similar to their physical one (see Illustration 9).[29] Increasingly, however, social media has been employed with considerable vigour by conservative organisations.

Illustration 9: South Australian Feminist Collective Facebook page (user tags obscured)

Source: Facebook. Used with permission

In the Australian context it is useful to know if these media have a political bias in their user base in examining if those on the 'left' of the political spectrum are more interested in online community activities than those on the 'right'. While this argument looks simplistic, there are foundations to the hypothesis we can see from theories of political action (that core beliefs about communitarian policy preferences will be exhibited in surface behaviours that are measurable; Sabatier & Jenkins-Smith, 1993) and simple observation that members of the Australian Greens are over-represented in the survey responses of Twitter, Facebook and blog users collected for this book. We can test this through seeing if there is a correlation between digital-media users' place on the political spectrum (inferred through party identification) and the number of different memberships they report. Taking the baseline respondents to the

---

29   Again, this does not mean this uptake is automatic. Petray's (2011: 927) work on indigenous activism using new media has argued that the comparative under-utilisation of these technologies reflects a cultural preference towards oral communication. This is irrespective of the potential value in channelling together a geographically distributed set of communities with similar interests.

Twitter and blog readers' studies (the non-political respondents) we can see there is no correlation between place on the political spectrum and the tendency towards being a 'joiner' (−0.002, n = 136).

Overall, generational characteristics appear to be a stronger factor on the political mix of social-media users (Greens voters are more likely to be younger overall; Phillips, 2010), however, we should also recall the thermostatic hypothesis presented at the start of this section: coming out of an era of Liberal Party political dominance, social media may serve as a site for counterpublics. If the former, the conservatism associated with ageing is likely to counterbalance this in the longer term. If the latter, it points more strongly to counter-organisation against majority opinion. One alternative explanation that we will turn to in the next chapter is that the predominance of the left online is the result of 'political correctness': a silencing of opinion out of step with the majority.

The opinion makers

The classic public-sphere model involves an organic process of the formation of public opinion. That is, a spontaneous process of the formation and mobilisation of public opinion from the bottom up. In this way, the public sphere acts as a regulator of authority through the identification of under-serviced issues, the generation of new ideas, and the reification of political interests. This view places considerable emphasis on those in the sphere of government to moderate and mediate between competing demands and ideas. The expansion of mass society (with mass education, political participation and enfranchisement) makes this a more complex task. It is difficult not simply because of the manipulation of rational publics by self-interested interest groups and factions, but also due to the scale of demands that need be synthesised (Power Inquiry, 2006).

From the bottom-up perspective, the complexity of the policy environment encourages the growth of intermediating bodies, which provide individuals with the expertise to synthesise and systematise policy preferences (Lehmbruch, 1983). While this provides a rational solution to the problem of complexity, it also introduces the principal-agent problem reviled by public choice economists and feared by political elites (that engagement with 'representative bodies' does not deliver the support of these constituencies because they are not aligned with these interests; Strolovitch, 2006: 894). The extent to which social media provides an alternative for individual citizens to directly express policy views appears limited to the 'charmed circle' of the engaged and educated.[30] In response we have seen experiments in the creation of public opinion through

---

30 As Ariadne Vromen's (2007) research demonstrates, this reaches across generations and the notion of an emerging, automatically engaged generation of the 'born digital' is overstated.

the development of virtual spaces, and new channels of opinion to elites. These social-media spaces represent an older paradigm of online politics associated with the 'electronic democracy' initiatives pioneered in the 1990s (Aikens, 1996). While systematic study of these initiatives remains to be undertaken,[31] we can explore this area through examining a number of case examples.

Yopinion

Yopinion.com.au ('Your Opinion') was an experiment by a number of undergraduate university students studying politics and government and backed by some 'angel' investors from familial social networks. Using a centralised discussion-focused website, *Yopinion* employed a range of media (text, video, social) to attract participation from younger Australians (under 25) for informed policy debate and information exchange. This reflects the deliberate formation of counterpublic public spheres by elites within this cohort. To facilitate discussion, the site's staff used the mechanism of 'leader' stories presenting contemporary policy issues, pacing the publication of these stories to encourage deliberative discussion in depth. This took inspiration from the type of policy coverage seen in news magazines: more detailed and neutral coverage aimed to allow the readers to take a position on the material presented. In this way the objectives of the site were strongly influence by the rationalism of Habermas's view of the public sphere (personal interview: Dougal Robinson, 12 March 2012).[32]

The site's success was modest, growing over time to attract about 700 members and closing in early 2012. Yopinion's staff used a variety of methods to engage with their potential audience, but found video and Facebook the most effective way to connect to their target audience. In a deliberate attempt to improve the tone of discussions (civility), they required posters to be anonymous. Possibly because of this, the site struggled with recruitment and conversion (from readers to commenters and writers), reducing its effectiveness and the ability of the operators to leverage its patronage into a long-term viable model (either through partnership with other organisations or to pitch summaries of its members' opinions as a representative sample). These problems show the difficulty in building a self-sustaining community from scratch: constant effort was required to produce activity on the site that, in the end, wore the organisers

---

31   This is a methodologically complex question and research will require care and attention to identify not just 'public' public spheres, but the use of new media *within* intermediating organisations to increase their consultation and capacity for representation of members. This latter area of activity allows representative groups (e.g. interest groups) to make strong claims about their capacity to 'deliver' the views of members to political elites.

32   Additionally, this deliberate choice was in response to what the founders' saw as the style of headline-driven writing in online news media in Australia, a problem exacerbated by the tendency for the effectiveness of online writing to be driven by click-through rates.

down financially. Failing to meet this 'critical mass' limited the founders' ability to free themselves from the intensive efforts of content generation, but also the ability to make a claim to legitimacy associated with the size of participating membership.

Tell 'em

Attempting to match limited resources with lower barriers to participation, *Tell 'em Australia* (www.tellem.net.au) is an example of an intervention into the Australian party system. Founded in late 2011, the website undertakes weekly polls of Australians against national and state-based issues. These polls are deliberately yes/no choices drawn from suggestions from site users and current affairs.[33] As results of the polls are intended to be sent to MPs, *Tell 'em Australia* collects participants' postcodes as the key means of verifying and reviewing the distribution of participants (*Tell 'em Australia*, 2011). While initially promoting the site through social media (particularly Twitter), the operators are aware of the problems associated with sample bias and the digital divide, attempting to target conventional media to promote their service beyond the world of social media.

While their site emulates the use of simple polling on the websites of national news organisations, the site operators see their position as independently attempting to frame their questions in a neutral way, facilitating agenda-setting from the participants through their input into question writing. The origins of the site lie in their personal conviction that the Australian political system is unresponsive to citizens, particularly due to the impact of parties' increased control over the policy position of MPs (personal interview: Christine Dodson, 6 January 2012). As a conduit between MPs and constituents, the site is the embodiment of the delegate model of representation seen in the motivations behind the formation of Senator Online, though without the heavy exceptions of participation (attendance, volunteering, financial donation) seen by that party (see Senator Online, Chapter 2). Citing a learning-by-doing philosophy, the site demonstrates how private individuals experiment with creating democratic fora at comparatively low cost and with the ability to create large communities of interest quickly (the site reached approximately 1200 individual survey respondents[34] within the first month of operations).

---

33 Seen as a leveller of participation between the highly engaged and those with lower levels of engagement.
34 Newspoll, by comparison, builds a deliberative sample of approximately 1800 respondents.

An electronic constituency surgery

The comparatively modest levels of participation in these 'third party' sites makes their impact to date modest at best. Attempts to increase the autonomy and responsiveness of MPs remains a windmill at which democratic reformers continue to tilt, regardless of the structural and historical tendency for centralisation in Australia (Mulé, 2001: 20; Jupp & Sawer, 2001: 262). While Tell 'em's founders' lack of experience inside the party system is reflected in their binary view of individual MPs versus party control, rather than also as active members of party and parliamentary decision-making, there does seem to be traction with some MPs expressing interest in the development of the service. Indeed, access to decision-makers is an important determinant in the success or failure of many of these projects, as participants make a rational choice to invest time based on the likelihood of policy impact (Walsh, 2007: 11). In one way, third-party sites like this can encourage those MPs seeking to challenge party policy with data derived from polling the electorate. This can only occur outside of the party machine. Previous attempts by MPs to use online fora and polling have encountered problems where these results were generated through Members' personal websites. A good example is that of former MP Mark Latham who, prior to his time as Labor leader, established a personal polling site for his electorate, *Direct Democracy in Werriwa*, as a means to overcome perceived disconnection between the public and elected representatives (Bishop, et al., 2002). The forum was discontinued when it became clear that it would serve only to place the MP at odds with party policy.

This problem has not stopped parliamentarians experimenting with building digital public spheres. Possibly the best known and longest running recent example would be Senator Kate Lundy's (ALP, ACT) Public Sphere events — with the name giving us a very clear view of the Senator's self-conscious engagement with the Habermasian ideal. While the examples above provide(d) ongoing digital spaces for participation, Lundy's events focused on the identification of, and deliberation on, specific policy issues in a time-limited manner using an array of technologies and social-media channels to provide a structured consultation process (including collaborative idea generation and limited voting to determine the idea agenda).

To do this the Lundy and her staff established a methodology that permitted comparatively open discussion (Lundy, 2009), but also focused on producing tangible policy-related outputs:

1. Preparation of the topic, including achieving 'buy in' from the relevant minister and key stakeholders — by nature this means that agenda setting remains somewhat removed from the discursive process and is pushed back into the elite-controlled initiation process.

2. Consultation, promotion and collection of comparatively unstructured initial feedback and input through a variety of formats.

3. Public Sphere 'Camp', a physical and virtual event aimed at drawing together and focusing discussions and recommendations.

4. Post-camp consultation and development of findings.

5. Reporting to the relevant minister.

Here, the flexibility of the platform tools is important: a channel can serve a number of roles within this methodology. Twitter, for example, can be a useful constituent of the discursive space in the early part of the process, while shifting to being a secondary data-collection tool in the physical meeting context. The use of physicality is interesting and important, reflecting international research that shows how commitment to the objectives of virtual communities can be strengthened through offline events and interactions (Rosen, et al., 2011).

To date Lundy has run three Public Sphere consultations within her area of specific interest (High Speed Bandwidth, Government 2.0, and ICT and the Creative Industries).[35] Participation in these events has increased over time, with the final event attracting 800 contributors. The impact of this participation on policy process is less clear, however, with ideas moving into the closed world of elite politics at this point. What this 'top-down' (or at least, top-initiated) model sacrifices is the enduring character of other e-democracy spaces for the promise of access to policy-makers. What this 'top-down' (or at least, top-initiated) model sacrifices is the enduring character of other e-democracy spaces for the promise of access to policy-makers. These initiatives are a good example of the use of an e-democracy platform to provide capacity to participants. As Lundy observes, this provides participants with a simple exchange: 'tell me what you think, and we'll provide a means by which we can package that up and deliver it in the most effective way to government.' The notion of this e-democracy initiative as a 'project' that can be 'delivered' to a public is misleading, however, with Lundy arguing that the fit between her use of a variety of social media in these projects and the topics themselves is a natural alignment of the audience with their 'natural' environment. Thus, following the observation that policy begets politics (Lowi, 1964), the Public Sphere initiatives' focus on the technology community served to facilitate the development of the technology as an act of co-creation. Clearly this presents questions about the capacity to regularise this practice and extend it outside of the technology context (participants in these examples had high levels of capability with the technology platforms coming into the exercise).

---

35 ALP NSW Parliamentary Secretary for Transport Penny Sharpe ran a 'NSWsphere' in 2009 using this model focusing on Government 2.0 for that state (Tindal, 2009).

The likelihood of this to be expanded more widely is questionable. While Lundy sees the presence of a number of 'tech savvy' parliamentarians as a key resource for members and senators interested in expanding their engagement with online public spheres, it is unclear if this would be elaborated to the extent that the public sphere initiatives have been to date. This has a lot to do with the question of motivation and the benefits of experimentation in new forms of constituent interaction. Interestingly, therefore, rather than the possibility that electoral marginality would encourage candidates to explore new means to increase 'alignment' with the public opinion in their constituencies, Lundy sees her comparatively safe seat as providing the freedom to engage in these experiments (personal interview: Kate Lundy, 12 March 2012). The notion of these activities as ongoing experiments appears problematic in terms of legitimising them as normal and routine ways to engage with the public, in the same way that other forums of elite-public consultation have been over time.

This reflects wider debates in Australian political parties regarding their level of engagement with the general public, of which the use of 'primaries' (pre-election candidate selection via ballot) is the most visible in recent years (van Onselen, 2009). At the ALP's national conference in 2011 the party accepted a proposal to further employ digital media to better engage members of the wider public through the creation of non-geographic branches (communities of interest), internet policy fora, and online memberships based on the community organising model (Crook, 2011). To this end the ALP has been successively investing in centralised ICT infrastructure over a number of years (Bitar, 2010) to build technical capacity. It remains uncertain if these developments lead toward a widening of the party's use of the discursive engagement model of Lundy's Public Spheres or more towards the market aggregation option of GetUp!

The more things change

Regardless of where you go, there you are. Social media has enabled Australians to create new public spaces for democratic and policy discourse as well as to 'virtualise' existing groups and communities of interest. In the process we can see that many of the 'usual suspects' are found online: the educated and emboldened majority, as well as the marginalised who seek for political identities and have expression into the wider public conversation. This reflects the power of the cultural explanation for technology adoption: that existing practices, discourses and power gradients are often reprinted on new technologies. At the same time there are clearly areas of deliberate and natural innovation in the use of digital media public spheres. Deliberate innovations can be seen in the way a range of groups and individuals from inside and outside the established political system have attempted to operationalise — knowingly or not — the idea of the discursive public sphere. Overall, there has been a massive expansion in highly visible public talk about politics that encourages individuals to see themselves as part of a discursive community. But, is this all that there could be? Does the new environment really embolden free talk? In Chapter 4 we look at the limits of free speech.

Chapter 4 — Anti-social media

I feel in the mood for a stupid and pointless argument in an online forum today.

— Walker, *How the Internet Brings Us Together* (2007)

One of the more important observations in political science is that the study of political action can reflect a bias towards the exercise of power (Schattschneider 1960: 71). The notion of subaltern (non-hegemonic) counter-publics, championed by Nancy Fraser, picks up on this concept, arguing for the need to identify areas of political dialogue and discussion that lie outside dominant political strata (1990). This is important in seeing the extent of opinion in the community, as well as being able to identify the genesis and conceptual DNA of new ideas that enter into the public sphere (John, 2003). The idea of the counter public is significant because it emphasises that, while some groups are on the edge of public discourse, they still exist within an intellectual community of interlocking ideas. Here Fraser draws a distinction between *publics* and *enclaves*: subaltern counter publics are not enclaves because they 'aspire to disseminate one's discourse into ever-widening arenas'. This is the desire for recognition and respect that rests within the human condition, as well as the important political work of ensuring recognition. For Fraser, these spaces may be places of periodic 'withdrawal and rergroupment' (1997: 82), and this allows for these voices to re-emerge into the wider discourse at a later time.

An example of tension between public and enclave in digital-media politics is illustrated by the use of an email discussion list to support the work of the Australian Women in Agriculture (AWiA) group (Pini, et al., 2004). The list was identified as a useful space for building technical expertise and individuals' confidence in engaging in public discourse (capacity building; 2004: 273–74). The comparatively homogeneous nature of the space was core to the process of building a political culture for the AWiA and re-crafting participants' political subjectivities (the active process of self-development, as opposed to the interpellation of one's political identity by external ideological institutions; Althusser, 1971: 127–88). Thus, the list served as a space for the deliberate fostering of political identities that ran counter to established stereotypes of farming women ('farm wives' implying marriage to the farm). In making this space, however, the researchers identified that the list contained its own internal power dynamics, and that these tensions saw 'non-standard' members leaving this list as the group focused more on promoting a core political identity of professional women in the farming sector.

In the social media context this raises questions about the way counter publics can use technology to develop and express their political positions. Ease of access and application provides these groups discursive infrastructure on a scale never seen. The more open and public the nature of the space created by technology increases the visibility of counter-public discourses to the majority: increasing their discoverability for potential members, normalising alternative perspectives and political identities, and reducing the ability of subgroups to control access to any particular space. We see evidence of this in the array of political positions and identities visible online, including those the wider public may find distasteful or threatening (such as groups opposed to the very discursive and political pluralism assumed by an expanded public sphere, such as extremist political organisations; Margolis and Moreno-Riaño, 2009: 86). Alternatively, this also limits the 'shelter' afforded by temporary enclaves from hostile perspectives or authoritarian actors who may wish to surveil or disrupt the formation of political and cultural opponents (Chase & Mulvenon, 2002). It is important to understand, therefore, the limits of tolerance in the Australian digital public sphere.

Amongst the chatter, a new silence?

The very participative nature of the digital-media environment leads us to see this communicative environment as open and expansive. Early debates about the regulation of online content popularised the view that internet technologies are uniquely resistant to top-down control. Heath Gilmore famously argued this freedom of speech is fundamental to the internet's core design,[1] in his oft-quoted observation that the 'Net interprets censorship as damage and routes around it' (cited in Elmer-Dewitt, 1993). Popular reporting of digital media is not generally framed in terms of what is *not* done or *not* said online, but as a catalyst of 'innovation engines' (Thorp & Goldstein, 2010: 13) or more commonly as a place where every perspective is visible and available (Shade, et al., 2005). But is this true? Does the combination of openness and anonymity also have a role in suppressing dissenting views and political subjectivities through the generation of disparaging meta-commentary, hostility and negativity that serves to delineate and reinforce 'popular opinion' within the flow of conversation?

The strange silence in some public spheres

To examine this question we can draw upon the 'spiral of silence' proposed by Elizabeth Noell-Neuman. This theory considers the way mass and interpersonal

---

1 The packet switching system that sees internet content routed through alternative network connections where a message or its component is lost in transmission.

communications interact to create and maintain public discourse with a stable set of 'acceptable' topics. Developed in the context of West German politics of the 1970s, the spiral talks about the way media systems generate a generally accepted zeitgeist (1974). This, in turn, encourages public discourse within 'popular' (acceptable) topics and discourages those views outside of the charmed circle.[2] Responsive to what is popular and accepted, this feeds back into the media system through market sensing (discussed in detail in Chapter 6). This, in turn, creates a self-reinforcing 'spiral' with each feedback loop narrowing and hardening this limited range of appropriate discursive topics.

As a testable theory, the spiral of silence has four components, it argues:

- That we fear social isolation and seek to avoid it.

- These fears are projected in the way we act and communicate. This can be explicit through speech, or implicit in our behaviours towards topics we find distasteful.

- Not only are these anxieties are communicated in our speech and action, but also the wider public has a 'quasi-statistical' sense of what views and opinions are and are not dominant. This has implications for individual behaviour: fearing social isolation people respond to their perceptions of mass opinion in ways that reinforce alignment with popular views and avoidance of unpopular ones.

- The *mass* media, which serves to both magnify (in terms of visibility) and reduce (in terms of what is repeated as being 'acceptable') public opinion.

The premise behind the spiral of silence is a meso-level one, linking together the interpersonal with institutional to explain observed phenomena. In doing so it can explain the narrowness of media representations of social diversity (Phillips, 2009), for example, as the spiral has a tendency to push towards a comfortable centre or average. The theory can also explain rapid 'shifts' in polling on public opinion, where suppressed viewpoints emerge due to a mass shift of individuals' perception of the majority opinion (thus freeing suppressed views) or as a result of the lowering of social risks associated with the expression of deviant perspectives.

This theory has relevance for both assessing social changes under a new communicative environment that provides alternative means to assess public opinion and for expressing unusual views with a degree of anonymity, as well as the neo-institutional view of media employed in this book (being concerned with the relationship between structure and agency). Like most social theory, however, it has roots in a particular political culture and milieu: that of a pluralistic, postwar West Germany, still recovering from the psychic shock

---

2   Deviant and heterodox views can exist in society but are hidden from public opinion.

of fascism and 'intolerant of intolerance' (Rosenfeld, 2010: 262). Thus, there are questions as to the value of this concept outside of its cultural, media and structural contexts (Scheufele & Moy, 2000).

Does the spiral turn down under?

The digital media has a range of characteristics that may challenge the underpinning basis of the spiral model. With both interpersonal communication and mass media characteristics, digital media allows for the development of communities of interest of intermediate sizes (larger than sustainable interpersonal networks, but smaller than mass-media audiences). Because of this we can ask if the suppressive power of social stigma is more or less relevant in this context. Certainly one of the strongest 'disciplining' effects of social media is the way that seemingly localised and immediate social interactions can, under specific circumstances become magnified and subject to scrutiny by mass audiences. As discussed in Chapter 2, social media exchanges have become 'scandals' for politicians, but it is also a reality for non-elites. Examples include a variety of forms of online harassment and victimisation where individual privacy is breached (AAP, 2012b).

Additionally we should ask: does digital media support or undermine the 'quasi-statistical sense' we get in interpersonal interactions about what is and is not an appropriate topic or argument? The social nature of the digital-media environment is not delivered solely through the use of databases to computerise interpersonal relationships and recreate social networks online, but also lies in the remediation of paralinguistic cues (non-verbal communication elements, like tone and facial expression). Where the online medium was once defined by its strict textual conventions (Chen & Hinton, 1999), successive generations of users have introduced and refined new forms of social signalling and forms of emotional communication (textual icons — such as emoticons and mood state indicators). This is not just a set of genre conventions that mark out playful engagement with a new social environment, for human communication has long seen the need for emotional indicators as a part of effective communication.

This points to a social ambiguity in flux, particularly in terms of social networking services' (SNS) 'publicity' (McNealy, 2012). These services encourage the sharing of personal information and the trivia of the day-to-day, which clashes with the trend to make profiles open to all web users (Boyd, 2011). Social expectations of these services remain fluid and it is unclear if these spaces are private, public, or 'private-public'. This latter category reflects the notion of a 'third place' where people can be 'alone together' in a community of fluctuating membership, but defined in terms of shared observation of external events (Shapira & Navon, 1991: 123–24). This is most commonly demonstrated in the social pretext we see on public transport where personal telephone conversations are politely ignored ('civic inattention'; Phillips & Smith, 2003: 86) provided they fall within a vague range of 'acceptable' behaviours (Wei & Leung, 1999: 25; Humphreys, 2005: 369). The difficulty lies in policing social boundaries in media that allow for mass observation and participation.

Increasingly, therefore, the online behaviour of individuals is being subject to routine surveillance that can limit the inventive and creative nature of these new spaces. The clearest example of this is the practice of potential employers to vet applicants based on searches against their names and requests for access to their SNS profiles. As this practice becomes common, job hunters are educated in avoiding posting material online that may have a negative impact on employment. The Career Builder website, for example, cautions against posting material that may 'clash with employer's values' or reveal your views on 'sensitive issues' (Dehne, 2008). These admonishments against disclosure are reiterated by governments. The Australian Communications and Media Authority's (ACMA) *Cyber(smart:)* website advises teenagers against recklessness regarding the employment implications of their online posts (ACMA, 2009).

These admonishments, and occasional media stories which feature the hapless who have fallen foul of routine employer surveillance of their social media (see, for example, Moses, 2009a; Whyte, 2011), reflect how online systems contribute to panopticism: Foucault's (1995: 285) insight into social regulation through the subject's internalisation of surveillance. In the context of the spiral of silence, this reflects how perceptions of majority opinion suppress the diversity of speech, through the accessibility of political speech by actors in the economic realm. In the case of youth cultures we can see how these forces are particularly powerful in the intersection of self-representation and social expectations regarding economic prerogatives. These disciplining forces interpellate young people into a narrow range of subjective desires (school tracking to employment), validate particular self-representation (largely focused on specific types of acceptable consumption; Best, 2009), while suppressing 'deviant' behaviour (sexual promiscuity, risk taking, drug use). Because of concerns that social media systems can freeze time, societal acceptance of the natural process of adolescent experimentation and distancing from parental authority is impaired: experimentation is not just a process of maturation, but a threat to your 'permanent record'. In this way CJ Pascoe (2011: 12) has argued that, while digital media presents new sources of risk and the resources to mitigate against it, there remains a similar 'dominant ordering of power' with regard to risk distribution.

Evidence for this can be found in the content analysis of wall posts discussed previously. Coding this content for misogynistic and sexist language[3] we can see that a considerable amount of material of this kind was posted on Facebook. This largely took the form of representing women as sexual objects or their sexual instrumentalisation (0.391 per cent of all posts), rather than statements about women's social role or position (0.092 per cent of all posts). While the quantum of posts of this nature is small overall, it is marked that almost 11 per cent of all posters in the sample group made one or more of these posts in the period measured. While men where the most likely to post this content (13.5 per cent), women were also represented (8 per cent) as regulators of their gender and sexuality.

At the most extreme end of the spectrum, however, very few clearly misogynistic comments were identified in the sample (0.021 per cent of posts, all from men). An example of this would be the group 'cutting your mum's car breaks [sic] when she cooks a bad dinner'. Importantly the majority of sexist statements are not personal utterances, but come from the membership of Facebook groups. This shows the role of social proof (support for individual behaviour assumed from others' participation in the same) in driving these attitudes: few of the posts were direct articulations by the sample group members but liking or joining groups with sexist titles and/or objectives. As we move from the nonymous space of Facebook to select, anonymous spaces we can see that this type of discourse can become more socially violent, such as the use of sexual images of young women in revenge[4] or 'tribute' picture[5] posts (Aston, 2012) to serve as an example of the way in which dominant gender relations are sustained and remediated.

Enforcing the acceptable

In addition to the collective processes of the spiral of silence, the digital-media environment has also given rise to a range of self-appointed regulators. Websites like *You said it ... ,*[6] *Fight Dem Back*, *Slackbastard* and *My iCrusade against Right Wing Extremists* patrol around the edges of Australian political dialogue online, exposing individuals and organisations they identify as having racist

---

3   'Misogyny', drawing upon Edward Armstrong's operationalised definition (2001) to include references to assault, rape and murder and sexism ('any phrase that may be interpreted to be treating men and women differently, simply on the basis of their sex') based on the work of Boxill, et al. to include references to social, workplace/professional and sexual instrumentalism (1997: 114–45).
4   For example, Hunter Moore's *Is Anyone Up?* website (now at http://yougotposted.com/).
5   The provision of a photograph of a person with the request for others in the forum to repost a photograph of the printed image following their ejaculation on it. See, for example, http://xhamster.com/search.php?q=tribute&qcat=pictures (NSFW).
6   Formally 'the Anti-bogan'; http://theantibogan.wordpress.com

and extremist views. Generally this takes the form of exposure and ridicule (see, for example, Illustration 10): reposting screenshots of offending material on their sites. *Slackbastard* (out of the Melbourne anarchist movement) and *You said it …* (from the Sydney socialist community) represent the best known of these types of site. The motivation of the founder of You said it …, 'the anti-bogan', for setting up the site was the perceived failure of Facebook and blogging networks to effectively police hate speech, racist and sexist comments:

> … we weren't getting very far. We were getting a lot of people banned, but once someone's profile is deleted they just start a new one and continue the public crap. So it was at that time I decided I would go the completely other way. Rather than attempt to censor all that crap I would try and expose it. If people really wanted an audience, I'd give them an audience.

The purpose of this exposure was to discourage this form of speech by raising the personal stakes involved and making these statements permanent, rather than change their views (personal interview: the anti-bogan, 20 July 2011).[7]

you said it...

@theantibogan

aussie freedom of speech and the people who abuse it   Home About/Contact Us Disclaimer Do You Feature Here? Stickers

Asians Continue to Cop 'Shit Driver' Tag

APRIL 17, 2012

tags: asian drivers, Australia, hoon drivers, ~~----~~ racism

FACEBOOK

theantibogan.wordpres
on Facebook

Like

1,655 people like
theantibogan.wordpress.com.

3 hours ago

Melbourne!!! Can't believe our shuttle driver was Asian a shit driver (standard) and got us here 1.5 hours before boarding and got road rage "fook off retarddd" — at Sydney Domestic Terimal.

Illustration 10: *'You said it …'* entry

Source: Facebook. Used with permission; user tags not obscured in original

---

7   The anti-bogan established another collaborative blog, *Is your mind made up* (http://mindmadeup.net) as a more educative channel.

The site did generate episodes of hostility. The provocative nature of the presentation of material on You said it … led, in 2011, to white supremacists 'hijacking' the anti-bogan's identity online to imply he was a paedophile, and friending the anti-bogan's students (Hilderbrand, 2011: 3). Interestingly it was his employment as a teacher that had led to the anti-bogan moving his anti-racism politics online in the first place becoming 'less vocal and less public'. The identification of his name by opponents was a direct result of him talking at an anti-racism event as 'the anti-bogan' and being photographed. The real identity of *Slackbastard*'s 'Andy Fleming' has been subject to speculation in Australian far-right blogs and discussion fora for some time (see, for example: Whitelaw Towers (2011)), with Fleming actively attempting to maintain his anonymity for reasons of personal safety (Fleming, 2012). This concern is not unfounded, with acts of violence committed against anti-fascist activists occasionally occurring in Australia (Begg, 1997).

Badges of shame, badges of honour

The impact (direct and indirect) of these sites is unclear. Individuals featured on You said it … are difficult to access for their views on the consequence of their appearance, with few agreeing to interviews.[8] This is telling about the impact of the site. At the extreme end, some featured have lost employment (de Brito, 2011). Even those who see themselves as developing activist identities online have found exposure threatening. For 'respondent A' the use of Facebook represented a new way in which he could engage in conservative politics online — seeing his profile and discussions as possibly provocative, but also as a catalyst for democratic debate. Following his comments being featured on You said it …, he changed the privacy settings of his profile to limit the visibility of his comments to friends only, but remained concerned that supporters of the site kept him under surveillance through fake profiles (personal interview: respondent A, 19 July 2011). In one way this demonstrates a basic difference of opinion of the nature of *publicity* on SNS. While the anti-bogan sees Facebook posts as public speech, respondent A saw greater ambiguity. One of his key criticisms of his exposure was that it took this content 'off site' and outside of the conventions of Facebook. For him this was inherently unfair. The short-term impact is that the ability for critics to penetrate these counter-public public spheres limits their effectiveness as sites for withdrawal, regrouping and microactivism.

While the silencing of some racist and non-hegemonic points of view is a result of these activities, there are also perverse outcomes. For those with more strident political opinions, being featured on the site can provide a 'sense of achievement'

---

8 By nature, those who have deleted or significantly altered their Facebook profile following this exposure are difficult to identify.

and vindication that their views are provoking the forces of political correctness. Following on from our observations about the role played by opinion leaders in social media (see Two-step flow, 2.0, Chapter 3), these individuals are not necessarily affected by the public silence of peers on their key issues, but see peer silence and the focus of sites like You said it … as demonstrating their importance as brave opinion leaders who speak for a suppressed counter public (Personal interview: respondent B, 4 July 2011) or representing evidence that their political opponents are counter-democratic forces (Personal interview: Nick Folks, Australian Protectionist Party, 18 June 2011). In having enforcement undertaken by political opponents, these sites can generate debate leading to conflict. The impact of this is to hollow out intermediate positions, which limits the possibility of rapprochement or dialogue.

L'Étranger: 'support Leb and Wog bashing day'[9]

The most visible and toxic aspect of anti-social media has been its use by 'hate groups': groups who advocate violence against ethnic and religious minorities. The 'rise' of these groups on SNS has featured in the media and they have been associated with outbreaks of racial violence (Pauli, 2009). While a negative social force, these groups also represent counter publics: giving voice and visibility to the dark parts of the public sphere. The extent to which the existence of racism and sectarianism is 'created' by these sites is unclear. Certainly the visibility of these groups makes them fodder for questionable journalistic trend pieces and tabloid sociology (Silverman, 2007: 118) that either purport to associate the rise of digital media with organised hate (*PM*, 2010) or identify these channels as a useful means to get around anti-vilification laws. As border control has been increasingly used to prevent the movement of spokespersons for extremist groups and ideologies, digital media has become a tool for these individuals to communicate with communities in states that actively restrict entry (Cunneen, 1997: 182–84). Even under the less, officially, 'politically-correct' period of the conservative government of John Howard (Simons & Fraser, 2010: 375), Australia continued to deny the entry of British Holocaust denier David Irving. High-profile, Australian-based Holocaust deniers, such as Fredrick Töben and the 'Adelaide Institute', have been similarly singled out for legal action by the Australian Human Rights Commission. The commission ordered the removal from Töben's site of some extreme claims about World War II genocides (Wainwright, 2009).

The changing nature of prejudice makes an objective determination of the 'level' of racism virtually impossible to determine, and this research has not

---

9   Context of text message sent in the lead up to the Cronulla violence in 2005.

been longitudinally collected in Australia.[10] Had this existed it might allow the identification of a simple correlation (if not causation) between digital media and these attitudes. But, this is unlikely. Australia has a long history with organised racist and far-right organisations (such as the League of Rights) stretching back to the 1930s (Greason, 1997: 190) and, to some extent, newly formed online and offline organisations represent the natural tendency in the far right for fluidity of organisational leadership, membership, and name (202–03). What digital media allow is the internationalisation of this activity, while employing social networking to localise political action. The leak of membership details of the international neo-Nazi group Blood and Honor in 2011 demonstrated the existence of global membership, including a small number of Australians (part of 'Operation Blitzkrieg', see WikiLeaks, Chapter 5). For Barbara Perry and Patrik Olsson (2009), this permits the comparatively fragmented (ideationally and socially) far right to form more coherent collective identities.

A spiral of hatred

One recent example of extreme political behaviour was the Cronulla 'riots' (December 2005), which consisted of two key outbreaks of violence: a 5000-strong violent demonstration to 'reclaim' the beach by the white population, and a smaller, 'retaliatory' attack against individuals and property. The immediate 'cause' of this violence was an altercation between two groups of beach users: Australians of ethnic origin and local lifesavers (Poynting, 2006). The role of digital media was highlighted through SMS messages that promoted violence (Tobin, 2006: 51).[11] Generally the media and elites have been quick to blame digital media as a catalyst for violence, possibly because that assumption deflects analysis away from more fundamental problems like entrenched racist attitudes. In the United Kingdom, violence following the shooting of a young black man in 2011 saw the government initially propose strict regulation of instant messaging services as a means of preventing the organisation of violence (Masnick, 2011).

The role of SMS and other digital media in the promotion of violence has, in this case, taken a back seat to concerns about the role of talkback radio in the days leading up to the crimes. In the case of Cronulla, John Hartley and Joshua Green (2006: 352) have argued that commercial media played an important role in fuelling dissent around these events through the characterisation of tensions

---

10 Dunn, et al. (2004) provide an excellent review of the shift from 'old racism' (based on views of the inherent superiority of some racial groups over others) and the rise of 'new racism' (based on views of cultural incomparability) in their quantification of racist attitudes in Australia.

11 For example: 'Every fucking aussie. Go to Cronulla Beach Sunday for some Leb and wog bashing Aussie Pride ok' and 'All leb / wog brothers. Sunday midday. Must be at North Cronulla Park. These skippy aussies want war. Bring ur guns and knives and lets show them how we do it'.

as assaults on the wider community or the essential Australian way of life. Violence was actively encouraged by 'shock jock' Alan Jones on 7 December,[12] who was later found to have violated the broadcasters' code (Commercial Radio Code of Practice) (Alberici, 2007). Thus, the violence was not a spontaneous act of creation that emerged from social networks, but was set against a backdrop of media reporting about tensions on the beach, as well as the use of digital media by participants in this discourse (both those promoting violence and those advocating calm).

This is supported by James Forrest's and Kevin Dunn's assessment of the nature of anti-out-group[13] prejudice in Queensland and New South Wales. Rather than a correlation of proximity, they find that 'the ability to make judgements about significant "others" or out-groups has been shown to relate more to abstract notions of self and national identity, reproduced in public by such as mainstream news media' (2006: 184). The recent violence is thus marked as different to historical outbreaks of anti-immigrant violence in Australia that have had more economic proximate causes (anti-Chinese riots on the goldfields pre-Federation, anti-southern European violence against strike breakers in the 1930s and 1940s; Collins, 2007: 64–65). While members of the far right may have taken credit for the 'uprising' (ABC, 2006) the more compelling evidence points to the rise of a background encouragement of aggressive cultural nationalism under the Howard government, liberally mixed with mass-media goading and alcohol.

There is, therefore, a difference between what occurs at the extreme end of the political spectrum and majority views. While survey research undertaken by Dunn, et al. (2004) identified that one in eight Australians agree that they 'are prejudiced against other cultures', this prejudice is not writ large in the social media. The Facebook wall post study identified a low proportion of overtly racist statements (such as the example in Illustration 11), the presence of which would indicate a country so racist that these views are normalised in online social conversation (Sianne Ngai's notion of 'casual racism' as demonstrating its social ordinariness; 2005: 386). Thus, in the sample of 29,660 wall posts, less than one-twentieth of one per cent (0.04 per cent) contained overt, casual racist or sectarian content.

---

12   '… the only language the Middle-Eastern youth understand is a good hiding … These Middle-Eastern people must be treated with a big stick …'
13   Defined as a group to which the majority do not belong and who are likely to attract distrust from the majority (Ferrante, 2011: 93).

Illustration 11: Example of 'casual racism' on Facebook (user tags obscured)

Source: Facebook

It's a guy thing?

It is important to ask if violence in online discourse impacts on the character of online political discussion. This is relevant given the gendered nature of politics in Australia. Gendering normalises Australian politics as an inherently masculine 'zero sum' activity and, correspondingly, explains the low level of women's participation as political elites (Crawford & Pini, 2010). In the context of the Australian political blogosphere, Mark Bahnisch (2006: 145) has talked about the dominance of masculine voices in this space (the majority of high-profile political bloggers in Australia are men), and the relationship between this and limited civility in these fora. Exploring this empirically, if we look at the respondents to the surveys undertaken into social media (Table 8) we can see a disproportionate response from men, particularly in the more 'open' social media of blogs and Twitter (as opposed to the comparatively enclosed space of Facebook). As these surveys include both active posters and 'lurkers', it is possible that the lack of non-male voices carries over into readership (there are, however, some methodological concerns about this, see the discussion of lurking, below).

	Political blog users (n = 488)	Political Twitter users (n = 222)	Political Facebook users (n = 592)	CANdo members (n = 97)
Male	63.75	72.97	59.45	77.32
Female	35.64	27.03	40.55	22.68

Table 8: Political social media, response rates by gender

Source: Author's research

While this could simply be an online mirroring of offline cultural norms, this does not neatly fit with the demonstrated use of digital media by women as effective sites for counter-public formation (as discussed above) and as willing participants in online survey research (Flaye, 2012). This may be explained by the over-representation of men in areas of technical and scientific professions, and as early adopters of new technologies (the latter tendency is declining over time, however; Murphy, 2011). As the presence of women in online discussions of politics remains small, this marginalises gender-specific concerns and associated agenda formation.[14] In addition, it may be possible to argue that, if women commonly find their online interlocutors are male, there exists a tendency for the presence of men to suppress (actively or through women self-censoring) women's voices.

Careful, he might hear you

This second proposition needs elaboration. Looking at discursive practices between men and women in an experimental setting, Annette Hannah and Tamar Murachver observed a propensity for women to speak less compared to their male interlocutors (2007: 286–88), adopting more 'facilitative' roles in conversation (short utterances, asking questions, etc.). Men just talk more, and it is socially acceptable for us do so. This appears to impact on those women who do choose to engage in online politics in the social media. If we look at the comparative willingness of men and women to engage in political speech where there exists social risk (revising the stranger on a train scenario) we see in Table 9 a considerable difference between those women who participate in political social media and those who do not in terms of willingness to talk. This difference is not found among men, reflecting our ongoing social and political dominance. We can argue that rather than feminise conversations, the non-participation of some women fails to challenge the aggressive and masculinised dialogue of Australian politics.

	Political		Non-political			
	Blog Readers (n = 491)	Twitter (n = 222)	Blog Readers (n = 74)	Twitter (n = 110)		
Male	61.09	67.3	*	76.81	Channel difference	
Female	52.57	76.67	45.71	43.9	Blog readers	Twitter
All	57.43	70.27	47.3	64.54	10.13	5.72
Gender difference	8.52	-9.37	na	32.91		

Table 9: Stranger on a train scenario, gender differences

Source: Author's research (* response rate too low)

---

14   Here we need to recognise the work of women bloggers and tweeters to encourage and facilitate female participation in these spaces. A good example would be the *Hoyden About Town* group blog (http://hoydenabouttown.com).

Considering this absence, we have to recognise that this 'non-participation' may not be the result of direct exclusion, but *active* non-participation. The most common form of this would be 'lurking': the presence as a reader in online fora, without substantive contribution (reading without posting). Problematically, there is some evidence that lurkers may be less likely to respond to survey requests than non-lurkers. In their study of active non-participators (based on carefully selected interview subjects), Blair Nonnecke and Jenny Preece observed that people lurk for a variety of reasons (2001: 6):

- desire for anonymity to preserve privacy and safety
- work-related constraints (employment risk)
- channel lacks value to the lurker in terms of the substantive content (a low 'signal to noise' ratio)
- shyness
- time limitations.[15]

Some of these factors appear to be particularly sensitive to gender effects, especially perceptions of risk.

It is important to also consider the average age difference between users of these services (from the survey: Facebook (37), blog readers (42), Twitter (44), CANdo (48)), which correlates negatively with increased women's representation. While this reflects a generational view of women's participation associated with increased levels of education and workplace participation by women (Aitkin, 1977: 34), the participation gap has not disappeared. This problem was also apparent to the founders of yopinion.com.au, (discussed in Chapter 3) who had difficulty motivating female members to 'convert' from lurkers[16] to topic authors (personal interview: Dougal Robinson, 12 March 2012). This may relate to young women's sense of political knowledge. The Australian Electoral Commission's Youth Electoral Study found that young men were 'more likely to report they had the knowledge to understand political issues, knowledge to understand parties, knowledge to make a decision when voting and knowledge to be able to vote' than women (Edwards, et al., 2006). Here we see how male dominance of the political stage can have intergenerational impacts in discouraging women's discursive participation.

---

15   It should be noted that Nonnecke and Preece's original paper also includes the consideration of the uses and gratifications model of media and consider positive reasons for lurking.
16   This concern was triggered by Robinson's reading about low levels of participation by women in editing Wikipedia (Cohen, Noam, 2011).

Ever thus? Incivility in political life

With the election of Australia's first female prime minister, Julia Gillard, in 2010, issues of gender and politeness have come into greater focus. As with with the presidency of Barack Obama, the breakthrough of a member of an under-represented group into high office is seen by some to have generated considerable vitriol from conservative members of the community. In the United States, the legitimacy of Obama has been subject to sustained attack by 'birthers' who deny Obama as a 'natural born' citizen of the United States — a proxy for his race (Hehmana, et al., 2011). In this country, the legitimacy of the Gillard government has also been attacked. At a Canberra rally to mark the end of the 'Convoy of No Confidence' protest organised by the trucking industry over the introduction of a tax on carbon dioxide, signs proclaimed the prime minister was the leader of the Australian Greens' 'bitch' and a 'witch' (Campbell, 2011). The presence of the leader of the Opposition at the event was seen as an endorsement of this aggressive style of political rhetoric. Indeed, this type of personal and gendered attack came on the back of an earlier uproar following the Coalition Senator Bill Heffernan describing the future prime minister as unsuited for leadership because she had not elected to have a family and remained 'deliberately barren' (AAP, 2007).

In the same time period, the leader of the Opposition had been subject to discussion of his Catholicism as the basis for a personal 'hatred of women' (Mitchell, 2011), described as a homophobe in posters displayed by government MPs, and subject to considerable popular media discussion of his genitals because of his sporting attire (Maguire, 2009). The then leader of the Australian Greens Bob Brown talked about News Limited as the 'hate media' that ran a campaign of ongoing and consistent attacks on his party and character (Grattan, 2011). This situation has continued, with the embattled MP Craig Thomson reading into Hansard hate mail[17] that called for his suicide or assassination in response to accusations that he had misused his corporate credit card prior to his election to parliament. The MP has accused the Opposition of inflaming this type of attack through their pursuit of the issue while it has been subject to formal investigation. As a result, the Acting Speaker of the Parliament, Anna Burke, has recently stated that MPs conduct is the lowest in the 14 years she has been in Parliament (AAP, 2012a).

---

17   'Go cut your wrists or, better still, hang yourself.'; 'You are dead. A bullet between the eyes will save taxpayers' money' (Thompson, Craig, 2012, *Hansard*, Canberra: Parliament of Australia: 4715).

Illustration 12: Prime Minister Gillard burnt in effigy, Eureka Dawn Vigil (3 December 2010)

Source: Photograph by Takver, (cc), image source: www.flickr.com/photos/takver/5226872939/in/ photostream/

At the heart of this type of discussion are concerns that uncivil and violent political dialogue undermine democratic practice through reducing the:

* quality of political dialogue and moving it towards invective and the trading of insults

* potential for speech to build consensus and form the basis of John Dryzek's deliberative democratic practice through turning political opponents into 'enemies' with whom consensus and agreement cannot be reached

* motivation of individual citizens with political interests to enter this hostile environment.

This type of argument walks a fine line between excessive conservatism through appeals to authority and tradition, and the need for speech to be facilitated through social rules that encourage, rather than discourage, participation.

Net nasties

Discounting the possibility that people in public life today are just a bunch of ass-hats of a kind not seen before, it is possible to see a link between the media environment and incivility. Concerns about media and the quality of discourse are not new. Current communication technology is commonly seen to impact on the quality of political communication. Just as television 'dumbed down' political communication due to the channel effects associated with the production of news (the sound-bite; Gaber, 2005: 26), digital media is associated with a coarsening of public life.

The direct relationship between digital media and political rudeness is unclear, and a number of (not necessarily mutually incomparable) causes are cited. At the organisational level, the changing nature of the news media (driven by economics as well as technology, see Chapter 6 for an extended discussion) is often cited as blending opinion with journalistic reporting (Robinson, 2006). In this context 'opinion' is associated with inflammatory and intemperate language, not bound by journalistic conventions of neutrality and balance. Indeed, a range of media commentators have made it clear that they are not journalists in defending themselves against attacks on their conduct (Gallop, 2011). As increasing numbers of opinion writers compete for attention in a crowded media space, there is more room for 'sexed up' copy and headlines to attract readers.

Similarly, in empowering the public to engage with reportage, online newspapers and other mainstream and alternative media are filled with increasing amounts of lightly regulated content that tends towards the more informal and offensive. The 'loose talk', which was once filtered by the Letters editor, is now found online (as seen in Illustration 13). While this is a function of anonymity and the movement of the medium from select to mass use (massification), the loss of personal accountability for rudeness is also driven by the tempo of modern publication cycles and the rapid obsolescence of political news online. This both creates the opportunities for incivility, as well as driving a cultural shift towards increasingly uncivil relations with strangers.

> ███████████████ says: 10:50am | 06/06/12
>
> @ █████████ - so you agree your article is a lie. You claim the minimum is $7.22/hr which is $274.36 a week — you're only out by 21.2%. That is for a 16 year old who can't drive by the way on his 'L's to work, so why would he own a car or have kids at that age anyway ??? Thank God you aren't in charge of pays at your workplace
>
> My figures come from an employer organisation — no made up bullshit union figures: http://www.masterpainters.com.au/files/11-07-05_20122_award_rates.pdf
>
> So you can see a 16 year old 1st year apprentice gets a minimum of $286.18 plus $61.90 fares allowance — that is, $427.08 a week. A long way away from your alleged $225.00 per week which you then corrected to $274.36 (and with fares of $61.90 = $336.26).
>
> Have another go you bullshit artist — ROFLMFAO !!!!!!!!!!!

Illustration 13: Comment on opinion piece published in *The Punch*

Source: *The Punch*, redrawn from original, user tag obscured

In considering the causes of incivility Tim Phillips and Philip Smith note the emphasis of research around the loss (and, by extension renewal) of social relations at the neighbourhood level (2003: 205). The work of people like Robert Putnam (as discussed in more detail in Chapter 5) has emphasised the value of enduring local social networks and aggregate this up to a societal pathology. This lies at odds with urban sociology, which has looked at how the massification of our cities leads to an increased regularity of interactions with strangers (90 per cent of Australians live in communities of more than 100,000 people; Berry, 2007: 222). Anonymity creates the potential for a high volume of low-level uncivil interactions, which in turn corrode social norms of behaviour. While traditional concerns about incivility have focused on the anonymity of 'the city' as a driver of incivility, Phillips 'and Smith's recent Australian survey has reoriented this focus on sites of movement: places where people are 'in motion' rather than 'in place' (particularly transport, 2006: 894). This makes sense as people in motion engage in 'drive by' incivility with lower social risk than when they are likely to remain proximate to their interlocutor for longer periods of time.

This social change is embedded in norms of behaviour and as institutional rules. In Australia, the institutional regulation of civility in political discourse has declined. This now has a legal basis that has expanded the idea of freedom of speech to include uncivil talk (Stone, 2011). In *Coleman v Power* (2004) the High Court overturned the sentence of a student charged with the use of insulting words under the Queensland *Vagrancy Act*. This case was focused on political speech as the insult was made in the course of an interaction with a police officer over the distribution of written material accusing the Queensland police force of being a corrupt institution. As Adrienne Stone argues, institutions in Australia are seeing themselves as having less of an enlightenment role in improving political speech through the regulation of its content or form.

Who are you to call names?

But, is this tale of woe and decline really true? Incivility in public life is nothing new in Australia. Former prime minister, Paul Keating, was famous for his creative use of invective; indeed violent language (and behaviour) dates to pre-Federation settlement and outbreaks of extreme political violence after Federation (such as riots between the communist 'red raggers' and the Soldiers Imperial League of Australia in 1919; Evans, 1992). While Illustration 13 (above) demonstrates uncivil online speech in the new generation of opinion websites (see I'm figgering on biggering, Chapter 6) a range of new conventions have developed on these comment sites that have increased the quality of such comment sections. These include pre-moderation, post-moderation (take-down), and the use of threaded conversations (either provided by the content-management system or via the adoption of the @[interlocutor] convention). The extent to which individual examples represent a social trend, therefore, is questionable.

In addition, there is the possibility that the digital-media landscape is competent at regulating the political speech of elites. As their speech is increasingly mediated and accessible to a wider audience, elites have found they have a reduced ability to control access to what has been said (Young, 2007a: 250–51). This is beneficial in increasing the availability of political information and reducing the capacity of elites to make different policy promises to different audiences. Mediation also broadens the likely consumption of political content and the range of contexts in which it will be consumed. This decreases the ability of speakers to ensure their context will be 'read' in a specific, known, and predictable localised context. In Australia, most senior politicians understand this and are increasingly cautious about the way they frame their statements, but not all in public life are professional politicians. In mid 2012, Tim Flannery's (Chief Commissioner of the Australian Climate Commission) offhanded comments at the end of a presentation on the health impacts of climate change in a medical conference were reported in a way that implied the Australian climate change policy would create the 'green job' of pulling teeth from the dead (Hambleton, 2012).[18] Thus, while many decry the blandness of contemporary political speech (Crabb, 2010), the multiplicity of potential audiences and contexts drives this caution in popular public discourse in a way not seen before.

In addition to this form of silencing, great care needs to be taken in any discussion of incivility and politics. The use of terms like 'rude', 'offensive' and 'uncivil' can be mobilised for political purposes. Accusations of rudeness in public life have been employed by political elites in response to persistent questioning on topics they prefer not to discuss (Wilkins, 2012), and by journalists with regard to their treatment by political elites (Massola, 2011). More systematically, Mills (2009) argues that the rhetoric of incivility is often mobilised as a way to characterise social 'out' groups. Through the definition of particular speech as inappropriate, this then forms a means by which the speech of certain groups can be discounted from political consideration. In the Australian context, Smith and Phillips (2001) have identified this in the way incivility in speech and action is associated with the notion of 'un-Australianness': not being part of the body politic of this country.

A recent example of how this type of characterisation denies the agency of whole groups of people can be found in some of the media reporting and associated commentary regarding an incident between the prime minister, leader of the Opposition, and a group of Indigenous protesters in early 2012. The context of this was a private function held *within* the precinct being used to celebrate the 40th anniversary of the Aboriginal Tent Embassy in Canberra. Following a tense confrontation between members of the gathering and the political figures, a considerable amount of reporting emphasised the disruptive nature of the Aboriginal protesters' actions, the rudeness of their behaviour and the threatening way the subgroup of protesters attempted to gain entry into the venue hosting the prime minister. What was not reported was that the prime minister's office elected to hold their private event 200 metres away from the Sovereignty Corroboree, a planned and advertised event.[19] Rather than reflecting on the bad taste of white political elites 'crashing' the venue of a significant Indigenous event, the popular response was to attack the actions of

18 Instead, in response to a question, Flannery suggested that mercury-filled fillings should be routinely removed from corpses prior to cremation to reduce environmental pollutants.
19 In addition, the role of the prime minister's office in 'tipping off' protesters about the presence of the leader of the Opposition at the event, and disparaging remarks about the Tent Embassy's contemporary relevance demonstrates a cynical manipulation of the protesters' emotions in this case (AAP, 2012a).

the protesters. At the extreme end of this disempowering rhetoric Andrew Bolt (2012) argued this served as a justification for the end of political reconciliation with all Indigenous people.[20]

Haters gonna hate

Over the last two decades the 'world' has increasingly begun encroaching on the free space of the digital environment. While dreams of cyberspace encourage thoughts of pure freedom, the social-media environment is social: it functions with some reference to the same social rules and norms of the offline world. While the comparative anonymity of the online environment tolerates increased diversity of discourse, the development of our online doppelgängers introduces new forms of social surveillance and self-representation. These SNS profiles and content trails permit experimentation with new political identities, but we've not escaped the 'meat space of real'. The most powerful agenda-setting systems — the combination of mass media and self-censorship — still appear to have powerful roles in restricting the true development of a weightless public sphere. Thus, as social media pushes public opinion 'up' to political elites, the elites, considered in chapters 5 and 6, still control a range of social and economic institutions and, they hope, continue to set the informational and ideological context in which these conversations occur.

---

20   Tony Abbott described the protesters as 'un-Australian' (Vasek, 2012).

Chapter 5 — All your base

Black and white and grey, all the colors of truth.

— George RR Martin, *A Game of Thrones* (1996: 464)

Jürgen Habermas's public sphere presents a tale of decline. In this story, the public sphere builds political legitimacy through fostering rational debate and the achievement of a degree of consensus based on the shared — if limited — agreed objectives of the bourgeois class. As a liberal idea, this includes a fear of unrestrained democratic practice associated with the growth of the mass enfranchisement: that majorities will suppress minority interests (Dryzek, 2002: 12). The problem of majority tyranny is countered by building process legitimacy through 'liberal constitutionalism': the protection of a set of individual rights via constitutional law and the focusing of political deliberation within institutions tasked for that purpose (courts, parliaments). Proponents of wider political deliberation remain concerned that constitutionalism undermines genuine political legitimacy through replacing the political objective of consensus-building with coalition-building (Dryzek, 2002: 18). This reflects a limited political pluralism (focusing on aggregation, rather than social and political diversification), which encourages the political calculus that, if you build a large enough faction to grab the spoils of the state, you need not engage in discursive practice.

This core debate has implications for individuals' relationship with political practice: hardening cynicism about the state as a site for 'transactional' politics, but also discouraging engagement in deliberative discussion as an *ir*rational way to produce policy outcomes. Thus, there is a tension between those who like politics bottom-up and those who see it as top-down. This chapter examines the use of digital media by a variety of political elites to assess the top-down use of these channels in Australian politics: looking at mass mobilisation to achieve political objectives. The chapter draws upon the definition of elite provided by John Higley and Michael Burton: 'persons who are able, by virtue of their strategic positions in powerful organizations and movements, to affect political outcomes regularly and substantially' (2006: 7). This captures two elements: that elites are those whose power can be identified by a regularity of impact, and they achieve this through the control of organisational *and/or* social movement resources. To this end we examine the way digital media has been employed in social movements, as well as more conventional institutions with regular political impacts.

The *new* new social movements

Possibly the most visible of all the digital-media politics in Australia has been the use of new political campaigning tactics employed by emerging online social movement organisations. The most prominent of these is the left-wing political organisation GetUp! that has become a significant new presence in the Australian political landscape through high visibility and fundraising success (Vromen & Coleman, 2011). Social movements exist in the space between the formal, institutional politics of elections (Chapter 2) and the diffused and disorganised discursive politics of the masses (Chapter 3). While a range of definitions exist, the most useful in this context is: 'organized, collective efforts to achieve social change that use noninstitutionalized tactics at least part of the time' (Burstein, et al. 1995: 137).[1] This definition captures their *liminal* nature. By nature they attempt to 'herd cats', using a range of resources and strategies without resort to the process of formally running as hierarchically structured political parties. This 'outsider' status allows them to promote specific policy issues without the need to compromise in the building of enduring political coalitions (Mansbridge, 2009: 161). Moreover, movements are more consistent in their political position over time than other organisations that have to make deals and build coalitions through compromise and mutual adjustment.

Because these are modernist political phenomena, the political role of social movements has a long history in Australian politics. The early workers movement challenged the authority of landowners and colonial parliaments and institutionalised the Australian Labor Party (ALP) and established a formal union structure around the time of Federation (Gauja, 2012: 171). The rise of non-class or industrially based movements (Huesca, 2000: 76), the 'new social movements' (NSM), was particularly visible in the 1960s and 1970s.[2] Their legacy is seen through a range of civil liberties laws (i.e. anti-discrimination) and institutions (i.e. the Family Court). Following Valdis Krebs's (2005) arguments about the changing nature of voter's electoral identification (from class to generational to 'social'), the NSMs differed to their predecessors in that their objectives were less tied to economic interests. This represents a difference in focus, rather than a fundamental shift in the political logic that drives social movement forms of organisation: the mobilisation of large numbers of individuals through networks and sub-organisations, attempts to affect change through a variety of formal (legislative, litigation) and informal (education, direct action) strategies, and the role of meaning-making in binding these movements together and achieving social change through cultural and symbolic political practices (Eyerman

---

1   Debates exist as to the appropriate definition for social movements, this is a function of their fluid structures and *ad hocratic* governance (as discussed by Rucht, 2004: 216). It is easier to define them as what they are not: parties, pressure groups, and disorganised publics.

2   Though, with the rise of women's liberation in the 19th century, clearly not a unique product of that era.

& Jamison, 1998: 7–8).[3] This allows us to investigate the status of these new forms of online social-movement organisation and ask in what way they are an extension of this tradition, where they differ and to what effect.

OSMOs-is

Online social movement organisations (OSMOs) are a new form of political organisation. They have developed in response to the opportunities for political organisation afforded by digital media and the nature of political participation of the social voter. These organisations can be found in nations around the English-speaking world,[4] and the establishment of the international, issue-oriented Change.org and Avaaz (www.avaaz.org) in 2007 added explicitly transnational versions to their ranks.

While there is a degree of variation to the approach and histories of these groups, they all have a number of similarities that relate to their shared genesis in the early work of the first of their kind: moveon.org. Formed by two business people in the final days of the US administration of Bill Clinton, moveon.org demonstrated the power of digital media to bring together unorganised citizens around a common cause. Starting with the promotion of a basic petition to congress to 'move on' from the Clinton sex scandal of the late 1990s, the Democratic party-supporting founders quickly saw the potential of the internet to organise protests and raise money from individual donors. This developed during the Republican administration of George Bush at a time when the climate of war and terrorism helped to galvanise a protest community around the site (Rohlinger & Brown, 2009).

Through the transfer of lessons related to this new model of political activist organisation, we can see that OSMOs have the following characteristics:

- They are *lightweight*, having very small numbers of staff relative to the numbers of members and campaigns they run (Stauber, 2009).

- They are *agile*. Due to their emphasis on online campaigning, these organisations develop and deploy their resources quickly. Hannah Lownsbrough sees one of the core strengths of these organisations in their ability to respond rapidly to issues of the day (2010: 75–76). They are able to capitalise on pre-existing media interest and agendas and this maximises the value of their resources (they need not invest in agenda construction), and the perceived relevance of the organisation to the issue's core audiences.

---

3 Note: symbolic political practice is different to 'symbolic policy' (rhetorical over practical policy outputs because of causal ambiguity) discussed above.

4 MoveOn.org in the United States (http://moveon.org), 38 Degrees in the United Kingdom (www.38degrees. org.uk), and ActionStation in New Zealand (www.actionstation.org.nz).

- OSMOs are noted for *innovation* and *creativity* in the design and implementation of their campaigns. This includes creative media messages to capture attention (see Illustration 14), as well as unusual strategies to achieve their objectives with an emphasis on the symbolic (i.e. raising funds to fly members of the stolen generation to hear the parliamentary apology in Canberra; Hill, 2010). Combined with their responsiveness this allows for rapid changes in their use of campaign tactics, increasing their effectiveness and unpredictability (Vromen & Coleman, 2011: 87).

- Participation is *low cost* or free for members. In this way these organisations employ nano-activism and paltry donation methods to provide easy 'buy-in' and sustain ongoing, low level participation over time (see Like my cause: Microactivism, Chapter 3). These organisations are inspired by new business models as much as conventional strategic repertoires of political action: such as 'freemium' pricing where the majority of participants are provided a basic service for no cost (e.g. petitioning in this case) with the minority opting in to pay for a more deluxe product (Heires, 2007).

Illustration 14: Still image from GetUp! election 2010 'enrol to vote' ad (5 July 2010)

Source: GetUp! Used with permission

Given the use of the term social movement organisation (SMO) (McCarthy & Zald, 1977), it is clear that this conception of OSMOs fits into the wider body of literature on NSM (Clark & Themudo, 2006: 50). SMOs represent formal organisations that act as 'the mobilizing structures of a social movement', and can be distinguished from other entities (such as supportive organisations, like churches and the media) by their focus on constituency mobilisation towards a collective objective (Kriesi, 1996: 152). OSMOs differ, however, from their direct predecessors in two ways. First, they are more expansive in the range of issues they advance. Under the traditional model, SMOs have a comparatively static and homogeneous constituency, which they have gathered for the purposes of promoting or defending their particular political interests. A good example of this would be Right to Life Australia (www.righttolife.com.au) an organisation that sits within the wider pro-life social movement, and works to mobilise this constituency towards a comparatively narrow set of subject areas (abortion, euthanasia). The wider focus of OSMOs means that these organisations are more likely to partner with traditional SMOs to undertake their campaigns, 'selling' their participation through their technical rather than subject-area expertise.

Second, it is not clear that OSMOs will be as likely to go through the social movement institutional life cycle (where SMOs bureaucratise and become 'insider' interest groups in the policy area over time). This is partially because of the lack of subject-specific expertise, but also the wide range of issues that they work on at any time.

Thus, the best way to consider them is as a hybrid between traditional SMOs and pure 'social movement platform providers'. OSMOs come out of historically specific political circumstances and, while broad in their political foci, are limited in the range of issues they are willing to promote. Pure platform providers (such as iPetitions, www.ipetitions.com) are focused only on the provision of advocacy tools, and are agnostic in the political use to which they are put (beyond a general orientation towards increased civic participation).

Let us look at some of these OSMOs and their work in the Australian context.

GetUp!

GetUp! was founded in 2005 by Jeremy Heimans and David Madden, two Australians with a background in policy scholarship through the Kennedy School of Government (a high-profile, North American 'scientific management' policy school) and with experience working with moveon.org (Dubecki, 2007). Today, the organisation claims over 600,000 members and has developed away from its roots in adjusting to local conditions.[5] Unlike the organic foundation of moveon. org, GetUp! took a path, which has come to be typical of similar Australian movements, in getting initial financial support from the union movement. This is significant, not simply in that it reflects our orientation towards institutions as the basis for political action, it also demonstrates the willingness of organised labour in this country to experiment with new forms of political organisation in light of the seemingly entrenched position of the then Coalition government of John Howard and the disarray of the ALP opposition at the time (Labor lost ground to the Coalition in the 2004 federal election and looked set for a long

---

5   Ariadne Vromen and William Coleman note that GetUp! invests more effort in member retention whereas moveon.org tends to have a higher rate of 'churn' (2011). Additionally, some earlier US-style strategies that are effective in that country (such as candidate surveys) were quickly seen as unproductive on implementation.

period in opposition at this time; Cavalier, 2005). GetUp!'s effectiveness (high visibility at a low cost) was quickly demonstrated, particularly regarding issues with which the ALP opposition was less publicly engaged on (such as anti-terror legislation in 2005, and the neo-paternalism of the Northern Territory 'intervention' on Indigenous people). In the work of GetUp! we can see the genesis of the Your Rights At Work campaign run by the union movement in 2007 (as discussed in more detail in Your Rights at Work: Success and failure?, this chapter).

The main focus of the organisation is running high-visibility campaigns that connect individuals, organisations and policy elites (often unwillingly), with GetUp! as the conduit for action. This commonly takes the form of using direct-email campaigns and petitions aimed at policy-makers and other elites, and through fundraising to support the promotion of the views of GetUp! members in the mainstream media (Vromen, 2008). This strategy works as a virtuous circle: demonstrating the success of the organisation aids in drawing in participants who see efficacy in membership. Thus, while digital media is the core of the organisation, its resources are largely spent in the 'old media' space of print and TV. For Penny O'Donnell (2009: 511) this demonstrates a form of member engagement or 'listening in television'. This is achieved through the use of a rapid response campaign model: email call, which includes the proposed creative material for placement ('get this ad on TV tomorrow'); members' response; ad buy; email to participants showing placement. In this rapid cycle of action, the organisation reaffirms to participants that they are 'heard'. This core methodology has been accompanied by other forms of creative and innovative campaigns, including the unexpectedly successful High Court challenge in the lead up to the 2010 federal election. The result was that 100,000 people were enabled to legally cast their vote (*Lawyers Weekly*, 2010).

As discussed in the introduction, these organisations have an ambiguous relationship with democratic values. While they provide individuals with a 'voice', this is often more focused outside than in. The extent to which the membership has influence over the governance and direction of the organisation is limited. GetUp! uses a suggestion form and regular surveys of members to inform its strategy, but this is not binding on the organisation's management (Rodan & Balnaves, 2010).[6] Membership, in this case, is therefore 'thin' (see Benjamin Barber's (1999) notion of engagement, discussed in Chapter 2). The organisation defines its focus as the realisation of 'progressive' values, defined simply as 'social justice, economic fairness and environmental sustainability' (GetUp!, undated b), making the selection of campaigns a combination of factors including the likelihood of traction with their members and the fit within these

---

6 The organisation also permits comments on its official blog (http://blog.getup.org.au), which has a comparatively light moderation policy: critical views of the organisation and its campaign can be found here.

loose ideological boundaries. Members 'opt in' to campaigns they support, and this allows them to demonstrate their preferences to the organisation over its executive decision-making. Where members have failed to respond to campaigns, they have been quickly abandoned.

These two membership strategies (opt in and withholding support) allow the organisation to campaign across a wide range of issues, without threatening members who do not support any particular issue or cause. This does, however, imply that commitment to the organisation is not strongly held by members, and that GetUp! has fostered an instrumental view of citizenship. In addition, because of the limited control members have over the organisation's direction, there are questions about the role of large donors in shaping the direction of the organisation: in the 2010 election cycle the organisation received over 60 per cent of its funding from large unit donors (Vromen & Coleman, 2011: 82). This questions the role that mass publics can have in an organisation where a small number of elite donors (institutions and individuals) make such a large financial contribution to the organisation.

This tension between the core and membership has been visible in the way GetUp! continues to experiment with new ways to more directly engage its members. This has taken the form of physical protests and gatherings to support its online protests (such as large rallies to support the campaign on the carbon tax), and less-successful attempts to foster local 'meet-up' style gatherings (Chen, 2011a). More recently the organisation has expanded how individuals can engage in political activity, through the creation of CommunityRun (www.communityrun.org). This platform site provides basic tools to build a localised campaign, allowing individuals to sign petitions and organisers to collect additional contact information for other forms of mobilisation. The success of this site is yet to be demonstrated, as it relies on considerably more effort from participants than other forms of activism. The organisation has been careful in ensuring the strategic direction of the service, with control over the tool through participant selection and the use of a Terms of Service 'shrinkwrap' licence that allows GetUp! to close accounts that are not used in line with the objectives of the organisation.[7] There is the potential that this could democratise the organisation, if the use of CommunityRun feeds into campaign choice made by the executive.

Similarly, the partnership model must be managed with caution. GetUp! offers considerable benefits to subject-expert SMOs looking to run campaigns, but carefully structures these agreements to ensure it does not lose its membership base to partner organisations. At its heart, GetUp!'s 'secret sauce' lies in its

---

7   The site forbids its use for campaigns that 'promote hatred, violence, discrimination or stereotypes based on race, gender, ethnicity, sexuality or religion' (GetUp!, undated a).

strategic repertoires and its large membership list, a list that it guards because it includes, not just email addresses, but data on policy interests, levels of participation, and — most importantly — members' tendency to respond to donation and participation requests. In partnering with interest groups, GetUp! provides a technology platform for running campaigns, considerable media expertise, and an existing constituency, but the intellectual property generated by the partnerships builds the organisation's database. This has led to tensions with partners who have seen their supporters being 'vacuumed' into GetUp!'s database (*Law Report*, 2008) and claims that short-term campaigns may not build partners' longer-term capacity. CommunityRun also adds petition signatories to GetUp!'s membership by default (with an opt-out option), another way that the organisation carefully develops its core political resource using a range of disaggregated strategies.

The anti-GetUp!s

On the conservative side we have seen the formation of a number of online social movements in response to, or in direct opposition to, the work of GetUp!. The most visible current movement was started by the South Australian Liberal Senator Cory Bernardi as the Community Action Network[8] or CANdo (www.cando.org.au). CANdo's formation was strongly influenced by the success of GetUp! in demonstrating the mobilising power of the internet for the political left. Where the organisation *initially* differed was in its emphasis on grassroots organisation through a more open and discursive mode of political activity (thus, the inclusion of CANdo's user base in discussions in Chapter 3). This was achieved through a turnkey social networking service (SNS) platform: Ning. Ning is a customisable SNS that can be rapidly set-up and deployed for a range of uses. The software provides for the creation and customisation of user profiles, personal blogging, and running discussion fora and online groups. The choice of Ning was, therefore, more ideologically attuned to Bernardi's preference for a decentralised network that would allow members to form subgroups and take action through these groups (vis the CommunityRun model), rather than the top-down model employed by GetUp! (personal interview: Senator Cory Bernardi, 23 June 2011).

This approach has limitations in replicating the mobilisation success of its antithesis. While CANdo managed to attract several thousand members quickly, this plateaued and did not automatically translate into political mobilisation. Based on a survey of membership at this time,[9] this problem existed irrespective of the desire of members to engage more actively with politics, their comparatively

8   Previously the Conservative Action Network.
9   This research was undertaken between 27 September and 28 November 2011. Using a number of CANdo profiles, site members were approached directly and through general appeals to participate in the survey. At the time of the study, the site had approximately 1700 members, making the sample size for the survey approximately 5.7 per cent.

homogeneous policy concerns (carbon taxation and immigration), and given their previous level of political experience. As can be seen in Figure 30, 'passive' activities (information seeking, socialisation and opinion expression) remain comparatively minor motivators for group membership, while Figure 31 shows the membership has not been inactive in offline and online politics in the near past.

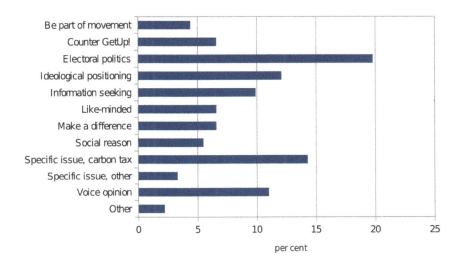

Figure 30: Reason for joining CANdo, self-reported (n = 98)

Source: Author's research

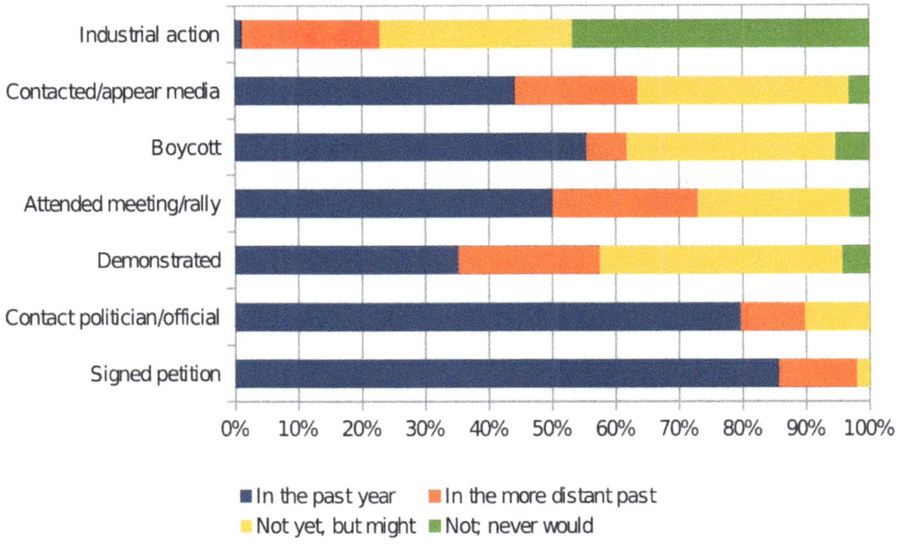

Figure 31: CANdo membership, political activity (n = 97)

Source: Author's research

The failure to thrive led to a significant redevelopment of the organisation at the end of 2011. Appointing an executive director with experience in online mobilisation in the Australian Monarchist League, the site was redesigned to more closely resemble that of the current configuration of GetUp!: focusing on a smaller number of key campaigns (an 'at a glance' or carousel site design), and pushing the discursive aspect of the original membership process further into the background. This format retains the use of members to indicate their interest in issues which can be then supported as featured campaigns, while maintaining the strategic focus of organisation through the use of a charter (www.cando.org. au/about/the-charter) that defines the range of political activities that fit within its rubric (personal interview: Jai Martinkovits, CANdo, 8 May 2012). Compared with GetUp!'s simple articulation of what it sees as progressiveness, the CANdo charter is an expansive document that includes general values statements (i.e. 'respect for the history of our great nation') and specific policy issues (i.e. low taxation, restored federalism). This makes CANdo a more focused organisation than GetUp!

Under the relaunched version of CANdo, the costs of membership are significantly reduced. Campaigns follow the GetUp! model, with an emphasis on direct messaging towards elites. This, more anonymous, nature of individual participation in CANdo is valuable in realising wider participation. The original model that put individual's profiles and views upfront attracted individuals who were very comfortable in expressing their policy positions (85 per cent would talk in the 'stranger on a train' scenario introduced in Two-step flow, 2.0, Chapter 3). Thus, the role of these sites in providing 'security and strength in numbers' to a majority of the public in 'the whisper zone' (unable to express their political views because of political correctness; personal interview: Senator Cory Bernardi, 23 June 2011) is more likely under the revised model.

At the time of writing, however, the prospects of this type of model remain unclear. Unlike GetUp!, CANdo has not managed to capture corporate or major donor support. While this is surprising given that a number of key campaigns would appear attractive to corporate or large-unit donors (opposition to the carbon tax and controls on gambling, for example), the (re)launch of the organisation, given the Labor party appears likely to lose power at the 2013 election, may limit the interest of potential donors in third party organisations rather than the incoming governing parties.

In addition, CANdo faces competition (ideological and for resources) from the rise of other, similar campaigning organisations, like the Australian Taxpayers' Alliance (ATA; www.taxpayers.org.au). Unlike CANdo's adoption of a centralised campaigning approach, however, the ATA remains focused on the cultivation of local organisations with a high degree of autonomy. Using the development of US political conservatives' self-aware identity, the ATA's founder sees this use of more active communication and physical networking as an effective longer-term strategy to develop activists from the conservative side of politics. In this way the rise of the Tea Party movement in the United States serves as a useful lesson that the development of movement culture can be more effective in mass mobilisation towards a shared objective that is sustainable over time. The ATA's avoidance of the GetUp!/CANdo approach is therefore a deliberate decision to stay away from clicktivism in an attempt to develop a self-sustaining political movement in Australia (personal interview: Tim Andrews, 22 May 2012).

Regardless of their differences, groups like GetUp!, CANdo and the ATA share their origins in developments in contemporary advocacy organisations in the United States. The strong focus on individual mobilisation, media management and agenda setting is combined with a more explicit view about the critical importance of fundraising as the basis for political success. While these organisations have a strong digital media focus, a difference lies in the role technology played in the genesis of the two groups. While GetUp! has its background in the work of moveon.org, CANdo and its related organisations in the new Australian conservative movement owe more to the strategies of 1980-era Republican party ginger groups like Grover Norquist's Americans for Tax Reform (Garnett & Lynch, 2003: 5). CANdo, Menzies House (discussed in Chapter 3) and the ATA all emerged from an explicit strategy of generating young conservative leaders and multiplying organisations that will cultivate a base of support and place pressure on existing institutions to adjust their policies accordingly.[10] This is a modification of an intermediating strategy through its explicit focus on cultivating a constituency ideationally. What this approach lacks — partially due to the funding difference — is the strong technological base of the original organisations, particularly in the establishment of good member management through well-developed (and expensive) organisational databases.

While the adoption of the moveon.org model could be read as that unholy beast of Australian cultural inferiority, the 'Americanisation' of our politics, the transfer of lessons from the United States to Australia has as much to do with the dynamism of that electoral system (in terms of the proliferation of elections, the resources that allow high-technology experimentation, and the social/regional/ religious diversity of the United States) as the development of a similar political opportunity structure across English-speaking countries. The decline of strong party membership and voter identification does not simply increase the size and importance of 'swing' voters, it opens parties to influence by organised activist organisations who mobilise groups to place pressure on party policy.

---

10   Tim Andrews previously worked for Norquist (Hills, 2011).

This opportunity is more prominent in the Coalition parties because they lack Labor's institutionalised union presence and factional system that places a counterweight on the effectiveness of these groups.

Strengths and weaknesses of the OSMOs

These new forms of political organisation demonstrate that there is something new under the sun. While interest groups and SMOs have existed for centuries, OSMOs are hybrids that are quantitatively and qualitatively different. There is a basic political logic that underpins their place in the social order. Social fragmentation and low levels of individual political efficacy create a type of citizen that Henrik Bang and Eva Sørensen call 'everyday makers' (1999): hit-and-run individuals who want to have a specific political impact without a commitment to long-term memberships or ongoing formal entities. In reaching out to these individuals — an unserved market segment — OSMOs sell activism to their members as an alternative to traditional party membership and politics (Marks, 2010).

As facilitative platforms they have to convince members that each campaign requires their attention and interest, and they employ creative marketing and knowledge of their membership to that effect. In this way, it is unsurprising that the original model for OSMOs came from individuals with business, rather than political backgrounds: the management of organisational 'publics' (stakeholders) is a core element of commercial marketing practice (Christopher, et al., 2002). This also explains their presence in English-speaking countries. OSMOs are a response to populations that have become fragmented and individualised by their immersion in neoliberalism.

OSMOs are therefore able to generate a considerable political impact through the rapid provision of a sense of solidarity in a fragmented social world. Their success lies in the ability to use modern, database-driven market segmentation tools to effectively match causes to particular constituencies. In doing so, they have to overcome a basic problem: how to create and sustain effective collective action. Employing moveon.org as a case study Marc Eaton (2010) has examined the way these organisations create communities 'top-down'. Whereas 'natural' communities are consumed and created simultaneously, this naturally limits the size to which these communities can grow before fragmentation. From an analysis of language, Eaton was able to demonstrate how OSMOs construct an 'imagined community' of progressive activists through its use of language and rhetoric. Noting that the most effective OSMOs to date do not foster 'horizontal' communication (between members), their use of top-down communication sells activist identities.

The future of these organisational structures is uncertain. Micah White (2011) sees the model of social change employed by OSMOs as inherently flawed: by embedding the logic of consumerism within the new activist model, the potential for this form of activity to deliver radical change is limited. This is because their notion of change is expressed outwards to institutional actors (governments, corporations), rather than including personal change by members. As has been observed, these politics are focused on self-gratification ('consummatory politics are profoundly conservative, emphasizing stasis') (Rosenberg, et al. 1988: 169). While this criticism has value, it does presume that OSMOs are interested in radical change.

This reflects the ongoing debate in social-movement literature about the tendency of researchers to disproportionately focus on radical causes. The consumerist basis of this activism has considerable advantages in dealing with the problem of collective action, but also presents the risk of comparatively weak attachment to the community 'sold' to members. Sensing this, these organisations have employed physical events to bolster member attachment, but their level of commitment to physical grassroots organising appears to decline after they have attempted to employ it. Australian OSMOs have recognised the need to develop more authentic opportunities for horizontal community building within their platforms. That both GetUp! and CANdo have had difficulty effectively employing more traditional types of member interaction may reflect less on a cynical application of imagined communities to achieve their broader objectives, as a low level of interest from members. The hollow rhetoric of community that Eaton saw employed top-down may just as readily be matched by limited real interest in the requirements of joining real political communities, from the bottom-up.

Digital media and movement (re)mobilisation

The rise of OSMOs does not mean that traditional social movements and SMOs have disappeared from the political landscape. Indeed, the social changes that focus politics on ideational and discursive practices, self-conscious political identity formation, and citizenship through social voting and the practices of the 'everyday maker' have far more in common with the politics of NSMs than other forms of political practice. So far we have seen examples of how SNSs have been quickly and readily adopted by organised and unorganised social-movement actors as a space for communication, solidarity and organisation (see Social media by the numbers, Chapter 3, for example). This reflects NSMs as early technology adopters of communications technology because their limited resource base and asymmetrical power relationship with oppositional elite institutions encourages the adoption of new technologies to create political opportunities (van de Donk, et al., 2004: 16).

This opportunity structure is particularly relevant in the context of the digital-media environment, where the architecture of digital-media systems facilitates the formation of social networks based on similar interests (enduring or temporary). Indeed, the classic definition of NSMs focused largely on their loose, non-hierarchical network structures of organisation (della Porta, 2009: 190). While it could be argued that the times in many ways suit the NSMs,[11] we have already discounted the idea of a media environment automatically producing particular political arrangements (Lister, et al., 2003: 177). This is most clear when considering that exemplar of the NSM literature: the anti-war movement's inability to sustain initial protests against the war in Iraq, regardless of strong opposition to the invasions. In this example, Damian Trewhella (2005: 8–11) has argued that, while key SMOs in the peace movement have employed digital media to promote protests, the predominant use of one-to-many channels (websites, email lists) failed to build on initial participation, particularly in the face of sustained domestic and foreign military propaganda and following the invasion of Iraq.[12]

Fostering intra-group communication and the use of social media to preserve commitment to the group reflects recent academic and popular discussion of the importance of 'social capital'. This stems from a body of literature that emerged in the late 1990s and early 2000s, driven by influential books like Robert Putnam's *Bowling Alone* (2000). For authors like Putnam, active communities which provide mutual welfare through strong social ties — social capital — are significant in the realisation of bottom-up social action (political and non-political).[13] Social capital is particularly relevant in the mobilisation and operation of social movements (as communities of interest), because this capital represents a reservoir of good will and network connections that can be mobilised very quickly for a variety of purposes. This reflects how social movements are observed to 'lie fallow' for long periods of time and then remobilise in reaction to changing political situations (threats and opportunities). Looking at three recent social movements' use of digital media can give a sense of the way technology is employed by individuals and SMOs, but also the role of social capital and trust in mobilising and sustaining these movements (Hutton and Connors, 1999: 11).

11 Particularly as the use of digital media has become less hierarchical in recent years: shifting away from centralised websites (Pickerill, 2001: 75) towards more fluid use of online media.
12 We should also add, however, in comparison with the 1960s and 1970s, that there is less support to the movement from the Opposition. Rick Kuhn (1997) points out that the support given to the fledgling anti-war movement in Australia was tied to long-standing opposition to conscription, an issue that is not present in recent conflicts.
13 In *Bowling Along*, the focus of this interest is that the measure of social capital is a useful marker of civic decline and social alienation in contemporary American life (see Plug in your USB coffee warmers, Chapter 3).

Occupy [your hometown here]

The Occupy movement captured considerable attention at the end of 2011 with a series of large protests and encampments around the world. The proximate causes for these mobilisations was the global financial crisis and perceived mismanagement of economic policy in response to the economic slump (industry bailouts in the United States, failure to introduce new financial industry regulation in the United Kingdom, austerity measures in Europe). This saw protesters mobilise to 'perform' their dissatisfaction with established elites, through the advocacy of direct action (occupations and other disruption) to highlight popular unrest in the economic status quo. Significantly, Occupy reflects the impressive ability for social movements to organise very quickly and broadly:[14] while SMOs have been important in focusing the movement and organising core protest infrastructure, the movement is significantly more than its vanguard organisers (Jackson & Chen, 2012) with 40 per cent of Australian participants considering Occupy the first movement they have taken part in.[15] This reflects the ability of Occupy to draw upon organisations, individuals and techniques that were active in the Global Justice protests of the 1990s.[16]

Occupy also presents an interesting case example in the use of technology by social movements. Australian participants used social media to discuss the Occupy movement and its political concerns (83.52 per cent).[17] From the outset, Occupy participants were conscious of the way in which digital media could be useful in spreading their messages and building solidarity. Most Occupy camps included activities and training aimed at increasing the reach and visibility of the movement, which served to hasten the transmission of key movement frames around the world, as well as develop a strong sense of activist solidarity. The use of social media distributed by protesters helps to sustain this togetherness, as channels like Twitter allow for the rapid distribution of real-time information about interactions with oppositional groups (normally police), and the visibility of protesters' hashtags helps to increase the sense of community among supporters (Juris, 2012). Occupy demonstrates the power of framing in building coalitions of political interest. In this case example, the rhetorical use of a very simple characterisation of the movement and its opponents (the 99 per cent versus the 1 per cent) was powerful in aligning the viewpoint of protesters with the wider public through existing political issues (the Qantas dispute with

14 Occupy Adelaide, Armidale, Brisbane, Burnie-Devonport, Cairns, Canberra, Darwin, Gippsland, Gold Coast, Hobart, Melbourne, Perth, Sydney and Townsville.
15 Source: Occupy Research Demographic and Political Participation Survey (http://occupyresearch.net/archive/03192012_OR_data_download_clean7_answers-txt.xlsx); n = 77.
16 Another social movement with a strong record of using new media for organising (Capling & Nossal, 2001: 443).
17 Source: Occupy Research Demographic and Political Participation Survey; n = 85.

management being a local example) and shifting away from the language of class warfare that is the stock-in-trade of many of the core SMOs that came from the socialist movement.

What NSMs like Occupy demonstrate is how willing individuals and small groups can combine resources towards a shared objective. This type of collective action rests on the ability of social networks to identify supporters and co-ordinate their resource base. At the core of the concept of social capital theory we can see that *trust* is relational in character. This makes trust situational and contextual. We see this in the research on Occupy Sydney. While participants had low levels of trust in political institutions and processes, they invested considerable trust in the movement itself (Figure 32).[18] For political campaigners, the interest in community also points to opportunities to engage in a new language of authenticity and mobilise political resources other than money (Rasmussen, 2007: 81).

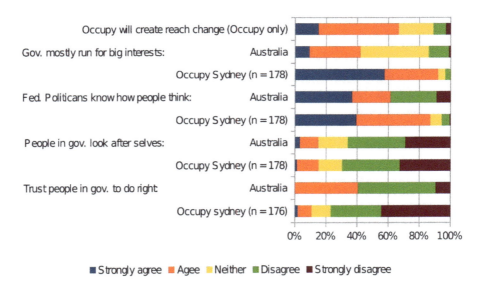

Figure 32: Occupy Sydney participants' levels of political trust, compared with Australian population

Source: Author's research, with Stewart Jackson

18 The research was conducted at the 5 November 'Rally to Re-occupy Sydney' event using a team of eight field interviewers who conducted the structured interviews face-to-face. The size of the rally has been estimated at between 400 (NSW Police Force, 2011) and 1500 (Smith, 2011) participants, making the sample size between 12 and 45 per cent of participants. A more detailed report on this research can be found in Stewart Jackson and Peter John Chen (2012).

The Occupy movement's use of technology to organise protest action is an example of the natural fit between network technologies and social movements as network organisations. Looking at the 5 November protest in Sydney, Table 10 shows how offline and online social networking represent the most significant form of promotional channel for the event. This is also generational in character. Table 11 illustrates SNS's role as a key promotional channel is negatively correlated with the age of participants.

Channel	Heard via*
Interpersonal	31%
Social networking service	30%
Group/organisational contact	26%
Mass media	24%
Website	21%
Poster/flyer/street	12%
Select/specialist media	4%
At another event	2%

* Respondents could suggest a variety of methods, therefore total will not add to 100 per cent

Table 10: Mobilisation channel (n = 180)

Source: Author's research, with Stewart Jackson

Age	14–30	31–45	46–60	61–83
Heard via SNS%	53	32	9	6
n	71	48	30	26

Table 11: Heard about protest via SNS, by age

Source: Author's research, with Stewart Jackson

By early 2012 participation in Occupy had declined to a number of small groups of encamped protesters around Australia. Unlike in Spain, where ongoing economic decline and government austerity has sustained popular protests (Associated Press, 2012), Occupy has returned to largely a dormant state. During late 2011 the movement experimented with new frames to revitalise participation (empty building seizures to protest cost-of-living issues, alignment with other industrial disputes). This demonstrates the limits of the movement in raising popular concern about social disadvantage when the relative depredation[19] of the wider public was less significant than in the United Kingdom, United States

---

19 Social movements can be driven by the perception of deprivation by participating groups (Blumberg, 2009: 17). This need not be absolute, but relative to other groups in society. In this way, motivation for participation may not come from the most disadvantaged. This concept would appear most relevant in the framing of the Occupy movement, where the idea of the 99 per cent aims to highlight the economic distance between the public and elites.

and Europe as communicated in the mass media that Australia was experiencing an economic 'miracle'. The ability to quickly reform, adjust their issues frames, and mobilise large numbers of people demonstrates the value of the 'cultural turn' in the study of social movements (Collins, 2004: 31): through the creation of cultural artefacts, movements preserve their ideology and identity over time. As Graham Meikle has observed in discussion of activist groups' use of the internet in the early 2000s, these techniques and cultural products are often picked up by movement pedagogues and shared in more general cultural events (conferences, festivals and 'tactical media labs'), demonstrating a tendency for new methods to 'leak out' of specific movements into the wider activist community over time (2004: 84).

Online anarchists and the democratisation of hacking

While Occupy can be seen in a long tradition of economic protest over the distribution of societal resources, the rise of digital media has generated its own, very specific policy issues, interest groups and movements. Examples include the rise of an online libertarian community opposed to the regulation of internet content that was active in the 1990s (Chen, 2003), movements aimed at increasing personal privacy that have been effective in getting these issues into the institutional policy-making process (Greenleaf, 1988: 7; 2008: 172) and, more recently, the formation of computer gamers as a coherent community of interest that has successfully argued for the introduction of an R18+ classification for games through a process of framing the use of computer games from the domain of children to an adult form of entertainment. Groups like Grow up Australia (www.growupaustralia.com) and gamers4croydon (www.gamers4croydon.org) have been able to use general social media and gamer-specific channels[20] to create a political identity around gamers, and mobilise action aimed at supporting regulatory reform and attacking opponents of change (LeMay, 2010).[21] The rapidity with which gamers have been able to undertake loosely coordinated action at different levels of the federal system is markedly different to the inability of previous fantasy ('pen and paper') role-playing gamer cultures to organise prior to the introduction of the internet (Larme, 2000). As with other recreational activities (e.g. fishing), these groups employ arguments about the economic size of their hobby to legitimise their community with policy makers. In doing so they were able to mobilise economic interests to support their campaign.[22]

---

20   Steam discussion fora. Steam is a game distribution service run by the Valve gaming company in the United States.
21   Gamers4croydon ran six candidates in the 2010 South Australian election in response to the Attorney-General's opposition to the R18+ classification proposal.
22   EB Games assisted Grow up Australia to collect 16,000 signatures on a pro-R18+ petition (Grow up Australia, 2010).

To date the most visible of these online social movements has been the rise of high-profile 'hackers'. In popular use, this term represents a vague set of activities that centre on the use of information and communications technologies for illegal activities. The political use of hacking is not a new practice. A high-profile Australian example dates to the 1980s in the effective use of the 'Wank' (Worms Against Nuclear Killers) attack on the US Department of Energy and NASA (Dreyfus, 1997).[23] While the methods may be identical to non-political hacking activity, these types of political activities are generally referred to as 'hacktivism'. Hacktivism is defined by Lincoln Dahlberg as direct action that aims to:

> ... bring excluded discourse to attention in the 'mainstream' public sphere, methods that include email spamming, denial-of-service attacks on internet servers, site defacements that leave behind protest messages and parody sites diverting attention to counter-discursive spaces. (2007: 841)

The use of these disruptive activities is in line with the logic of radical political organisations that are less powerful than their adversaries. This pattern of adoption conforms to the view that social movements look for political opportunities that fit their particular interests and capacity to act. In addition, the use of illegal forms of protest and direct action has been seen as more likely to occur in repressive environments where social movements have a tendency to see the political in more conspiratorial terms (Heberle, 1951: 386). In the context of hacktivism, therefore, it is relevant that these actions have focused on protests against entrenched policy positions where there has been a high level of elite consensus (globalisation and deregulation, and the War on Terror). In reviewing the longer history of radical politics online, Jenny Pickerill (2006: 268) sees the choice of online activism as a response to the shift in power away from 'the street' and towards sites of elite presence and value. Protests therefore move to the online sphere as political institutions become less responsive to older forms of protest action.

WikiLeaks

Hacktivism in Australia has had its largest impacts in two areas: discursive and direct. The discursive has been achieved largely through the work of the organisation WikiLeaks, run by the Australian Julian Assange. Not a domestically focused organisation, WikiLeaks operates on a principle of radical openness (Flew & Wilson, 2012: 173): providing a hosting service for leaked material from a wide variety of sources. In many ways, WikiLeaks operates as

---

23   A worm is a computer program that moves through a network with the aim of creating disruption or damage. Worms are similar to computer viruses, but rather than 'infecting' another program, they are stand-alone programs. Worms and viruses are software commonly classified under the title of 'malware'.

an intermediary between whistleblowers and journalists as the organisation releases material unedited and in its raw form (see New audiences, new partners, Chapter 6). But seeing the organisation as purely a content host and platform for third parties (such as, for example, Pastebin; http://pastebin.com) is incorrect. In recent years the organisation has moved from the periphery of political discourse to direct conflict with the most realist of policy domains: international policy making and the US security state. The most significant of challenges was the staggered (to maximise the length of time these documents received media coverage)[24] release, beginning in 2010, of hundreds of thousands of pages of classified documents that are believed to have been provided by a low-ranking, US military-intelligence analyst (Poulsen & Zetter, 2010).[25] WikiLeaks' high-profile interventions have been focused on maximising its impact on issues surrounding the war, through the timing and framing of the release of its material (significantly, the 'Collateral murder' video showing US military firing on civilians and journalists in 2007; BBC, 2010). These releases have had an incidental impact on Australia, through attacking the conduct of military and intelligence operations that successive Australian governments support.

Anonymous

The second area has been active in the realm of Australian politics and the mobilisation of opposition to proposed regulation of internet content by the Labor government. Using hacktivist techniques of disruption and high-visibility protest, 'Operation titstorm' in early 2010 had a significant, if temporary, impact in taking down key Australian Government websites (including Parliament) using distributed denial-of-service attacks (DDOS) (Hardy, 2010: 474–75).[26] These attacks were proposed and managed through the loose hacker collective called Anonymous, which organises around particular operations based on the interest of participants. Through the development of tools for the formation of ad hoc networks participating in DDOS attacks (e.g. software programs like the Low Orbit Ion Cannon (LOIC)), these tactics have been increasingly common in recent years and groups like Anonymous have refined their attack strategies and the related promotion of them within the media. The drama and 'high-tech' nature of these direct actions are still novel enough to attract strong media coverage of successful actions. In this way, these actions retain the dramaturgical character of street protests.[27]

---

24 A learned strategy by the organisation following earlier tendencies to simply 'dump' complete sets of records in one release.
25 The prosecution of whom has become a *cause célèbre* in parts of the online community.
26 'Flooding' websites with access requests to reduce their performance or 'crash' the servers and prevent legitimate access to them.
27 Dramaturgy, in this context, picks up on the way that protests are 'staged' or performed for their audiences (be that in the street, or through media).

The social meaning of these tactics remains unclear and is in flux, both inside and outside of the 'hacker community' (see below). While there are increasing moves to securitise issues of computer intrusion and misuse (the creation of an interpretive frame which sees the threat as requiring an extraordinary response; Vultee, 2007; Pauli, 2011), it is clear that some (but certainly not all) perpetrators may not understand the significance of their crime in the eyes of the law. While Australian law tends to tolerate temporary disruption to physical infrastructure for the purposes of public protest (e.g. marches and rallies; NSW Council for Civil Liberties, 2010), participation in a DDOS has been classified as a form of terrorism. Here we see the logic behind the shift from 'the street' to cyberspace as a response to elite signalling of the significance of the virtual over the physical realm. But this signalling is not universal. Unlike the comparatively harsh treatment of direct-action protesters (particularly in the environmental and animal-rights policy areas) in the United States in recent years (Potter, 2011), members of the Australian judiciary remain cautious about excessive regulation in this area. An Australasian sentenced for participation in Titstorm was given a comparatively mild sentence by the magistrate on the basis of his ignorance of the significance of his participation (Ryan, 2010). The implication, as with the prosecution of online piracy, is that increasing the punitive nature of penalties may be ineffective in preventing these attacks in the medium term (Doloswala & Dadich, 2011), particularly where participation is facilitated through easy-to-use tools like the LOIC.

The value of direct action remains in relationship with its impact and visibility. The most significant opportunity for impact will be the disruption of key infrastructure and time-sensitive events. Participation in these types of actions may become more potentially significant if initial moves to online voting by New South Wales in the most recent state election are expanded. There is little evidence, however, that these attacks have influenced the outcome of any election to date (political party sites have been defaced during election periods). The use of these attacks, given the negative message they send about those who employ them, are likely to be counterproductive as a political strategy. Additionally, it should be noted that the majority of (known) politically motivated computer intrusions fall outside of election periods.[28] This is for a range of reasons, including the tendency for these to be motivated by a comparatively small set of policy issues (such as computer-content regulation in recent years), but also the relatively short window of time that election campaigns present to design and undertake a co-ordinated attack on websites. While the number of incidents may be small, however, preventing access to online political information during election campaigning is clearly an assault on the basic tenets of the electoral

---

28 An incident was reported in 1997 against the Liberal Party website, while another report in 2007 appears to have been a photoshopped version of the site and therefore a hoax (http://news.com.au, 2007).

process,[29] denying candidates from engaging in free speech, and voters from accessing this information (an interference with political liberty[30]). Another, just as rarely occurring, form of computer misuse has been illegal access to politicians' email. To date these incidences have been largely[31] restricted to within parliamentary settings (Tucker, 2004; Jenkins, 2010), and have been addressed by internal review and discipline.

'You weary giants of flesh and steel'

In the case of WikiLeaks and Anonymous we can see both similarity of purpose and a diversity of political perspectives and concerns. While the work of WikiLeaks and Anonymous have roots in the individualism and meritocratic nature of the computer programming culture of the Californian university scene of the 1970s (Castells, 2001: 60; Coyer, et al., 2007: 164), the political directions in which these two groups have moved is quite different. WikiLeaks seeks to directly challenge the authority of governments and corporations on a supranational level, seeing the ability of online organisations and publics to rise above restraints over global issues within jurisdictions. Anonymous, on the other hand 'comes from cyberspace'[32] to tell everyone to just piss the hell off. The majority of its major campaigns have focused on targets (corporate, religious and government) that have attempted to place regulations of the free action of individuals online. This represents a form of 'cyber-separatism', which seeks, not a new approach to resolving political problems, but a withdrawal from conventional forms of political community (Mayer-Schönberger, 2003). This is a new form of the classical approach to utopian thought that looks for escape from rather than reform of existing political problems; it also sits squarely within the meritocratic perspective that others are not fit to judge the behaviour of the online community aside from their own (in regulating the behaviour of individuals online, two 'Operation Darknets' have been conducted by Anonymous to attack online paedophilia networks; Gallagher, 2011).

Hacktivist groups like Anonymous are often referred to as 'e-movements' because their activities are restricted to the electronic media environment (Friedland & Rogerson, 2009). This type of distinction, however, may be problematic. While Anonymous is most famous for its online attacks, like most social movements it is hard to unambiguously define. The cultural aspects of the movement make it hard for a core group to hold control of its social definition. This is most obvious

---

29 In mid 2011, Anonymous claimed to have leaked detailed count data from the NSW state election. The NSW electoral commission responded that the data was from a public server and therefore not secret (Hopewell, 2011).

30 A light version of which is recognised in s327 of the Act.

31 Though malicious editing of wiki content is sometimes reported as 'hacking' (see, for example, Keane, 2010).

32 Borrowing John Barlow's 1996 evocative opening phrase from his *Declaration of Independence of Cyberspace*.

in the expansive use of the *V for Vendetta* (Guy Fawkes)[33] masks in a range of physical protests across an increasing political sphere. To some extent this has been the result of encouragement by Anonymous to supporters to undertake physical events in support of its operations (such as anti-Scientology protests in 2008; Ramadge, 2008). Over time, the use of the mask has gained wider association with anti-establishment politics that reflects a generational change in both the focus of political action and its organisation.

This demonstrates how social movements demonstrate the difficulty of controlling ideas and tactics. As hacktivist methods become more visible in the public arena, there has been a shift away from separatist ideological homogeneity among their practitioners. Governments have been increasingly employing these techniques as part of their active intelligence-gathering, cyber-warfare strategies, and general harassment against political opponents.[34] Additionally, 'patriotic' hacking against perceived national enemies has been popular in countries like China and Russia in recent years (Muncaster, 2012).

In response to hacks against national security interests by Anonymous and associated groups in the United States, a range of other hackers announced their intention to identify members of these groups (Mills, 2012). This demonstrates how movement tactics can quickly spread to other organisations in the digital environment, particularly where organisations have the resources to rapidly acquire technologies they may lack. In the case of governmental response to the rise of independent cyber-attacks, the United States has been active in using law enforcement to coopt members of the movement, particularly given the tendency for cyberactivism to face legal sanctions (Hardy, 2010). Thus, while we will continue to see hacktivist politics come from the cyber-separatists, these tactics will be increasingly employed by a range of political actors (Stephey, 2008), including governments and corporations.[35]

Your Rights at Work: Success and failure?

While Occupy and Anonymous represent anarchic social movements of the NSM generation, the use of digital media campaigning by traditional, institutionalised social movements may represent the most effective examples of online campaign organisation to date in Australia. The Your Rights at Work

---

33 As popularised by the graphic novel and film. This bears little (if any) relationship with the original sectarian political motivation of Fawkes and his co-conspirators.

34 Of particular note would be the use of DDOS by supporters of the Russian regime against political opponents within the country (Roberts & Etling, 2011), and as part of military actions against Georgia in 2008 (Danchev, 2008).

35 As can be seen recently emerging in the UK scandal over telephone message interception by employees of News Corporation, including accessing messages of key cabinet ministers during a time of war (Whittaker, 2011).

(YRaW) campaign played a notable role in the 2007 federal election through the mobilisation of resources in support of the election of the ALP, as well as framing debates around issues that favoured the then Opposition. While much of the $30 million campaign focused on traditional use of media and physical events, there was promotion of the online aspect of strategy. Through e-petitions and email lists, the official campaign site (www.rightsatwork.com.au) generated over 600,000 unique visits, built a mailing list of 190,000 people and collected nearly 90,000 signatures on a petition against the Government's laws. The GetUp! style of targeted and time-limited fundraising strategy was also employed, successfully raising money for billboards and print advertising purchases during the campaign (Muir 2008: 77–79). This demonstrated how the union movement had carefully studied the lessons of the OSMOs to integrate into their wider campaign strategy.

While, on the surface, this campaign was about achieving the policy objectives of the Labour movement through a change of government, it also served to reinforce in the eyes of the ALP that their union base had power outside of their political wing. This was important as the Opposition were not initially opposed to the reforms (Bramble & Kuhn, 2011: 137). YRaW demonstrated that unions mobilise citizens in a way that parties no longer can. Shaun Wilson's and Benjamin Spies-Butcher's analysis of the 2007 election campaign demonstrated how the issue of industrial relations was of increased salience for electors,[36] and that increased activity in protests and rallies (up from 3 to 8 percent of the 12-million-strong membership base) (2011: s317–19). This latter approach increased physical participation in the campaign to vote out the incumbent government by just under one million people.

Outside of the role of the campaign in changing government, YRaW's impact was more modest: in government Labor did not 'rip up' the WorkChoices legislation, but introduced a series of amendments to moderate the legislation (Barnes & Lafferty, 2010: 4–5). While the Australian union movement had little choice but to campaign hard against WorkChoices because of the impact of the legislation on the union movement overall, its considerable investment in this campaign achieved limited policy benefits. The institutionalised campaign of the union movement serves as a good example of how social movements can employ digital media to achieve brute-force success. The combination of considerable economic resources and institutionalised access to power through the union movements' ties with the ALP appears to provide a more significant set of resources than that provided by diffused social networks and political capital.

---

36 Barbara Pocock and Karen Brown highlight the role of framing the impacts on individuals, and particularly women and families, in this process of framing the salience of the dispute (2009: 168).

The campaign also demonstrates that it is easier to 'push a falling fence' than achieve a lasting influence. The union movement in Australia is not well positioned to be able to halt the more general trend towards considerable liberalisation of labour laws in this country in the future. This is significant with regard to how effective SMOs are at mobilising members of the public into action, but also the responsiveness of political elites to more radical calls for change. Gabriel Almond and Sidney Verba described this in terms of the nation's 'civic culture' or its underlying working principles that shaped political practice and the formal institutional containers it works through:

> ... the ways in which political elites make decisions, their norms and attitudes, as well as the norms and attitudes of the ordinary citizen, his relations to government and to his fellow citizens — are subtler cultural components. [sic] (1963: 3)

That Australian elites respond in a limited transactional way to the mobilisation by social movement organisations demonstrates that they have little faith in their ability to deliver a lasting ideational change in the populous. While the modest impacts of Occupy point to some truth in this elite perspective, the inability of the Labor government to sustain its support base following the 2007 election also indicates that the public places some stock in trust, authenticity and honesty over simple majoritarianism.

Rise of the l337s

The digital-media environment resents challenges to existing elites in society, public and private. The opportunities afforded by new technology to develop new political and media organisations has broken down some of the barriers to entry into the political environment, with a range of young, hungry, political entrepreneurs clambering through the breach to launch online campaigning organisations and digital media ventures. The success of these new actors has been varied, but, at times, the NSMs have demonstrated how to revitalise individual participation in a way many had thought impossible. These organisations have liberated political resources and influenced the outcome of policy debates through a canny use of mass membership, money and old-fashioned political propaganda. In doing so they have encouraged counter-mobilisation and the spread of new movement tactics to their political opponents. The 'corporatisation' of social movement politics may blunt the radical edge of the new OSMOs, but this vacuum has been quickly filled by new, radical groups who have taken direct action to a new level of sophistication and, in doing so, challenged some of the most powerful military-intelligence institutions in the world, while partnering with other centres of power to get their message across to the public. In Chapter 6 we look at the shape of the media industry under the radical digital media political economy.

Chapter 6 — Elite digital media and digital media elites

Audiences know what to expect, and that is all they are prepared to believe in.

— The Player, *Rosencrantz and Guildenstern Are Dead* (Stoppard, 1967)

Information is power and the 'mainstream media' in Australia — the established, commercial news organisations — are the most significant institutions in shaping public opinion. This occurs at two levels. The first is through the creation of information that forms the basis of democratic dialogue. While the classic model of the public sphere saw local information as filtering up to national elites, the modern public sphere requires news media to provide information upon which informed debate and deliberation can take place. In this, media organisations are often the origin of many of the issues that form the grist for the mill of public opinion, serving as engines in the generation of popular discourse in this country. The second, and equally important, level is through the framing and focusing of attention on particular issues. Media organisations act as both conduit for other's content (such as the material produced by campaigners in parties and social movements), and produce their own frames of preferred interpretation for the information they transmit (Young, 2011a: 102–03).

The political-economy model of news media

Under the liberal democratic model of Australian politics, a free market based media is essential to regulate the conduct of elite public institutions (the legislature and the executive) through providing a means by which the public observe the elite's behaviour. This formulation supposes a classic principal–agent problem, where the 'agents' of the public — politicians and bureaucrats — are difficult for voters to watch directly because of the complexity of their work, distance from their constituents, and the public's lack of specialist skills to oversight their behaviour. 'Solving' this problem, the private sector nature of the media is significant, because it provides this oversight of the governmental sphere *without* being dependent upon it for resources (Errington and Miragliotta, 2011: 4–11).

Through these resources, specialists (journalists) scrutinise the work of elected and salaried elites. This 'free press' provides voters and citizens with the information they need to make informed choices during elections, combined with the informational role of political parties and active citizens they form part of the political system as an information system. The commercial basis of media does not simply insulate the media against government interference (as do political traditions that protect free speech and publication in democratic nations), but the need for media to make a profit calibrates the media towards the public's areas of concern: a competitive media acts thermostatically to sense and respond to the public's interest through 'market sensing'.

Stories of decline

Under this (idealised) view of the nature of democratic practice, the single biggest impact of the rise of electronic and digital media following World War II has been its erosion of the economic basis of journalism and the free press. This is because the arrival of radio, television and, most recently, the internet, have tended to undermine the financial viability of newspapers and news magazines, leading to the contraction of titles and consolidation of ownership (Figure 33). This has been driven by a significant reduction in the circulation of print titles (Figure 34) regardless of the rapid increase in the total adult population, combined with an inability of the print industry to adapt to new sustainable business models in the short term (Macnamara, 2010b).

In Australia's media–politics arena, Rodney Tiffen (in Jones, 2005) has argued that this led to the belief in 'the influence of "media mates" on coverage' by political elites, and the distortion of policy towards positions favouring media proprietors (Dyer, 2010). While this focused on a limited number of domestic news owners (the Murdoch and the Packer families) in the 1980s, over time the globalisation of News Limited (holding a 65 per cent share of national and metropolitan circulation in 2011; Finkelstein, 2012: 59) has shifted this down to the role of individual editors within consolidated media corporations (McKnight, 2012: 38–46; Josephi, 2011: 20).[1] In 2012, attempts by Gina Rinehart to assert editorial influence over a weakened Fairfax organisation rekindled the political interest in the role of individual proprietors in shaping the editorial focus of newspapers in Australia.

---

1 This is also the case in the electronic media, where reforms to cross-media ownership laws in the mid-2000s encouraged a shift from proprietors to corporate ownership (Pusey and McCutcheon, 2011).

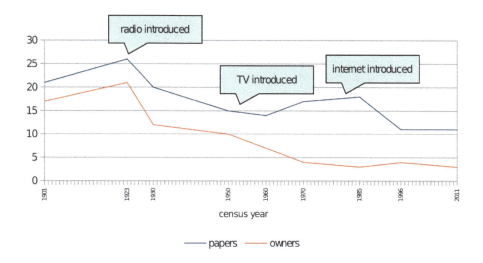

Figure 33: Changes in the metro and national newspaper industry, 1901–2011

Source: Finkelstein, 2012 (rescaled and annotated)

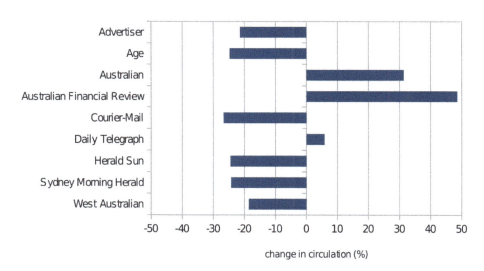

Figure 34: Percentage change in newspaper circulation 1977–2012

Source: Rosenbloom, 2012

This industry consolidation also has a direct impact on the work of journalists through the reduction of resources available to them, while also undermining the market-sensing model through a significant reduction in the level of competition. The importance of this particular industry has been highlighted because print, it has been argued, is the preserve of 'quality journalism' (Birnbauer, 2012: 83). The impact of this economic squeeze creates a negative cycle, because cost cutting sees a shift away from areas of news production that are seen as high-cost (specialist journalism, like investigative and technical analysis). Following the liberal-democratic media model presented above, this has a number of knock-on effects leading to concerns regarding the reduction in the quality of our democracy.

While the internet is often cited as *the* source of the decline (Finkelstein, 2012: 55), in Australia there was significant consolidation of media ownership during the 1960s, with a contraction in titles in the 1970s. This reflected the impact of radio and television on the consumption habits of Australians, which led to a weakening of the economic position of print, through increased competition for consumers and advertising revenue (Radio Adelaide, 2004). The rise of the internet has further reduced the profitability of print publications, and narrowed their economic base (fundamentally in subscriptions and advertising). This significantly changes the political economy of the news media as more media compete for declining audiences and advertising revenue.

Media in an age of 'attention' economics

Following a neo-institutional reading of the impact of structures on social institutions, scholars of media politics have long speculated as to the reasons commercial media organisations diverge in practice from the purist view of them as democratic institutions. The most famous of these perspectives is the 'propaganda model' proposed by Edward Herman and Noam Chomsky (1988). The propaganda model argues that a series of 'filters' shape what is produced by commercial media organisations by nature of the capitalist system of production in which they are embedded. The profit motive, the need to appeal to large audiences, reliance on advertising, and the relationship with other social elites for access to information (journalist–source relations; Tiffen, 1989: 95–124) narrows the type of news that is likely to be covered by the media, with a preference towards market-friendly, advertiser-friendly, and reader-friendly copy that is unlikely to significantly challenge the status quo. Thus, rather than capitalist production producing a neutral press, this model sees the media as having a specific, in-built, conservative and pro-market bias. For Paul Taylor, this means that the mainstream media's watchdog role is constrained by its desire to retain its relationships with existing elites: 'Even at its most critical, the media commentariat who purport to hold power to account are increasingly difficult to distinguish from the corporate apparatchiks' (2011: xi).

Given the time distance between today's visualised media organisations and the research of Herman and Chomsky, it is important to ask if the new business environment undermines these tendencies. Indeed, there is a trend for digital media entrepreneurs to argue that they represent a new type of business enterprise that is fundamentally different from pre-existing ones. This has a range of dimensions, from the purely technical, to a basic shift away from the need for capital to be invested in plant towards its investment in intellectual property. At the political level, arguing basic difference has been useful in seeking regulatory advantages from governments, such as exemptions from taxation for online transactions (Winn and Wright, 2001: 18.2) and exclusion from existing content regulations (Chen, 2003). Tarleton Gillespie (2010) argues, however, that this overdraws the basic truth that as businesses, these digital-media organisations are more like their forebears in their commercial orientation and desire to develop sustainable business models based on mass appeal. Indeed, while the notion of the 'free press' independent from government influence is commonly seen as a core democratic principle, authors like Eric Louw (2010) argue that this is more reflective of the same type of 'hands-off arguments' made by an emerging enlightenment media class against the old power elites of the aristocracy. Cyber-separatism, it seems, is a longer and more complex history than our previous discussions may have indicated.

This leads us to consider to what extent the political economy of contemporary media reflects practices aligned with Herman and Chomsky's model, and ultimately the 'pressures [that] mount to strike a different balance between safe and controversial, between socially and financially valuable, between niche and wide appeal' (259).

The 'googlearchy'

In the attention economy, being noticed amongst a blizzard of competing media is fundamental. For all the openness of the digital environment to new publications and voices, discoverability is a function of the impact any media voice will have. In a provocative analysis of the 'myth' of a democratic digital environment, Matthew Hindman talks about the importance of search engines as key drivers of online visibility (2008: 54). On one level this is not controversial. While the core role of search engines in finding information online has declined relative to social search functions through social networking services (SNSs) and other social media, since Hindman published his book, search engines represent the most common 'kicking-off point' for attempts to obtain information online.

In Australia this process is most commonly represented by Google. Australia, in line with its long and ineffective policy attempts to limit media consolidation, has seen Google take an impressive 85 to 95 per cent of the market share for internet searching (Stafford, 2010; Cowling, 2011a). If you search online in Australia, you 'google it'.

The implications of this are not simply in the capacity for Google to represent a new 'super gatekeeper' over online information, but, as Hindman points out, how search engines like Google operate to deliver the results of search requests. Rather than simply matching results to the content of the pages found, Google uses a range of measures including cross-linking and site popularity to rank results (their trademarked 'pagerank' algorithm). This means that popular pages have an advantage in remaining popular, and that larger media organisations with a higher level of intra-organisational cross-linking are more likely to dominate search outputs. The commercial nature of mainstream online content providers combines with the commercial objectives of Google (who seek to provide results against which advertising placements will be matched) to reinforce the dominance of a small number of media organisations.

Importantly, this is not simply an outcome for causal consumers of political media, but is also true of the smaller number of highly motivated and interested political news 'junkies'. Using our 2010 election study data introduced in Chapter 2, Figure 35 shows the origin of news content (political, non-political and mixed). While public media (particularly the ABC) contains a comparatively strong market share for mixed content (predominantly homepage visits, which contain political and non-political headlines and summaries) the considerable shift in consumption between the pre-election and election period reflects the impact of search results in directing consumers towards commercial content over public broadcasters. Over the last decade we have seen the ABC moving into the provision of textual news stories, reflecting the comparatively low cost of the organisation to 'repurpose' material and create quasi newspapers off its news site (www.abc.net.au/news). What the googlearchy demonstrates, however, is how commercial media have advantages in discoverability over their public cousins.

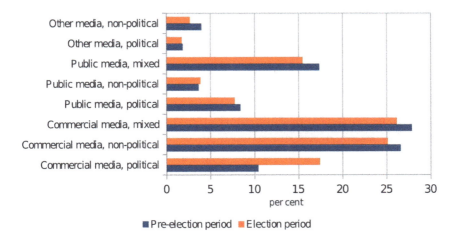

Figure 35: Online news media source, 2010 election

Source: Author's research, with Ariadne Vromen

Cooking the golden goose/biting the hand that feeds

While the googlarchy funnels large numbers of views to news homepages belonging to corporations, media proprietors have not necessarily seen this as a cause of celebration. Speaking of the way search engine companies like Google place advertising against search results and news extracts, Rupert Murdoch has attacked these organisations as being engaged in little more than online 'piracy' and theft of the profits of his intellectual property (Levine, 2011: 114). The upshot of this has been that media organisations have been forced to experiment in new ways to pay for online content (such as the use of 'paywalls' around content in the online version of the *Australian*, the value of which remains unclear at this time; Browne, 2012: 187), and increasing use of low-cost, syndicated content focused on lifestyle and celebrity. The former removes the content from the wider readership towards a narrower economic elite; the latter has eroded the quality of newspapers, particularly, in their online form.

As advertising has moved from newspapers to other forms of media, this narrows the diversity of advertisers who fund news, and rebalances the economic basis of newspapers away from a large number of small advertisers (particularly via classifieds) to a much smaller array of larger buyers (Finkelstein, 2012: 77). Following the propaganda model, this has made commercial media even more sensitive to the concerns of its advertisers in the way that the 'wrapper' surrounding advertising (journalism) impacts on the substance of the media: ads. A recent example of the impact of the contraction of the advertising market was highlighted by the ABC's *Media Watch* program in September 2011. Following a feature story in the *Sunday Times* (WA) real estate section about people who sell their homes without the aid of an agent, the paper faced an advertiser backlash. With the loss of classified advertising, real estate sections have become major economic earners for newspapers. This increased the power of those advertisers relative to that of the paper's editorial. For the *Sunday Times*, then, the threat of a boycott (or worse − threats of shifting to an industry-owned online real estate website) saw the management of the paper offer the industry both an apology, but also, the following week, an in-depth feature on the benefits of agents in the sale process was published. The political implications of this are not clear, nor was the impact of housing costs on the living standards of Australians considered in this interaction between the industry and a media sector it sees as a cheerleader for its business activities.

Garbage in, garbage out

As the economic basis of journalism contracts, proprietors and owners are under increased pressure to raise the productivity of their remaining staff. While some aspects of the digital-media environment allow for substantially increased productivity of equal (or higher) quality (expanded access to online information (Tiffen, 2012: 25–26), reduced cost of telecommunications, electronic word processing, greater ability to produce graphics and illustrations, etc.) at some point the ongoing push for productivity impacts upon journalistic standards. In many areas this is seen in the additional reduction in diversity of reporting: such as the use of identical reports from news services in the few remaining 'competing' media markets (Johnston and Forde, 2009), or the sharing of television footage ('vision') by all free-to-air broadcasters in a particular market. Other examples simply mean increasing staff output through reducing quality of the product. Commonly referred to as 'churnalism' (Mann, 2008: 5.2–25.3), high productivity news production has reduced the time spent in the critical investigation of the issues being reported.[2] At times this is reflected in the application of 'standard operating procedure' (SOP) forms of reporting (the use of routine heuristics and writing practices to 'churn out' a story to a journalistic-writing formula), at others in the significant reprinting of material provided by the most well-funded or organised source in a story.

Information subsidies and the growth of PR

For sources wanting to shape the way their issues and concerns are presented, the effective use of public relations (PR) training and material has been a growth

---

2 In an admission of hypocrisy, however, it's important to acknowledge that productivity formulae, such as that used to determine forced redundancies at my university in 2012, equally encourage churn in the academic setting. Let's hope this isn't representative of it.

area under the current media political economy. This practice represents the use of 'information subsidies': lowering the cost of media production through the provision of pre-packaged material that can be slotted directly into a story (or, in extreme examples, as whole stories). While the classic example of this practice is the well-written press release (a document that is written and structured in a way that it requires minimal changes for republicaiton as a news story), these practices have developed over time into increasingly sophisticated use of multimedia (such as the provision of video 'packages' for television broadcast), and the use of dubious corporate surveys to provide the hook for stories (Zoch and Molleda, 2009: 254). These latter techniques can be effective as the demands of churnalism reduce the time journalists have to investigate the source, veracity and reliability of the data presented therein.

Information subsidies are effective when designed around the needs of media organisations and professionals. As staff productivity has been driven up, these needs are simply the ability to produce acceptable copy in the quickest time possible. While the use of information subsidies is not new (indeed, the use of such material is a journalistic norm and expected practice; Stanyer, 2001: 162), there is evidence that the impact of PR material on the content of news output has increased in recent years. Through the use of content analysis Bacon, et al. (2010) identified that 55 per cent of the content of 10 of Australia's major newspapers[3] was based on PR material (media releases or some other form of information subsidy). These findings are matched by survey data where journalists report an increased reliance on PR material in the production of stories: 55 per cent relied on PR material for the generation of a 'majority' of stories in 2008, up from 20 per cent in 2006 (Johnston and Forde, 2009).

While this has significant implications for the way that organisations outside of the media can employ information subsidies to have a substantive impact on the content and framing of journalistic reports, we must recognise that this is often focused on areas of commercial activity, rather than the political sphere. Unsurprisingly, it is the consumer-driven technology reporting about new products and services that is the most likely to be driven by PR (77 per cent of stories). Of the 11 news categories studied, politics was the least likely to be driven by this type of material (37 per cent of stories).[4]

The logic of the 'PR state'

While 'only' one third of stories containing or driven by PR material may look considerable, the high watermark set by the information and communications technology (ICT) industry may simply serve as a target for some in the political

---

3   The *Australian Financial Review*, *Advertiser* (Adelaide), *Courier-Mail* (Brisbane), *Daily Telegraph*, *Herald Sun*, *Mercury* (Hobart), *Australian*, *Age*, *Sydney Morning Herald* and *West Australian*.
4   Information technology was the most likely to be driven by PR.

world. Over the last 40 years, governments have been increasingly employing media professionals to manage their relations with journalists (Barnes, 2005: 20–22).[5] This is a deliberate process of creating capacity in government to generate information subsidies to achieve favourable press coverage and the nature of the reporting of government affairs. At one end of the spectrum this is a purely political act: attempting to control public opinion through shaping what is (and is not) reported in the media. At the other this represents the appropriate use of public resources: shaping communication to ensure effective communication of government initiatives, or realise policies that are informational in nature (such as social-marketing campaigns aimed at achieving specific policy outcomes).

With the decline in employment opportunities for journalists in the news media, it is unsurprising that more journalists and media professionals work for government than in the private media (Pearson and Patching, 2008: 6). The specialisation of media liaisons and officers, communications planners and writers in the public sector reflects a growing sophistication of government management of information, combined with more instrumental desire to maintain good coverage of the work of elites. While exact numbers are difficult to determine (as these professionals operate under a wide variety of job titles), we can estimate this by looking at a range of indicators. By 2009, about 20 per cent of the members of the Public Relations Institute of Australia worked for government (PRIA, 2011) with survey research pushing PR employment in the public sector as high as 30 per cent (De Bussy and Wolf, 2009).[6] Looking at other measures of the increased use of professional communications techniques in government, Young (2007a) provides an indication through estimates of the increase in advertising expenditure by the Commonwealth. This expenditure has increased in real terms by a factor of three over the last 20 years.

This has led some theorists to see the development of a far more problematic outcome: the rise of the 'PR state'. This term was coined by Oscar Gandy (1982) to identity the trend towards the expanding number of information specialists in the US government. Importantly, however, the PR state is more than simply 'spin', but also reflects the expanding role of communication professions in the 'formulation and implementation of public policy'. This has been seen in the Australian context, with Ian Ward (2003) arguing that Australian governments have adopted the type of pro-active media-management approach which sees the formation of good public policy placed secondary to questions about the ability of policy to be 'sold' to the public. This leads governments to the adoption of policies that are more easily communicated (and therefore are likely

---

5   Whitlam's 'It's time' campaign is often seen as a good example of the introduction of modern campaigning techniques in Australia, as discussed in Chapter 2.
6   This excludes the number of PR professionals who work for government through private sector consultancies.

to be simplistic) and to avoid those that are seen as complex, have aspects that are easily exploited by the Opposition or other opponents of the policy or government, or that require significant framing to communicate effectively and are therefore innovative in nature. KISS — keep it simple, stupid — rules this type of communicative and policy-making logic.

One of the problems here is that PR is often seen purely in terms of propaganda: in this case the use of government resources to convince the public of a particular point of view. While this is clearly the point of high-profile expenditures of public resources around policy issues (the GST, WorkChoices, mining and carbon taxation), these high-visibility activities do not define the range of government communication practices. To some extent, there is ambiguity in the way in which political elites and practitioners see the role of PR. Glenny's (2008: 164–65) review of policy documents surrounding public sector communications has identified that these directive documents commonly frame PR in terms of one-way communication between government and stakeholder publics. This is at odds with conventional industry definitions of the practice, which focus more on information exchange and the facilitation of dialogue towards shared understanding and adjustment between key stakeholders (the 'mutual satisfaction' model of PR; Moffit, 1994).

While the use of PR as propaganda in this way is widely condemned (the politics of 'spin'), contemporary political and media logic reinforces its use, even reluctantly. This was a problem for the former prime minister Kevin Rudd, who famously talked about restricting the level of partisan and propagandistic government advertising declaring it a 'cancer' on democratic practice because it disproportionately favoured incumbent administrations (Griffiths, 2010). While this may have been a position of principle, the limitations of governments denying themselves the use of government advertising and PR came to the fore in the public debate over the Resource Super Profits Tax (RSPT). Following the announcement of this taxation package, mining-industry advertising quickly framed the debate, leading the government to concede that their failure to promote the policy allowed opposition to build and dominate the media (AAP, 2010b). By the time the government changed its position and introduced a propaganda campaign of its own, the damage to the RSPT policy (and Rudd's leadership) had been done. Under the prime ministership of Julia Gillard, the policy had to be significantly re-negotiated and the origins of the policy in the detailed and methodical review of taxation (the Henry Tax Review) was significantly lost to the pressures of policy-making on the run.

This explains the political logic of moving from reactive to proactive media management strategies. Allowing oppositional voices to dominate the use of advertising and PR early in the proposal or implementation of a policy critically allows them time to define the nature of the issue and frame its interpretation.

Framing, once embedded in the way a policy is discussed, is difficult (and more expensive) to dislodge. Regardless, therefore, of the good intentions of any government (the most recent to talk about restricting public advertising being the then incoming Coalition government of Barry O'Farrell in NSW; AAP, 2009), ensuring that issues are framed in the favour of the government of the day becomes a normal process (SOP) of risk avoidance. One experienced public servant clearly articulates this shift :

> The older defensive approach was largely response-based ... preparation of question time briefs or briefs to respond to critical media stories. The proactive work ... Over the last decade the requirement to manage risk in the public sector has become more obvious and this requires a forward-looking approach — one that anticipates problems. (Andrew Podger, cited in Australian Government, 2005)

This is not simply a reflection of the professionalisation of issues management in government to provide for the type of 'rapid response' model honed in the United Kingdom by New Labour under Tony Blair (which aimed to 'shut down' negative stories before they could develop; Beech, 2006: 109), or a reflection of the way in which PR has moved up the organisational chain to become part of the strategic-planning process (Allen, 2012). This reflects the perception of the news cycle as so rapid as to require constant attention by press officers and media minders. Lose control of a story early, as in the case of the RSPT, and you might just lose government.

Now, now, now!

The diversification of media over the last century has also impacted on the way Australians define what is relevant political news and information. By the 1980s consolidation led to a contraction in titles through the end of morning and afternoon editions, leaving the evening news largely the domain of afternoon 'drive-time' radio and evening news broadcasts. This positioned newspapers at the start of the day's news distribution cycle (and, therein, they set the day's media agenda for radio and television). Where newspapers were once the key 'breakers' of news, their position in the temporal flow of the daily news cycle has changed with the rise of more immediate sources for breaking news: first the electronic broadcast media, then newspapers themselves, reborn through their online editions, attempting to increase the frequency of viewership through continually updating their homepages throughout the day and night.

For many commentators, this reflects the acceleration of the news cycle. This acceleration reflects a popular understanding that the definition of 'news' is in terms of what is most immediate and up-to-date (Macnamara, 2010a: 214), as opposed to what might be most important. As electronic and digital media increasingly allow for a constant flow of information, this shortens the time for professional journalists to produce content seen as relevant to their consuming public. While this is commonly decried as part of the decline in the quality of journalistic output, due to the lack of time for reflection, a disproportionate emphasis on immediate events over careful evaluation of what may be relevant in the wider content of the story, or through requiring political elites to respond to events in real time (Blair, 2007) are also contributors to the decline. This, however, is not a new tendency. The regularisation of news production in line with the need for commercial media to produce a reliable revenue stream creates the notion of news as a continual flow of events — as opposed to irregular and ad hoc happenings. For the same reasons, media organisations invented and have honed opinion polling over the last 100 years: allowing them to control the flow of news through creating 'reportable' events on a regular basis.

New audiences, new partners

While the digital-media environment has exerted pressure on conventional media organisations to produce more at lower cost, the economic basis of media production is not the sole determinant of the output of these organisations. Constructivists understand structures of economic incentive as being moderated by social norms and expectations. In the case of journalism, a strong professional tradition and a 'noble' self-perception as public advocates and watchdogs (Simons, 2007: 245) tussles with managerial imperatives to drive down standards for increased output (Edy and Snidow, 2011: 830). Thus journalists, as professionals with a sense of a coherent set of skills and norms of behaviour, have not simply responded through 'churnalism', but also by attempts to develop new methods of news production that retain quality. This includes the use of social media to assist in the generation of leads, verification of facts, and greater inclusion of readers in the production of news (Robinson, 2011: 40). In this, way social media allows readers to become Axel Brun's 'producers' (as discussed in Chapter 1) through micro-participation in media production.

This has begun to filter up. Recently, the Fairfax organisation attempted to make routine this method of participation from sources through the establishment of Newso (www.newso.com.au), an institutional source management website that allows invited contributors to provide quotes, suggestions and input into an organisation-wide sourcing tool (Jamieson, 2012). The purpose of this experiment is to trial ways that working journalists can access 'banks' of content for incorporation in their stories. Outside the walls of the established media, the idea that information subsidies need not be the preserve of parties, government and large corporations is demonstrated by the way in which WikiLeaks has become more adroit (although not without some friction at the personal level;

Lundberg, 2011: 2) at working with journalists to ensure that their release of raw material is timed and co-ordinated with mainstream, respected news organisations in a way to give the material (and the organisation) maximum impact and exposure. This follows a number of years in which the organisation assumed that simply 'dumping' material would lead to it being picked up by a hungry media (3–4). In this way, organisations like WikiLeaks have adjusted their media strategy to maximise the value of their material for the mainstream media, assuming their logics of news production processes and expectations at the same time.

Thus we see how performance expectations are not just internalised in the journalistic community, but also across the various stakeholder publics who produce and consume news content. The clearest way this can be expressed directly is by readers, rather than the indirect market-sensing approach of consumer demand. One area where the public has been increasingly active in defending standards and quality in the commercial press (as discussed in Chapter 3's consideration of the role of bloggers as critics of journalistic practice) is through direct interaction between audiences, journalists and editors. This takes two forms. First, just as public institutions have become the subject of more visible popular discussion and criticism, the media industry itself is actively discussed in these new public spheres. This takes the form of commentary within the context of particular issues or stories (e.g. Illustration 15), as well as the formation of oversight communities made up of monitorial citizens (see The long form opinionistas: The Australian 'blogosphere', Chapter 3) who are interested in the exercise of influence in private as well as public institutions. Examples of the latter can be seen in specialist media blogs and news services like Pure Poison (http://blogs.crikey.com.au/purepoison) and mUmBRELLA (http://mumbrella.com.au), as well as less sympathetic critics like Australian's Worst Journalist (www.australiasworstjournalist.com.au).

The extent to which this form of oversight impacts upon the behaviour of media organisations is unclear. In talking about proposals for statutory regulation (thus, subject to a strong motivation to defend self-regulation) the former editor-in-chief of the *Sydney Morning Herald* recently argued that this form of scrutiny is an increasingly important external constraint on the behaviour of media (2012), and acts as a powerful regulator of media standards in Australia.[7] Certainly, powerful media organisations have been sensitive to online criticism about their conduct and professional standards (Neighbour, 2011). But this has not always led to media organisations taking on criticism in productive ways.

---

7   Peter Fray was talking in the context of the report of the Independent Media Inquiry's recommendations that a new, more powerful regulator of news media be introduced in Australia.

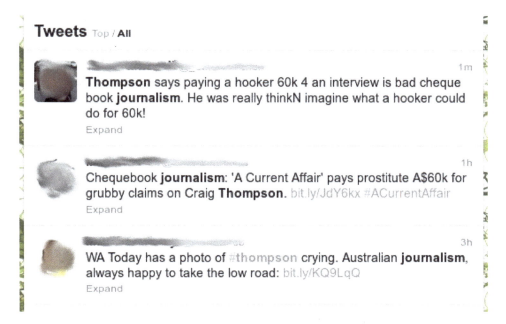

Illustration 15: Story commentary on Twitter regarding the Craig Thomson affair (24 May 2012) (user tags obscured)

Source: Twitter

Examples of this include tweeted accusations that the editorial position of the *Australian* newspaper was hostile to coverage of mainstream climate change science, which led to threats of litigation against the tweeter: journalist and academic Julie Posetti in 2010 (ABC, 2010). Similar criticism by academic and commentator Robert Manne that the *Australian* is a campaigning paper which follows a strong political agenda on issues like the environment and attacks on the Australian Greens (2011) was rebutted in a succession of articles and editorials (Hamilton, 2012), escalating to legal action (Crook, 2012). More broadly, the mismatch between the Canberra press gallery's interpretation of Gillard's criticism of the Leader of the Opposition's views of women in public and that of the widespread social-media praise for her 9 October 2012 speech demonstrated how out of touch these 'insiders' could be (Dunlop, 2012).[8] Rather than recalibration of their interpretation of the social impact of this speech, the media elites reacted churlishly to accusations they were in a bubble (Maley, 2012). It is questionable if established media are responding as much as

---

8 Following a move by the Opposition to censure the then speaker of the House of Representatives, the Prime Minister engaged in a wideranging attack against the Leader of the Opposition regarding views on the status of women.

reacting (Flew and Wilson, 2010: 137), with media organisations resorting to defensiveness and litigation, techniques that were once employed against them by older, entrenched elites.

Another question we need to ask is the extent to which this form of participation expands or narrows the substantive content of media. While material sourced by journalists from social media has been important in elaborating breaking news (Murthy, 2010), the relatively narrow democratic base of politically interested social-media users (see Chapter 3) highlights the enduring problem of the digital divide. Interestingly, this reaffirms the core of the propaganda model: that the economic base that supports middle-class consumption of new products and services creates a charmed circle of media content and journalism produced by, and aimed at, the needs and expectations of this class. Chris Nash, however, argues that the advantage that some bloggers have is their separation from the 'hothouse' environment of the Canberra press gallery (2008). Citing the way the work of Possum Comitatus (Possum Pollytics; http://blogs.crikey.com.au/pollytics) moved from 'external critic' to respected analyst in the eyes of some members of the mainstream media, he sees the power of anonymity and externality in shaking off constraints of journalist–source relations (fear of being 'punished' by sources of coverage).

Who's following whom?

One of the more interesting outcomes of the changing economic model for news media has been how journalists have seen opportunities to strengthen their organisational and economic positions through the use of digital media. Social media, in particular, has become a popular way that individual journalists have built (and demonstrate) strong personal followings. Examples of this include Latika Bourke, who won a Walkley Young Journalist of the Year award in 2010, in part for her innovative use of social media in reporting. In addition to the development of a personal audience, Bourke has established a reputation for online interaction with her readers and political elites. This example represents not simply an example of innovation in the adoption of technology (over the last two years, political journalists of all types have been rapid adopters of the medium), but also the use of personal branding strategies to protect and enhance employment prospects by journalists in an age of increasing uncertainty. Personal branding in this case is a deliberate and planned approach to promoting the attributes and characteristics of an individual to a market, using known techniques developed for the sale of conventional products (product development, communication and advertising, market analysis; Lair, et al., 2005: 209).

Like blogs before it (*Media Report*, 2007; Murphy and Burgess, 2004), journalists have found Twitter to be an attractive digital-media channel because of its neat fit with their tempo of work (journalists have been quick to substitute Twitter posts for 'vox pop' interviews and quote tweets directly in stories, as well as using Twitter traffic to source interview questions and story ideas; Sheales, 2012):[9] an emphasis on timeliness and novelty that come in-built into the channel; and, its compact format (excellent for both short-form journalism and conventional television screen resolution). The use of short messaging services (internet and mobile telephone) can also be seen, however, as reinforcing a perception of closeness between media and political elites. While tweets are performed 'in public', the ability for particular journalists to solicit responses from elites serves to demonstrate their 'currency' and standing in the media community. That this is done in the wider view of an enlarged online community shows how contemporary politics is friendly to the 'media dramaturgy' of the age (Bard and Soderqvist, 2002: 204). In acting the role of 'insiders' (which they are not), journalists perform their importance to their stakeholders (peers, publics and elites). Joe Atkinson identifies this as the:

> ... self-serving 'watchdog' fantasies some political journalists hold about themselves: as a fearless posse of 'inside dopesters', guardians of truth and justice, infallible spin-detectors, and duty-bound to intervene in the political process against politicians and spin doctors on behalf of an easily hoodwinked public. (2005: 17)

This becomes a circular process as journalists and politicians 'must' also perform their significance through the adoption of these technologies, even if they are sceptical of their value (Gillard, for example, has expressed concern at the medium's triviality and limited value, while maintaining an active Twitter account through her office).

Looking at the dynamics of this relationship, Peter Brent (2011) undertook a lengthy participant observation of the use of digital media by journalists and politicians in the Australian federal parliament. This study was well timed, taking place during the period in which this medium came to be salient in the Australian context, driven by minute-by-minute coverage of two leadership #spills (Rudd and Turnbull) which represent the apex of the notion of insider politics (knowledge about the machinations of the 'machine men' of politics). He observes:

> Who do politicians and their staff follow on Twitter? The same as everyone else interested in politics: the journalist, particularly the

---

9   Or as stories, in May 2012 the Government Whip, Joel Fitzgibbon, became the subject of a story based on accusations of 'treason' against the prime minister, accusations he refuted with a tweet of support for the PM (Maiden, 2012).

Canberra press gallery. In the chamber in question time, MPs can be seen spending a lot of time reading their internet-enabled mobile phones … From enquiries I have determined that at least some of the time is spent on Twitter. The parliamentarians are not tuning to the #QT [question time] hashtag, but are watching those tweeters they follow. And the most frenetic activity, at this time, comes from the press gallery. (58)

Through the use of private and public micro-messaging, politicians and journalists maintain and sustain their professional–personal relationships (see Illustration 16). Journalists report unsourced messages during key 'crisis' events as being from key insider 'sources', demonstrating their special access to the political class (sometimes through literally comparing SMS messages on television; *Media Watch*, 2010). Similarly, politicians rely on reciprocal exchanges to keep them informed about other political goings on from outside of their immediate party/circle/faction/clique (Davis, 2010: 80).

Illustration 16: Politician–journalist social interactions on Twitter

Source: Twitter

The question, therefore, is the extent to which the visibility of this relationship by 'outsiders' alters the nature of this relationship. In many ways these interactions are nothing new: journalist–source relations have long been a complex 'game' of dominance and trust that has been played out by these two groups of 'frenemies'. Politicians need journalists to distribute and collect information, and journalists need politicians for content (Tiffen, 1989). The shift from private relationships to include more publicly performed ones does increase journalistic standing, but also presents the opportunity for interventions by non-elite voices in these conversational threads. There is evidence that some of the discursive environments online provide counterweights to the notion of digital media as reinforcing the existing media visibility of entrenched elites.

In an analysis of the Australian political use of Twitter, minor party figures, like the Greens, are identified as more highly represented than major parties (Grant, et al., 2010: 597). This is because they are more likely to engage in conversational (as opposed to broadcast) posts through this medium. This tendency for diversification needs to be tempered, however, in that their representation is 'higher' only to the extent that their representation in posts closely matches their primary vote, rather than being significantly under-represented in conventional media. This is another representation of how institutionalised journalism's emphasis on 'horse race' reporting tends to focus excessively on the parties of government, a tendency that becomes problematic where elections produce more complex outcomes (such as the 2010 election), or where the election outcome is determined well in advance.[10]

Corporate tolerance of personal twitter profiles by working journalists may be short lived. In the United Kingdom, a number of media organisations have attempted to regulate these channels (placing restrictions on content, exerting 'ownership' of profiles; Halliday, 2012). News organisations, therefore, have a mixed response to the rise of personal branding. On one level, the use of high-profile writers and columnists are institutional selling points, with their headshots featuring on key pages of the paper to demonstrate the quality of their prose.

On another level, these 'star' writers are more expensive, demanding and autonomous than suits the modern corporate media. Martin Gilens and Craig Hertzman (2000) argue that the rise of media corporations shifts the focus of news bias towards corporate over individual proprietor's political interests. Organisational initiatives like Newso, therefore, can also be seen as a challenge to the capacity of journalists to control their sources and maintain their personal brands. If source relations become institutionalised, this will serve to make the production of news routine, and reduce the expertise required to produce copy, further eroding the professional basis of journalism in Australia.

---

10   Thus, for example, there was a tendency for media to cover the 2011 New South Wales election as a competitive race, regardless of the implausibility of the return of the ALP to power. In both cases, limited scrutiny of minor parties and independents can be seen as a failure of journalism when using the 'functionalist' measure of media as a significant contributor to electors' understanding of relevant candidates and parties.

The development of news stories written by computer has also been viewed internationally with concern because of this. To date this has been limited to formulaic reporting in sports and business (Lohr, 2011).

Media [from/on] the margins

While robo-journalism and institutional source management have relevance to the fordisation of media production, the economic model of media in the digital environment is not simple. One of the interesting products of the rise of online commerce has been the rebirth of craft culture and small-scale production that is often of marginal commercial viability, but driven by motivations other than profit (cost-recovery, gift economics, propaganda and political purposes). Online communities of artists (such as www.deviantart.com) and craft workers (such as www.etsy.com) have demonstrated that the massification of the online environment also has room for select markets and small audiences to be serviced, while the imperishability and discoverability of online content allows for the reuse and resale of material over longer product lifecycles than would have traditionally been envisaged (the so-called 'long tail' phenomena that allows economic value from back catalogues and electronic data; Shirky, 2008).

This is also the case in the political-media space in Australia, with a wide range of small publications that seek to service select communities and work with modest budgets. The popularity of increasingly powerful free, content-management systems (CMS) simplifies the establishment of these ventures, as one person can host a wide range of different sites using the same installation and host. Additionally, through the use of a mix of original and syndicated content, a few individuals can compile unique offerings to their readerships through careful customisation to their target audiences.

Recent start-ups of this kind can be found across the political spectrum, including the conservative news, commentary and opinion website *Australian Conservative* (http://australianconservative.com) and the progressive online journal *Independent Australia* (www.independentaustralia.net). The wide variety of these publications (from think tank spin-off like *New Matilda* (http://newmatilda.com) to personal newspapers published by individuals, as seen in Illustration 17) make the simple characterisation of these publications impossible, but they collectively show a willingness to engage with media production practices as primary producers, as well as the difficulties in sustaining (if not establishing) new online-media ventures.

Illustration 17: Personal newspaper drawn from political content, published using paper.li

Source: Paper.li. Used with permission

Movement media: Indymedia

One way to maintain a digital media venture is through the use of platform, rather than editorially driven, models of production: rather than use a hierarchical model of production, allow open access to the publishing engine and encourage interested parties to post their content and allow social filtering to determine what is of value to the readership. The most famous example of this in Australia would be the left-wing alternative media service Indymedia (www.indymedia.org.au), which now has collectives in Brisbane, Melbourne, Perth and Sydney. Initially established in the United States and arising from the Global Social Justice protests of the late 1990s, Indymedia Melbourne was founded in 2000 as part of the S11 (11 September) anti-globalisation protests focused on the World Economic Forum (Gibson, et al., 2004: 188). The focus of Indymedia's establishment in Australia is also informed by the type of concern that drives the propaganda model: that corporate media, by nature of ownership, production processes and orientation towards the private sector, is unable and unwilling to report on anti-corporate protests and events in a fair manner (Bruns, 2005: 82–84).

The non-commercial nature of outlets like Indymedia often give them a wider scope of issue coverage than the mainstream media. As a media form embedded within activist networks, this tends to be focused on political content of interest to movement organisers and members, rather than 'general news'. Thus, for example, Indymedia and Socialist Alliance's *Green Left Weekly* (which has a significant online edition; www.greenleft.org.au) provided the Australian and international Occupy movements with more serious coverage than that afforded by commercial media, which displayed a familiar hostility to physical protest movements (Crawford, 2006: 237–40) and largely adopted the view that the comparatively good economic performance of Australia made the movement an example of self-indulgent youth protest (Devine, 2011).

From margins to mainstream: Crikey

While pessimism about the future of commercial news media in Australia abounds, the online news site Crikey demonstrates that specialist, online, commercial, media ventures are possible. Formed in 2000 by Stephen Mayne following his high-profile falling out with the Liberal Victorian state government under Jeff Kennett (for which he worked as a PR staffer), the site has origins in a mix Australia's tradition of 'larrikin' journalism (independent, disrespectful of authority, and humorous; Vine, 2009: 109–12) and a willingness to experiment with uncertain practices, including use of reader contributions and the publication of anonymous 'insider' stories. Significantly, using the paid-subscription model, Crikey has demonstrated it is possible for paywalls around content to be effective in building wholly digital-media ventures.

Over time, Crikey has developed into a mainstream and journalistic enterprise. With increasing numbers of staff, the venture has changed hands (showing, unlike single- and multiple-author blogs, its ability to survive transition from the status of a founders' hobby). In doing so, however, greater commercial-management rigour has come into place. Crikey has shed some of its 'publish and be damned'[11] attitude and become a more conventional journalistic enterprise (Morieson, 2011). Interestingly, as Crikey has moved out of the insider-gossip-oriented space, new ventures like Vexnews (founded by Andrew Landeryou; www.vexnews.com) have taken its place.

In recent years, Crikey has expanded to carry more detailed reporting, some of which was undertaken through unconventional and innovative arrangements. The organisation has begun collaborating with a range of academics to provide investigative and other forms of journalism on specific topics. Examples include:

---

11   Mayne had to sell his home to pay for defamation in 2003 (Shiel, 2003).

- Collaboration with Professor Wendy Bacon and the Australian Centre for Independent Journalism on research into the practices of media organisations in the use of PR material (Foreign Aid, Spinning the Media, 2010; www.crikey.com.au/spinning-the-media, www.crikey.com.au/topic/who-profits-from-our-foreign-aid).

- Collaboration with staff and students at Swinburne University to undertake a detailed analysis of Victorian Government annual reports (the then Labor government 'dumped' over 200 annual reports in one day in an attempt to bury negative news by overwhelming state journalists; www.crikey.com.au/the-brumby-dump) (Swinburne University of Technology, 2010).

- Sponsorship of a research and writing project headed by the well-known ex-blogger Dr Mark Bahnisch on the politics of coal seam gas (CSG) extraction in Queensland in the lead-up to the 2012 state election (FAQ Research; http://faqresearch.com). This initiative is interesting in that, rather than drawing on institutional resources, the FAQ Research project[12] was funded largely by requests for readers' donations.

In addition to these partnerships, Crikey has attempted to employ 'crowd sourcing' techniques in the production of articles (for example, asking readers to examine political donation reports; Young, Sally, 2011: 228).[13]

This demonstrates how some Australian news-media organisations are attempting to experiment with alternative business models in the production of expensive news content. To date, these experiments and projects have been limited, and their ability to substitute for established, predictable and reliable news production practices (staffing and syndication) may be limited. The lethargic time frame of academic work is not always well suited to news-production requirements and (as discussed with regards to *The Conversation* below), there is evidence that academic institutions are looking to pull more journalistic content 'in house'.

The ability for independent ventures to raise substantial funds from readers is also questionable. For FAQ Research's CSG project, initial donations from Crikey and the organisers' social networks were substantial. This level of donation, however, particularly from new readers drawn into the project through the process of fieldwork, did not carry through the life of the project. Additional difficulties come from the multiplicity of roles that project participants have to take on. Combining the interpersonal process of fundraising with the more disinterested one of the neutral journalist can create tensions, particularly where the political positions of donors is not matched with the eventual content being

---

12 This coincided with the closure of the long-running blog Larvatus Prodeo, a decision associated with the authors' view of the rise of alternative spaces for debate like Facebook and Twitter (Bahnisch, 2012).

13 A strategy that was employed with some success by the *Guardian* in the United Kingdom parliamentary expenses scandal (http://mps-expenses.guardian.co.uk).

produced. This was a problem in reporting of CSG, which has brought together an unusual coalition between urban Greens and rural farming communities (personal interview: Pandora Karavan, FAQ Research, 18 March 2012).

Never pick a fight with someone who ...: On Line Opinion

Like Crikey, the political opinion website *On Line Opinion* (www.onlineopinion. com.au) was an early entry into the alternative media space. Started by businessman and former Queensland Liberal Party official Graham Young in 1999 as a not-for-profit organisation, the site provides a space for the publication of opinion articles and associated discussion on a range of political, social and scientific issues of the day. Young's motivation was in response to the observation that 'Australia lacked an open forum where people from all sides of a political point of view could come and express themselves'. In addition, Young saw the site in terms of the modern public sphere: correcting perceived problems in the coverage of science by newspapers (he has a personal scepticism towards mainstream climate science, for example), and the formation of public opinion through commissioning and reporting on online focus groups. His choice of opinion column writing was both pragmatic and political. Pragmatically it allowed for the generation of content without paying writers.[14] Politically, the model is inclusive, allowing individuals with public standing and those who are comparatively unknown to participate, but retaining editorial oversight of the content produced (Young and Brown, 2003).

This editorial model made *On Line Opinion* different to the anarchic model of Indymedia, and the more risky strategy of Crikey with regard to litigation. The low-cost nature of the site's business model has, however, meant that it has been susceptible to the capricious nature of online-advertising revenue (personal correspondence: Graham Young, 4 January 2012), and the risk presented by advertiser boycotts. In early 2011, *On Line Opinion* published an article hostile to same-sex marriage.[15] This led to the withdrawal of advertising by a number of major corporations, considerably reducing the advertising income (Young, Graham, 2011). While this led to debate about the merits of having published the offending article, and the moderation process on *On Line Opinion* (Kim, 2011), the case demonstrates how susceptible small and alternative online publishers can be. While the low-cost business model may allow ease of entry into the marketplace, the correspondingly limited revenue stream means these publications can be at continual risk of closure. This problem was demonstrated

---

14   The journal has published an average of over 1000 articles per year (*National Forum*, 2011).
15   Muehlenberg, Bill, 2010, 'Dismantling a homosexual marriage myth', *On Line Opinion*, 25 November, www.onlineopinion.com.au/view.asp?article=11268&page=0/ accessed: 3 January 2012.

with the closure and re-establishment of *New Matilda*,[16] which struggled with readership numbers (Bass, 2010) and the ability to convert readers into paying subscribers for a free product (Jamieson, 2010). While the use of 'angel' investors to support these ventures has been one way that significant new money can be found, the willingness of individuals to support loss-making ventures in the medium (let alone the short-term) is questionable.

I'm figgering on biggering

The political economy of online media presents a complex picture. While large media organisations are under pressure to cut costs and discover new ways to 'monetise' their online content (a technical term for 'make a profit'), disaggregation into smaller units aimed at specialist audiences, and the nimbleness required to develop new publishing and production models, appears no less fraught with problems. While the mainstream commercial media is often dismissive of their small rivals, the larger organisations do watch for developments in the alternative media and blogger communities. Indeed, if political bloggers were really the sad, parental-basement-dwelling losers they are often presented as being (during hostilities between psephologists and the *Australian* over the interpretation of NewsPoll data, it editorialised in 2007: 'The self appointed experts online come instead from the extreme Left, populated as many sites are by sheltered academics and failed journalists who would not get a job on a real newspaper'), it would not behove the quality media to respond to their criticisms. In 2010 the *Australian* employed one of the more high profile psephological bloggers it had singled out for criticism in 2007: Dr Peter Brent, formally of http://mumble.com.au.

This demonstrates how the institutional media has responded to the development of user-generated content and digital-media ventures: moving from outward hostility to alternative publishers who are critics or competitors, to cherry picking talent and emulating platforms. An example of the latter has been the proliferation of 'commentariat'-type websites developed by institutional media organisations — *Unleashed* (later *The Drum*; ABC), *The Punch* (News Corporation), and *National Times* (Fairfax). Recently, even the higher education sector has become a direct publisher, through the establishment of *The Conversation* (http://theconversation.edu.au), a site for the publication of popular press articles by academics. The implications of this are varied, but

---

16   While a left-wing publication that spun off its policy wing to become The Centre for Policy Development think tank, the founder John Menadue AO shared similar motivations to Young in its establishment (Cordell, 2010). On its takeover by Duncan Turpie in 2007, the publication moved from a subscription to advertising model (Simons, 2010), and moved to a subscription drive model on restart in 2011. This shows the uncertain state of the business models sustaining these publications in Australia and internationally.

have been largely negative for some of the smaller and non-profit publishers who see their markets and business models targeted by large institutional players with considerable resources and exposure. *On Line Opinion* is an illustration of this tendency. Having reached a high-water mark of about 170,000 unique visitors in late 2006 (source: Google Analytics, courtesy of Graham Young),[17] the introduction of competition from the national broadcaster and two major newspaper companies in 2007[18] and 2009[19] align with a slow and steady decline in traffic for the site (losing more than half its traffic, and correspondingly, attention to its advertisers). This competition for attention is matched with competition for authors, who now have a far wider range of online publications for which to provide content.

The new public ownership problem

The power problem of the relative size of digital-media ventures is not limited to the commercial world. Eric Beecher, publisher of Crikey, has been critical of the ABC becoming involved in online opinion publishing, citing this as an area of active commercial competition from a range of non-government companies, large and small and with different editorial positions (Sinclair, 2010). This argument, that public broadcasters should concentrate on areas of clear market failure, has been seen in recent debates in the United Kingdom about the scale of operations of the ABC's role-model, the BBC (BBC, 2009) by executives of News Corporation. This revisits an old debate about public provision of media in a democracy: that these media organisations run the risk of distorting democratic practice through providing a state-centric media company (state propaganda), undermining the economic basis of commercial news production, and distorting the capacity for market-sensing as a result (Janda, et al., 2008: 182). The problem that this view has always presented is that it is difficult for public broadcasters to determine where market failure may be (particularly if it requires divestment in the assumption that its activities are commercially viable), and the political pressure on these organisations to match their cultural charter obligations with 'popularity' to justify their impost on the public purse. A rational public-media policy would automatically spin off any successful program or venture into the public sector, but this is not always organisationally or politically viable.

On this front, *The Conversation* is a troubling development, not because there is no need for quality reporting of the work of Australian researchers and scholars (which, we can see includes areas of market failure), but in the way it draws content away from mainstream and alternative media with established readerships. *The Conversation* is a non-profit company owned by a range of

---

17   This includes unique visitors for both the *On Line Opinion* articles and the separate forums sub-domain.
18   ABC's *Unleashed* in late 2007, later to be expanded and relaunched as *The Drum* in late 2009.
19   News Corporation's *The Punch* in mid 2009, and Fairfax's *National Times* in late 2009.

Australian universities.[20] It employs editorial staff to maintain its website and help academics produce news stories in plain language. While the editorial staff of *The Conversation* see the importance of its work in attempting to stem the decline in the quality of public-sphere debate (*The Science Show*, 2012) it is interesting that, rather than provide information subsidies to existing media (and therein reduce the cost of quality content in self-sustaining ventures), *The Conversation* possesses a number of years of subsidised funding to create a new site for quality content aimed at educated and elite audiences. In this way *The Conversation* has implications for the partnership models that exist between the academy and private providers (as discussed in From margins to mainstream: Crikey, this chapter), demonstrating that new, publicly funded ventures are not just a threat to the established interests of the media barons, but play in the creative space of the start-ups as well. That *The Conversation* stems from a perception of market failure, then, makes its potential impact on small and start-up commercial online media more ironic.

Elites and e-lites

The political economy of the news media is in flux, shifting between old and new business models. In expanding the capacity for members of the public to engage in oversight of their actions, social media has eroded the costs of principle oversight of distant institutional agents, allowing for enhanced social regulation of the behaviour of elites. At the same time, these forces have further reduced the capacity of some elite groups: particularly in shifting the political economy of media away from those organisations and proprietors who traditionally engaged in the production of costly political content. This has 'trickled down' to make the workplaces of the content makers more insecure, with flow-on effects on how they position themselves in this uncertain environment through building protections around their professional standing and relationships with other elites.

The upshot of this has been a more pluralistic, faster-paced political environment where political resources are no longer contained in specific institutions as much as in temporary alignments of actors and organisations. The use of new technology serves to drive these dynamics, as well as being involved in making them precarious in the first place. In all of this, one, final elite set of institutions requires investigation, the one that has been able to largely resist the impacts of this digital-media economy and retain its financial and power base over the last decade through the old tools of authority and law. In Chapter 7, therefore, we will examine the public sector in this new environment.

---

20   This does not include the University of Sydney, my employer.

Chapter 7 — Policy in an age of information

Evelyn, a dog, having undergone
Further modification
Pondered the significance of short-person behavior
In pedal-depressed panchromatic resonance
And other highly ambient domains ...
'Arf', she said.

— Frank Zappa

Computers and government: An intimate history

Governments have a long history with information and communications technologies (ICT). From the computerisation of census tabulation, to military calculation and code breaking, it was government need that drove the initial development of mainframe computers and networking technologies around the world. In Australia, computerisation was supported by governments as part of the nation-building activities of the Commonwealth, with the objective of developing an industrial economy. For example, the production of the CSIR Mark 1 mainframe in the late 1940s (one of the first computers in the world) was an early initiative of what would become the CSIRO (Pass and Hornsby, 2006), just as telecommunication services were largely provided by the public sector up until the late 1990s (Arnold, 2004). Given this long history of work with ICT, it should not be surprising that governments, as large organisations with an expansive range of operations and a considerable numbers of 'clients', have looked to new technology to assist in the day-to-day management of their activities. Indeed, the notion of *bureaucracy* ('rule from the desk') talks about a standardisation and automation of the process of government that developed alongside the nation-state itself (Williams, 2008: 52).

In the recent Australian context, the 1990s saw a renewed public sector interest in technology acquisition as part of a deliberate attempt to move away from this standardised model of bureaucratic rule and service delivery. With accelerating public uptake of the internet in Australia, governments of all types became interested in its use to deliver services, provide information to the community, and serve as a channel for interaction with citizens. Larger agencies have predominantly been attracted to the use of these technologies for enhanced service delivery and cost-reduction purposes, and Australia was seen as a leader in electronic and online service delivery[1] through much of the period of the Coalition government under John Howard (United Nations, 2005: 25). Initiatives like the introduction of the Australian Taxation Office's taxation lodgement application (eTax) and the Bureau of Statistics's online eCensus tool demonstrate how online services can assist citizens' to comply with government regulation through automation, while benefiting government through the digitisation of paper forms. These developments have seen Australians increasingly interacting with government using online service portals (OECD, 2009).[2]

In addition to simply meeting the contemporary needs of a citizenry increasingly comfortable with online transactions (Thomas, 2004: 267), we can also see that these initiatives adhere to the priorities and concerns of the new public management (NPM) era under successive Labor and Coalition governments. NPM represents the self-conscious adoption of ideas from the private sector to reform government management and service delivery. This is achieved through the separation of policy development and program implementation (often associated with outsourcing and privatisation) and the greater use of performance management through market and market-like tools (contracting, internal markets and market testing; Denhardt and Denhardt, 2011: 12–13). Under NPM, computers and new communication technologies become important in the modernisation of 'back office' activities as well acting as a conduit through which services can be delivered. While these aspects of the new IT agenda need not be related, in reality the practice of system modernisation is a prerequisite for contracting, either through greater attention to determining service-delivery standards via data collection of existing practices or via the integration of new technologies with 'legacy' (pre-existing) databases.

The shift towards increased use by Australian governments of online service delivery is ongoing. While some authorities have made advances in delivering complex services through new channels,[3] the systematic adoption of electronic and online service delivery in Australia is variable. While comparatively simple translations of offline processes represented the 'low hanging fruit' of online modernisation in the late 1990s and early 2000s (bill payments, simple bookings systems; Canadian e-Business Initiative, 2004), more complex service

---

1   The distinction between 'electronic' and 'online' in this context being that computerisation (electronic) does not necessarily lead to service delivery provided online (think the one-stop-shop electronic kiosk model popular at the turn of the century; Kelso, et al, 2001). Normally, electronic service delivery preceded online provision, but, in some cases in the 1990s, a shift to online provision necessitated the regularisation and automation of processes that were still undertaken manually.

2   The extent of Australia's success may be queried to some degree, as many of the initiatives represent 'low-hanging fruit' (automation rather than substantive transformation). Australia's record of cross-jurisdictional services remains more limited.

3   An example is in areas like the administration of vehicle registration, which often requires sophisticated integration of ownership, payment and safety systems (that may include third-party validation of compliance).

transformations like electronic health records have been harder to implement because of the wide range of participants in the process (public servants and private providers), the need to protect against risk ('real', such as data intrusion, as well as less-well-defined political risks) and the complexity of implementation (Dearne, 2012). Qiuyan Fan (2011: 933) has discussed how the patchy implementation of e-government makes it difficult for service delivery to be 'joined up' and integrated into single point of entry service systems that allow citizens to access services without having to navigate through a myriad of agencies and levels of government. This demonstrates how the complexity of Australia's public sector (including aspects of federalism and the legal requirements to undertake some functions in specific ways; Barrett, 2003: 11) makes the public sector unique for business process re-engineering.

Rather than discuss the development of government e-services in detail,[4] this chapter focuses on the way that new technology (and new thinking about the technology of government) shapes the public sector. This focus on meta-policy (policy frameworks and heuristics that shape the design of other, subordinate policy; Dror, 1971: 74) allows us to see the broader impact of digital technology on thinking about policy design and implementation in Australia today. This has two components: the first focuses on the impacts of an increasingly sophisticated and 'data-driven' public sector on the design and implementation of public policy, the second focuses on new ideas to employ the creative energy of the online environment to 'rewire' government with the same ideas and energy of the dotcom start-up businesses: Government 2.0 (Gov 2.0).

The new scientific management

The digital-media environment allows for the production and analysis of large amounts of data as transactions and interactions (internal and external to government) become automated, and storage and processing costs fall. Just as the private sector has begun to 'mine' its existing transaction data for new ways to sell products and profile their consumers (Hill, 2012), governments have a wide array of points of interaction with members of the public that deposit data into public-sector owned or controlled databases. Routine interactions with the government that were once stored in seldom-to-be-opened filing cabinets now produce easy-to-access data points maintained over long time periods.[5] While this presents concern about the ability of the state to have intrusive amounts of information about individuals (Chen, 2005a), in policy terms this data can

---

4   A good, systematic assessment of the development of electronic and online service-delivery systems is provided by Paul Henman (2010).

5   Unlike many private organisations, governments have long 'warehoused' data because of legal requirements to hold records and due to the longevity of public institutions.

be moved and analysed with ease to understand more about the administration and impact of public policy than ever before. It is unsurprising then that there is considerable interest in the liberation of this data to drive policy development and improve program implementation (Aichholzer and Burkert, 2004: 335). This is the age of data-driven policy-making: a focus on solving policy problems through the use of the type of large data sets produced by government's regulation of the population to provide natural experiments into the effectiveness of policies (Esty and Rushing, 2007).

The desire to make the art of government more of a science is not new. Plato's *Republic* calls for philosophers to become kings and vice versa. Beyond the personal qualities of leadership, he proposed that this ability to engage in disciplined thought must be matched with practical management training (Reeve, 1988: 191–95). In the modern era, the lessons of World War II pointed to the ability for a greatly expanded and interventionist managerial state to be able to achieve incredible results. Following the 'failure' of the welfare state model (circa 1970s) and the mixed successes of the subsequent Ronald Regan and Margaret Thatcher 'revolutions' (1980s), a renewed interest in scientific management in government was championed by the New Labour administration of Tony Blair in the United Kingdom. Calling for the use of 'evidence-based' decision-making, Blair argued for a 'third way' between state-centric governance and free-market deregulation. Rather than develop policy on the basis of abstract political or economic theory, governments should be more rigorous in their approach to the design of public policy based on structured decision-making and the use of empirical data.[6] This type of approach remains popular with advocates of structured and rigorous decision-making in government, such as the Institute of Public Administration Australia (2012), itself a product of the formalisation of the policy 'sciences'.

An evidence-based Australian politics?

While not unique, the idea of a more technocratic administration was embraced by the Labor government under Kevin Rudd. The reasons for this are more than simply Rudd's background as a chief administrator in the Queensland public sector. Evidence-based policy (EBP) suited the reformist government for two reasons. The first served as a response to perceptions of an increasingly partisan public sector during the era of John Howard's Coalition government (Miragliotta, et al., 2009: 137).[7] The second reason was through the transfer of ideas that Rudd brought to government as an inheritor of the third-way vision of the United Kingdom (*Lateline*, 2007). The Rudd government's penchant for detailed policy

---

6   The extent to which New Labour followed this idea is , however, debatable (Hay in Dillow, 2007: 8).
7   The loss of permanence of the senior executive service began under the previous Labor government (Mulgan, 1998).

reviews (which were criticised as representing a 'do nothing' government; Eltham, 2012) were examples of this approach to policy development. This may have been unfair, but EBP requires the political discipline to reflect when intemperate voices might call for action. For an effective implementation of EBP, Gary Banks (2009) has argued the prerequisites are for an independent public sector to employ good research methodologies, producing clear and transparent data. This reflects the spread of research expertise outside of the academy and the ability of large public institutions to fund practical research activities (Bogenschneider and Corbett, 2010: 91). In addition, the authorising environment of the political class needs to be receptive to the core principle of 'whatever works' policy, rather than driven by ideological (or other) motivations.

The limitations of this approach to government are clear in the rapid downfall of the Rudd government and many of the policy ideas championed by his various reviewers. The most obvious policies have been in the areas of climate change and taxation reform, where the political realisation of the proposals developed by independent experts was considerably more difficult than simply generating the 'best' technical solution to the problems at hand. The government found 'selling' its policy prescriptions and technical assessments to the general public increasingly difficult in a cluttered media environment, where any limitation in the research methodology could be exploited to create doubt. This problem should have been predicted, given the history of climate change politics to date (Zajko, 2011). In addition, while the government championed the credentials and standing of the experts selected to engage in these inquiries, this appeal to independent expertise provided minimal political capital (possibly as a result of excessive cynicism about the state of the public sector, as indicated by Miragliotta, et al., above). Thus, we need to add popular willingness to accept appeals to technical authority to Banks's list of prerequisites for success.

This example shows how Deborah Stone's (1998) argument about the political value of ambiguity is still important: ambiguity allows coalitions to form and be sustained because the specific costs and benefits of policy are not made clear. The elaboration of policy outcomes and costs makes these results clear, making EBP the antithesis of this proven political strategy. While good policy is often seen as having a foundation in a solid and reasoned causal theory that shows how government action is likely to affect change (Birkland, 2011: 241–42), it is easier to communicate simple linear 'stories' than more complex theories and ideas in the current abbreviated media news cycle. This is problematic in policy areas where the public value produced sits at the aggregate, rather than individual, level. Examples of this include public health initiatives and areas of economic redistribution where citizens must weigh collective outcomes over their personal experience. In these cases, the tendency towards confirmation bias (looking for evidence to support one's pre-established position) is enhanced when the group's views are polarised. Additionally, the ability to sort rigorously argued material from furphies declines when the quantum of information is increased (Beecher-Monas, 2007: 23–24). In the recent experience of EBP in Australia, it is evident that structured policy analysis does not produce structured public debate.

Having backed down on a number of key EBP-driven policy areas, the Rudd administration then faced the second dilemma of this type of technocratic model of government: if policy *should* be made in this way, how can a government justify *selectivity* in the use of evidence. As Rudd's argument that climate change represented the 'great moral challenge of our time', the decision to shelve the Emissions Trading Scheme demonstrated a lack of commitment, not simply to the policy area, but the use of EBP more generally. The ad hoc and noncommittal use of evidence, therefore, opens up the elite to claims of relativism and employing data only when it serves their political objectives. In the experience of EBP in Australia, Don Harding (2008) argues that in some policy areas evidence was stretched to fit the policy preferences of government, leading to the selection of policy based on weak evidence, which is harder to defend.[8] Similarly, Michael Coory (2004: 582) has argued that the selection of likely future scenarios has been driven by elite preferences towards the particular policy instruments and outcomes these projections are likely to support.[9]

The opportunities and demands of data

While EBP continues to struggle against the competing logics of political realism and communicative capacity, the idea of data-driven public policy has not gone away. Under the governments of Rudd and his Labour successor, Julia Gillard, a renewed interest in shaping the performance and behaviour of markets came with the opportunity presented by the global financial crisis (Rudd, 2009). This marked a break with the consistent push towards de-regulation in Anglo countries. While wholesale re-regulation of markets and industries has not occurred, these governments have increasingly focused on the role of market regulation to improve social outcomes inside and outside of the public sector.

The concept of markets refers to real and virtual spaces where buyers and sellers come together voluntarily to exchange goods and services, with the shape and nature of exchanges determined by the factors of supply and demand. In the contemporary policy environment, markets are seen as good regulators of social provision because they can be used to disaggregate a range of choices to individuals, who are deemed to be in the best position to make consumption

---

8   His case example being the failure of the 'FuelWatch' system to monitor and publicise fuel prices nationally.
9   Coory's case example focused on the use of 'worst case' healthcare costs associated with the aging of the population that favoured the use of marketplace responses over state provision of care.

choices. The 'grassroots' nature of these interactions means that governments need not regulate exchange relationships where individuals have an interest in ensuring they receive the best outcome.

This, of course, is a fanciful view of markets, which have a tendency towards asymmetrical power relations, with resultant impacts on the price, quality, and suitability of the services received. In cases of market failure in private fuel and grocery items (in this case, inflated pricing through reduced competition and likely price collusion; Waters, 2012), Labor has proposed market transparency policies (the Grocery Watch and FuelWatch schemes) to increase the ability of consumers to make informed choices more easily. The capacity of the state to make these policies has increased as the cost of the collection, aggregation and promotion of pricing information has fallen considerably through the use of information and communications technologies across the economy.

These two initiatives employed the idea of increased marketplace transparency to reduce the cost of supply. If the market was not providing systems by which competition would drive down the prices of these staples, the government would do so using new technology to achieve their objectives. Unsurprisingly, the proposed market transparency policies collapsed under the weight of resistance from the private sector (Burke, 2009), who benefit from the inability of their consumers to have comprehensive information about comparative pricing.[10]

In areas where the government has direct authority, the use of more market information to empower individual choice has been more effectively (actually) implemented. Possibly the most high-profile example would be the use of performance data to influence school performance through the My School website (http://myschool.edu.au). Using new national standardised data collection and testing, the site serves to allow education consumers to select from public and private schools based on their assessment of performance provided through the site. This demonstrates how the NPMs' ideas of internal markets (comparison between public schools) and market testing (comparison with private providers of similar products) are being employed in areas where wholesale outsourcing and privatisation are unlikely to occur. Thus, the government supports parental choice through ensuring information is available upon which informed decisions can be made. Similar tools are to be introduced for University performance (Gilmore, 2012) and proposed for hospital services.

---

10   A number of non-government price-watch websites have been established following this policy failure, including Grocer Watch (www.grocerwatch.com) and the NRMA's Petrol Price page (www.mynrma.com.au/motoring/car-care/fuel-prices.htm).

Who benefits?

While the provision of information may be a substitute for top-down regulation, it does not negate the need for minimum standards of performance. Markets provide innovation and choice, but are most responsive to the most profitable and/or informed segment of their customers who have the capacity to act on the information provided. This capacity is not distributed evenly across the social gradient, with the educated and wealthy more likely to gain advantages under these systems for a variety of reasons (Berg and Gornitzka, 2012: 171). This is a good example of what Frank Bannister and Regina Connolly (2011) identify as the societal risk of e-transparency: failure to recognise the context in which data will be interpreted and employed in the public realm. Where concerns about the release of sensitive information are well-known policy problems associated with populist laws (such as criminal registers; Pager, 2003), debates about government data release and the potential for aggregation and mining remain formative. Michael Gurstein (2011) has identified how privileged social groups employ government data to support their economic privilege in developing and developed nations: demonstrating that while the provision of more data may appear value neutral on the surface, the context of use needs consideration.

The problem with many of these initiatives lies in their unwillingness to recognise how decision-making can be supported across the spectrum of users. While the introduction of the My School website was accompanied by assurances that this would not produce 'league tables' that reduced the range of variables on the site into a simple list, thereby stigmatising some schools unfairly and leading to a 'death spiral' or enrolment declines and recruitment problems (McGraw, 2010), mainstream media organisations quickly used the data to produce lists comparing schools, just as they have done in the past with other indicators (such as graduate entry rates). While the My School site design seeks to mitigate this through a number of means (use of captcha to prevent site scraping,[11] as well as 'how to interpret' information in the school reports), league tables serve a part of the community: the need for more simple decision-making heuristics to deal with the increased complexity of the shift towards greater choice in the provision of public services. We also see here the limited ability of the government to disintermediate their communication with members of the public: digital data is harder to control than its analogue predecessor.

What gets measured gets managed

The visibility of these data releases is designed to shift the attention of public managers to improve their performance. This is achieved by pressure being placed on them to perform by their clients and peers, as well as being internal

---

11   Using a script to access a site and harvest its data for reuse.

performance indicators for promotion and performance-based pay. The ability of these systems to accurately match the range of work areas of public employees generally defines their utility (Rosenberg, et al., 2010: 202–05). If significant aspects of a task are opaque to data collection, the market-information model runs the risk of a lopsided attention towards activities with clear performance indicators attached. The introduction of the standardised testing to support My School has led to concerns that this diverts the attention of school administrators and teachers to 'teach to the test' (Rout, 2011; Barry, 2012), which is seen by many educators as a retrograde step back to an excessive focus on the '3 Rs'.

This also has an important time dimension. In a desire to liberate data from legacy systems and make it increasingly transparent, there is a potential that activities that are easy to quantify and which deliver short-term results become the emphasis of managers. Thus, where the public service was once seen as a counterweight to the short-term orientation of the political class because of its independence and insulation from direct criticism (Alesina and Tabellini, 2008: 427), successive reforms and the use of these measures may narrow bureaucratic attention as public servants become directly accountable for their performance in real time. This is in line with NPMs' encouragement of public-sector managers to move out of the background and engage with members of the public more directly to create 'public value' through engagement and entrepreneurship (Moore, 1995). Managerialism's focus on standardised management techniques drawn from the private sector also runs the risk of importing short-term horizons over concerns about organisational sustainability.

On this front, there is Australian evidence that the use of market mechanisms may produce short-term boosts in performance and diversity of service delivery, but that these effects decline over time (Considine, et al., 2011). In response to the problems of standardised data demands from the 'top' of the political system reducing the value of data to generate innovation at the local level, Dunleavy, et al. (2006) have argued that this era of digital governance can be more effectively managed through the critical adoption of 'needs-based holism'.

This type of comprehensive management process looks to the state as a powerful agent in data integration and matching to solve localised and/or policy domain-specific problems. The value proposition of this model is the inverse of the current federal approach to quasi-market information provision: largely, datasets should be liberated from a wide range of centralised government agencies to support local evidence-based policies, rather than have defined data collected at the local level for standardised reporting at the national level. This focuses on the reality that most citizen-centric policy is relational in character and that the comparators people use in their lived experience tends to be community based (physical or of-interest).

Rewiring the state: Gov 2.0

While data-driven policy and EBP tend to be ideas generated from within the public sector, recent years have seen the emergence of a new paradigm for government reform running in parallel with these approaches. Inspired by the expansive growth of web-centric firms in the last decade, Gov 2.0 proposes that the practices and technologies of Silicon Valley's successful start-ups should be used within government as a catalyst for service modernisation through co-creation with stakeholders.

The notion of Gov 2.0 remains an amorphous concept subject to competing definitions (Bardsley, 2010). The term has its origins in another socio-technological change, the introduction of what is called 'web 2.0' in the mid 2000s. Web 2.0 itself is not a specific technology,[12] but an approach to developing interactive services for the internet. Christoph Schroth and Till Janner (2007: 36–37) talk about web 2.0 as a 'philosophy' of design that focuses on the creation of 'mutually maximising collective intelligence and adding value for each participant by formalised and dynamic information sharing and creation'. In practice, this sees websites and digital-media applications as providing the capacity of co-creation with their users. This is a more full implementation of the idea of 'active audiences', as discussed previously.

Web 2.0 is often illustrated in popular parlance by talking about the 'read-write web': an emerging internet where users are able to interact with the material online, to contribute to it, modify it, reuse it and, thereby, create collective goods. Examples like YouTube and Wikipedia show how comparatively simple-to-use technology 'platforms' can be used by the public to build considerable information repositories of great value, simply by linking together individuals and providing toolsets for creation. This links to observations about the shifting capacity of members of the public to participate in policy dialogue. As Helen Margetts (2009: 6–16) has argued, computer networks have served to increase the degree of interaction between policy makers and stakeholders, particularly those who may have been less able to establish and maintain formal and physical organisational ties with government. From the perspective of policy networks, the facilitation of these exchange relationships can be empowering for actors who are more likely to have non-tangible political resources, such as information and skills.

---

12   Though, in its early iterations it was commonly associated with the web-development methods described as AJAX (asynchronous JavaScript and XML). These allowed webpages, once static 'repositories', to become interactive and dynamic.

Gov 2.0.au

In Australia, following similar high-level endorsement of the idea as seen with the presidency of Barack Obama in the United States, the then Rudd–Labor government created the Government 2.0 Taskforce to investigate the utility of the idea. Presenting an enthusiastic report to government, the Taskforce defined Gov 2.0 as:

> … a public policy shift to create a culture of openness and transparency, where government is willing to engage with and listen to its citizens; and to make available the vast national resource of non-sensitive public sector information (PSI). Government 2.0 empowers citizens and public servants alike to directly collaborate in their own governance by harnessing the opportunities presented by technology. (2010: 1)

In specifically calling on the adoption of Gov 2.0 by the Commonwealth public sector, the taskforce highlighted three areas for reform: opening of the public sector's culture to greater levels of transparency and engagement with the public; explicit use of web 2.0 technologies by government organisations to achieve the former and produce collaborative outcomes; and, the release of increasing amounts of public sector information into the digital commons.

This take on the promise of Gov 2.0 has been pushed by the thinker most commonly associated with the term, and the originator of the term web 2.0: technology publisher Tim O'Reilly (O'Reilly Media).[13] O'Reilly draws upon examples from the technology sector to demonstrate the power of web 2.0 design in creating innovation and value (2009b). Given the dominance of NPM meta-policy in Australia, the report and its emphasis on cooption of private sector strategies to create public value fell on fertile ground. Lindsay Tanner, one of the ministers responsible for the taskforce, made an unfavourable comparison between the performance of public sector organisations in providing correspondence to members of the public and fast-food restaurants in his 1999 technology and policy book *Open Australia*. In 2011, he reiterated this by emphasising the relationship between Gov 2.0 and the lessons to be drawn from sectors with traditions of innovation (CeBIT, 2011).

New or new-new?

Gov 2.0 focuses on shaping government in ways to encourage the creation of self-regulating, problem-oriented communities of interest. In championing this model, Gov 2.0 presents an interesting proposal for recasting the role of government in Australia from one of provision to that of a gardener: tending the

---

13   Matthew Allen (2009) argues that O'Reilly has ongoing importance in the use of the term web 2.0 in the way he uses his media profile to sustain and shape its popular meaning over time.

productive platforms (data sets, and APIs[14]) from which empowered citizens can draw. The emphasis on the use of data to enhance service delivery and decision-making fits within the tradition of scientific management. In broad terms this notion of electronically facilitated democratic practice is not new. In popular fiction, the notion of automatic and automated decision-making systems emerged with the development of information theory and pre-eminence of technocratic decision-making, as illustrated in novels such as *The Machine Stops* by EM Forster (1909). With the introduction of pre-internet computer networking, ideas like 'teledemocracy' gained currency (Taylor, 1998) in the 1960s: recognising the inherent role of information and communication in political decision-making, while (implicitly and explicitly) incorporating normative assumptions and aspirations about the place of technology in structuring and rationalising social processes and politics.

In practice, Australia has had a mixed history of experimentation with new forms of democratic decision-making employing digital media, with many initial 'electronic democracy' initiatives (such as online discussion fora employed by local and state governments) being quickly wound back or cancelled. The majority of these initiatives are what are best described as 'programmatic e-democracy': top-down initiatives designed and implemented by government organisations in the same manner as any other service (as discussed in An electronic constituency surgery, Chapter 3). As such, they often sit within public service delivery paradigms, such as the automation of existing services (online petitions, for example) or applications of existing policy models (such as jurisdictional consultation manuals). To generalise, many of these initiatives at the local, state and federal level have be deemed to be unsuccessful, largely due to low levels of take up (Griffiths, 2002; Blackhouse, 2007).

The underlying causes of failure are often due to: excessive planned-risk avoidance that reduces the utility of the service (such as strict participation control, or functional limitations due to the — not unfounded — fear of system misuse); a tendency to place systems within government domain spaces, rather than undertake partnerships with civic groups to place them in existing organisational settings; and, limited stakeholder commitment to the initiatives (Anderson and Bishop, 2005). The last factor often sees these initiatives never exiting 'pilot' testing, and having no outwardly visible connection to policy-making processes. Partially this is the result of limited interest in the idea of e-democracy compared with the investment in e-service delivery (thereby instrumentalising the perception of government–citizen interactions). It also, however, stems from the failure of advocates of these 'Gov 1.0' ideas to learn from their lack of success, (such as Stephen Clift who visited Australia frequently in

---

14 Technical specifications that allow for data interoperability, the ability to use another organisation's data in a meaningful manner.

the late 1990s and early 2000s to talk about his experiences with one of the first high profile e-democracy projects, Minnesota E-Democracy; http://forums.e-democracy.org[15]) whereby the technologies of these initial online virtual spaces were emulated by governments, but often without observing the situation of the projects in their unique cultural contexts.

Self-regulating communities of creativity

Following these lessons of failure, Gov 2.0 is interesting in that it sidesteps direct engagement with the formal policy process to move more directly to implementation: emphasis is placed on the use of data, building new means for engagement and citizen oversight, and developing tools that increase the flow of information from government datasets into the public domain. The read–write nature of Gov 2.0 is significant in how it encourages the elaboration of public datasets to increase their value (such as overlaying data on maps, 'mash-ups' of multiple datasets to produce new insights, or adding user-generated data to 'official' information), and the formation of temporary groups working on issues of mutual concern, drawn from a range of sectors. Gov 2.0 appears, therefore, to be aligned with Henrik Bang's idea (as discussed in Strengths and weaknesses of the OSMOs, Chapter 5) of citizenship that focuses on ends-oriented and time-limited interactions with government. Social media works well in this context with a concentration on the formation of user communities' interest in the use of PSI. By using tools that are less strictly, or not at all, controlled by government, Gov 2.0 aims to avoid the natural risk aversion that led to many of the e-democracy initiatives remaining hidden from public view and disconnected from policy-making (personal interview: Steve Davis, 10 January 2012). This picks up on Mary Griffiths' observation that this can lead to 'free flows of ungovernability': openness is hard to control from the top-down and attempting to wind back on the provision of PSI is difficult when there are stakeholder communities organised around its provision (2002: 8–9).

This allows us to ask to what extent Gov 2.0, through the fostering of spaces for civic interaction and the data for a range of purposes (including rational dialogue), provides for the development of genuine and generative public engagement within the sphere of government. There is more potential in these aspects of the plan because of the relative autonomy of new data-driven civil society actors. The core difference between Gov 2.0 and earlier e-democracy initiatives is that, in the past, online engagement was seen largely as a task of 'place making' (as in *Field of Dreams*; Universal Pictures, 1989) by government, focusing on the development of tools, rather than communities. Social media in the public sector can be seen as providing significant potential for the development of 'corporate

---

15 A project run out of civil society in a state with a distributed population.

dialogue' between stakeholders and government authorities (Bonsón, et al., 2012: 125–26, 130–31). As dialogue often occurs in public spaces, its conduct is regulated by citizens who are part of these communities.

The 'hobbification' of Gov 2.0

In the move from e-democracy to Gov 2.0, the power relationship between participants is equalised. As co-creation activities, Gov 2.0 projects create mutual dependencies among participants. This is at considerable odds to the way in which top-down e-democracy initiatives have been more structured than the offline policy process. Indeed, the reluctance of organised groups (pressure groups, industry associations) to participate in many e-democracy activities is because the use of structure undermined their capacity to go outside of the formal policy cycle to have an impact on outcomes (for example, strategic arena shifting; Holyoke et al., 2012). Co-creation presents a challenging dynamic for governments, which places governance issues at the project level with ambiguous and context-dependent accountability and performance measures. Following the era of NPM, in which policy delivery through networks saw 'increasing control over less' and the use of 'rubber levers' to effect change, Gov 2.0 will present challenges to the public manager, but not unique ones.

What is interesting for the public manager is how Gov 2.0 leads to interactions with an array of participants. While NGOs and the private sector are well represented in NPM activities, Gov 2.0 draws increasing numbers of amateurs and individuals into the co-creation process. While this can lead to weak attachment to projects, it also changes the way citizens engage with government creativity. To fill the commitment gap, interest has been shown in the use of 'gamification'. Gamification serves to increase rates of participation across a range of activities normally considered serious chores (Weaver, 2011: 21). A good example of this would be NASA's planet hunters 'game' which involves citizens in searching for exoplanets around stars, using data provided by the space agency and challenging the public to find the largest number of new extra-solar planets (www.planethunters.org).

While an ambiguous concept, gamification generally involves the use of game mechanics (competition, intangible rewards) in activities that were not normally deemed to be playful in nature. These 'serious games' commonly serve a public good, and can be employed to encourage participation or adherence to an activity where other rewards are difficult to deliver or provide equitably. Alenka Poplin sees the implementation of serious games under the rubric of 'playful public participation' (2011: 204–05), a function of the changing nature of the citizen's relation to the state, but also a characteristic of the difficulty of the attention economy. Playful public participation sustains interest in the involvement of constructive games through a high-level of entertainment in the process of the simulation. The extent to which this model 'scales' from simple hit-and-run activities to more complex policy and program activity remains in doubt, however. Poplin suggests that game mechanics should be simple to ensure the most rapid movement from initiation to participation.

The rats in the walls

While some of the claims of Gov 2.0 fail to excite jaded public servants conditioned to 'paradigm changing' reform every few years, the idea has advocates from within government. These individuals and groups can be found across government, but Gov 2.0's focus on open data and information exchange resonates with agencies that have public information roles (in the same way that the initial deployment of government websites in the early 1990s were commonly driven by department library and IT units).[16] Former parliamentary librarian Roxanne Missingham (2011: 426–27), for example, sees the bottom-up nature of web 2.0 technologies as instrumental in accelerating their adoption in government. This has been supported by independent online communities of public servants who have been interested in innovation in government, like Ozloop (http://apsozloop.ning.com).[17] Just as we saw in the movement of activist techniques for political protest through conferences and events (as discussed in Online anarchists and the democratisation of hacking, Chapter 4), the distribution of Gov 2.0 ideas through programming 'camps' and other training sessions is being facilitated by activists.

Following a model popularised in the ICT community, groups like the Australian Gov 2.0 Community[18] have run programming events that bring computer programmers (public sector, private sector, professional and amateur) and data owners (agencies) together to engage in creative competitions to develop new applications for PSI. These gatherings ('hackathons' or 'hackfests') have been popular in the open-source community as focusing events that motivate the community of contributors to projects, and by major technology firms to encourage and support their developers. Usable products and product ideas have resulted from these events, but they are more likely to be useful in

16 Sometimes without senior management being aware. This did lead to a proliferation of sites and standards in the 1990s that required rationalisation as the cost of maintaining the functionality and accuracy of many of these sites became apparent.

17 The foundation of this was in response to the limits of online collaboration and information sharing within agencies. Ozloop follows a model established in the United States (www.govloop.com). The use of social networking services (SNS) for public servants allows the 'noddling of behaviour' associated with the innovative use of technology to distribute information and collaboration (personal interview: Steve Davis, 10 January 2012).

18 Situated around a google group discussion board: http://groups.google.com/forum/?hl=en&fromgroups#!forum/gov20canberra Recently a ning SNS has been established (http://gov20australia.ning.com) for this community.

developing ideas, demonstrating the possibility of toolsets and data repositories, and promoting specific organisations, technologies and groups.[19] This can be achieved at comparatively low cost by the host organisation (the provision of space, food, and prizes commonly of lower total value that that produced at the event). The Gov 2.0 community has used this model in Australia (2010 and 2012) through forming partnerships between private ICT companies, government agencies with data sets of interest, and the network of programmers interested in using government data.

Illustration 18: 2012 Govhack (1 June 2012)

Source: Photograph by Gavin Tapp (cc), image source: www.flickr.com/photos/92795775@N00/7314896154/in/set-72157629999887028/

These events demonstrate that network forms of organisation meet in the intersection between the disaggregated and atomistic culture of computer programmers and hackers, and the tendency for policy to be increasingly produced from policy networks rather than structured hierarchical groups. The importance of advocates of Gov 2.0 also lies in demonstrating that this type of

---

19   For example, the use of laptop accelerometers as input devices (as opposed to their original function as safety features to protect hard drives against sudden movement) emerged from an event like this. These are now integral to a range of consumer-ICT products.

co-creation can be undertaken effectively and without the introduction of new forms of risk (Matthews; 2009: 21–22), a barrier to the implementation of Gov 2.0 that is more acute in the public sector than is found in the private.

The outsiders

While the Gov 2.0 Taskforce solidified the legitimacy of the concept in government, advocates of this model have been working outside of government to promote the value of open data. One of the best examples of this is OpenAustralia (www. openaustralia.org; part of the OpenAustralia Foundation), a website that aims to promote civic awareness of parliament and parliamentarians by employing available government data (such as Hansard transcripts and a member's register of interests) and value-adding them to improve accessibility and use by members of the public (Bellamy, et al., 2011: 21–22). Based on the popular *They Work for You* site in the United Kingdom (www.theyworkforyou.com), OpenAustralia demonstrates both the ease of emulation of effective models across and between jurisdictions, as well as the existence of a loose international movement of reformers interested in applying digital media to improve, enhance and reform democratic practices.

There are questions, however, as to the transferability of some ideas. While Australia and the United Kingdom share the traditions of Westminster, Australia's party model virtually eliminates the autonomy of members of parliament in the casting of their vote. Whereas their British counterparts are more likely to exercise a free vote (and therefore, as in the United States, can be subject to scrutiny based on their parliamentary record), the novelty of this in the Australian context limits the value of sites that increase transparency of existing parliamentary data. Moving away from strict reliance on government data,[20] the foundation has also imported a 'bottom-up' model for collecting and archiving copies of political leaflets online (www.electionleaflets.org.au).[21] The limitations of the bottom-up collection of these records to date has been their partial nature and limited geographical coverage, as well as a focus on one type of transitory, election material only.

What lies beneath

Due to the uncritical adoption of ideas from Gov 2.0 in Australia, there is a tendency for the direct importation of a range of political norms and assumptions that need to be explored if we are to understand the politics of Gov 2.0 as a meta-

---

20 Which can be problematic in ensuring that services remain functional if the data structure provided by the host organisation changes.

21 Recently the foundation, with the support of the Gov 2.0 Taskforce, developed an alert service for planning applications that aggregates data from a range of local government websites (www.planningalerts. org.au).

policy (Bardsley, 2010: 67). Richard Heeks, writing about the transfer of ICT technology initiatives between different political cultures, sees these programs as 'carriers of context' (2005: 58). He employs case analysis to demonstrate the unintended transfer of the assumptions of systems designers. While focused on explaining the considerable under-performance of government electronic and online service delivery projects because of misfits between administrative and political cultures, this work highlights how underlying computer code can be important in structuring the behaviours of individuals who use these systems (Giddens, 1984). As Lawrence Lessig (ongoing) has argued, the core technical standards of systems can shape outcomes in specific ways through control over what systems can and cannot do. Employing the expression 'code is law' he argues for ICT to be seen through a lens of soft determinism. Given this, it is important to recognise the context ideas about Gov 2.0 might carry. This will provide indications of the political, as well as practical, implications of the idea for Australian public life.

Here come the eCitizens, ready or not

The first point of consideration is the way in which Gov 2.0 constructs citizenship. In his discussion of the potential benefits of the idea, O'Reilly (2009a) is clear in seeing the relationship between the state and the citizen as not one of top-down service provision (which he refers to as 'vending-machine government'), but as fundamentally participative: citizenship is not restricted to procedural participation in elections and services. In this way, the citizen should not see government as the guarantee of a minimum set of rights (democratic) or benefits, but as a place for self-actualisation. This argument reflects a classical notion of the liberal state, such as the public sphere as a site of freedom, as expressed by Hannah Arendt (discussed in Chapter 3). This notion also depends on the active and informed citizen, and one who is able to recognise their own needs, and act upon them in a meaningful way. The separation between the political and apolitical citizen has been theorised considered in a rationalist tradition of theorising American citizenship in a way that has seen the passive citizen as one who has made a rational decision because of their essential satisfaction with the status quo (see Dahl's (1961) notion of *Homo Politicus* and *Homo Civicus*). That this idea has influenced the concept of Gov 2.0 is evidenced by O'Reilly's use of classic texts in American politics as the basis for his arguments (2009b).

At the core of Gov 2.0 lies a reliance on the revised classical, political liberalism of the internet economy. Comparatively under-regulated, transnational and with a Darwinian attitude towards success and failure, the internet's social and business ethos sits neatly with the liberal state of the classical period of the public sphere, but in an era where the capabilities of individuals (real or artificial) to amass considerable and disproportionate economic and social power is magnified by technology. This presents a concern about the impact of this set of ideologically invested technologies into the domestic context — particularly as this draws largely from a political environment without the Australian focus on egalitarianism as a positive task of government. It is not clear that open platforms will contribute to goals of social empowerment as much as furthering the knowledge gap that stems from the stratification of the educational opportunities that we see emerging as a result of unequal access to the information and training that builds information literacies.

Additionally, in an environment dominated by government-as-platform, we run the risk of seeing those who fail to build on these platforms as being unwilling to engage in the self-help available to them. This has key cultural impacts. As Andrew Kernohan notes: 'In an inegalitarian culture, many of the beliefs that people take up from their cultural environment are based on beliefs about the moral inequality of persons ... If people base their ends in life on these false evaluations, their highest-order interest in coming to know the good will have been harmed' (1998: 88). In examining neo-liberal education policies, Becky Francis has argued that the failure to take up 'obvious' opportunities discursively recreates these recalcitrants as 'the undeserving poor' (2006). Given the importance of education and information literacies in being able to shape (rather than use) the new toolsets available to the e-citizen, the declining importance of minimal procedural forms of democratic practice as representing 'good citizenship' leads to concerns about a widening participation gap between stratified groups of political and apolitical people in society (see the discussion of Dahl, below).

Bootstrap government

A second concern, and a flip side of the first, is the view that Gov 2.0 has of the nature of the state. In O'Reilly's (2009b) discussion of 'government as a platform', he argues that government should see itself in the same manner as a web 2.0 provider: as a basis upon which civic action can be undertaken, rather than as a distributor, regulator, or arena. This lies at the core of the argument about the value of the concept. As discussed in Chapter 1, many advocates of Gov 2.0 cite the power of the internet to overcome classic collective action problems (Wilkinson and Huberman, 2007). As has been observed:

> Many cases of technology employed in collective action appear to strain, if not outright violate one or another tenet ... the classic binary free-riding decision metric is not obvious [and] the pursuit of collective action occurs either completely or largely in the absence of formal organization. (Bimber, et al., 2005: 371)

These arguments have merit, and the power of collaborative co-creation, in circumstances where it has worked, has been shown to be remarkable in the output of projects, but also the ability to mobilise large numbers of productive participants (Ortega and González-Barahona, 2007).

It is necessary to question the quality of evidence that is presented as the basis for this model, however. The examples that are cited as exemplar 'bottom-up' projects are initiatives such as Wikipedia, the Firefox web browser, and the Libreoffice/ OpenOffice.org productivity suite. Each of these began as, or ran parallel to, conventional projects that were then 'open-sourced' (Nupedia, Netscape Navigator, StarOffice). In addition, some of the key institutional supporters for these projects have been commercial interests that had economic motivations to increase competition in the marketplace (such as Google's support for Firefox to open up new markets to its search engine, or Sun's support for OpenOffice. org to reduce the market dominance of Microsoft's key cash cow products).[22] Thus, while co-creation is a powerful generator of activity and value (each of these projects gained considerably in public value from distributed bottom-up participation), the role of institutions in developing these initiatives needs to be highlighted. This is not just in the role of fostering their initial development, but also in the way strategic decisions were important in identifying market failures that could be exploited by new, open-source offerings.

Adhocracy's limits

In addition to the generative question, we need to question what implications the open-source model has as a governance model, a significant question in the way software projects are run, and a critical one when dealing with the use of public resources. Governance in this context is commonly associated with the adhocratic organising model: one where the structure and processes of decision-making are designed from routines, or from scratch, according to each situation. This suits volunteer activities, but produces great variability in the decision-making process. Given the strengths and limitations of this model, it is not surprising that the most effective projects are those that are divisible into discrete tasks that can be delivered incrementally (e.g. Linux distributions and their use of 'rolling updates'), rather than projects that require cohesive structure or vision (such as the *A Million Penguins* wikibook initiative, which was ultimately described as 'unreadable'; Mason and Thomas, 2008). Given their rejection of conventional government-management styles and processes, it is not

---

22   This point needs development. Certainly, the role of Google in encouraging the development of browsers to rival the dominant Internet Explorer did not have commercial value to Google only, but also served to develop the web platform. Internet Explorer, as a once near-monopoly provider of web access, entered a prolonged phase during which it was not developed. OpenOffice.org helped to push the case for open standards for documents, which has had an impact on existing market players, but this largely benefited insurgent projects.

surprising that what is attractive about adhocracy to proponents of Gov 2.0 is its ends orientation (Hayes, 2001: 128). Processes in this model are generally a secondary consideration to the adoption of 'what works'.

The de-emphasis of process and leadership is problematic for government, particularly in places where resource allocation and legal proceduralism are required (i.e. most of government activity, as conventionally defined). Additionally, as Francis Rouke and Paul Schulman (1989) observe, the historical use of adhocracy by governments tends to be found in commissions of inquiry, investigations into disaster, and responses to sudden systemic shocks that signal a period of exception, where normal processes and procedures have broken down (see also, Mendonça, et al., 2007). The problem with these organisational systems, they contend, comes in the lack of accountability these decision-making arrangements bring and the relatively arbitrary treatment of rights by decision makers.

This is present in some of the exemplars citied by O'Reilly, such as the Apple iPhone. In recent years, Apple has been criticised for its internal processes of reviewing and approving applications that can run on its platforms. The company has been criticised for taking a conservative approach to the approval of material with adult content (including restricting graphic novels of classic literature) and refusing to publish political cartoons (Tate, 2010).[23] Critics of Steve Jobs' company's approach to censorship is that it lacks rigour in process. Responses have been arbitrary and based on aggregate popular opinion in the marketplace. This latter tendency has been seen in the differential treatment of adult graphic novels, with strong preference given to those that display heteronormative content. Arguments that the internet, by nature, automatically disintermediates hierarchies (social, economic, political) has not been born out in practice: the iTunes/App Store model itself represents a process of reintermediation and the reinsertion of Apple as an intermediary because it has control over a key point in the distribution chain at which rents can be accessed.

Time, again

Developing from the point above is the idea that Gov 2.0 has to be recognised as the transmission of approaches and models from the leading edge of online business practice. The focus on web 2.0 business models as the key technical example of what Gov 2.0 might look like in practice presents problems, largely because of the uncertain nature of 'success' in the web 2.0 environment. The interactive and flexible photo-sharing service Flickr is an example of how unstable online properties and services can be: lauded in 2007 as a web 2.0

---

23   Should this surprise us? Consider the example of the physical public-private space: the shopping mall, and its owners' tolerance of unregulated speech-acts.

pioneer (an online content aggregation, storage, indexing, social networking, and editing service) which insulated Yahoo! against its search rival Google (Sterling, 2007); by 2010 its fortunes were flagging as casual photo sharing moved rapidly to Facebook.

Governments have history, whereas the internet has very little. Thus, the promotion of Gov 2.0 carries a strong valorisation of the work of the private sector in creating public goods, omitting those who have crashed out along the way. O'Reilly identifies the best examples of platform providers as those economically successful parts of the ICT industry:

> ... every big winner has been a platform company: someone whose success has enabled others, who've built on their work and multiplied its impact. Microsoft put 'a PC on every desk and in every home,' the internet connected those PCs, Google enabled a generation of ad-supported startups, Apple turned the phone market upside down by letting developers loose to invent applications no phone company would ever have thought of. In each case, the platform provider raised the bar, and created opportunities for others to exploit.

More recently, O'Reilly (2010) has drawn an even stronger analogy between Gov 2.0 as a bountiful 'supermarket' full of products, compared with Gov 1.0 as a soviet system of supply.

This reliance on a specific section of the private sector as a paradigm for public production is a problematic for a number of reasons. First, the analogy is weak. The examples employed overstate the similarities of the business models that made these companies successful; for example Google's open-access tools that are most likely to be used in Gov 2.0 mashups, such as Google Maps, are not a major part of the company's core economic strength (its vanilla search is). Second, it implies 'platform' is an open and participative concept, which is not necessarily the case. There are considerable differences between the provision of software for undifferentiated clone computers created by Microsoft and the locked-down environment of Apple under Jobs' most recent tenure (Zittrain, 2008: 3). Additionally, while Google may have 'enabled a generation of ad-supported startups', it eats its young when it feels the need (for example, the acquisitions of YouTube, Blogger, Picasa, and the online documents suite components among many others).

Publicising or privatising?

The final point of consideration is the extent to which Gov 2.0 asks government to emulate the dotcom heroes. If we look at the definition of Gov 2.0 developed by the consulting firm Gartner, it is defined as 'the use of IT to socialize and commoditize government services, processes and data'. (Di Maio, 2009). This is conveyed in the taskforce report, which characterises one of the three pillars of Gov 2.0 as the release of public sector information with 'additional rights of access, rights to freely reuse, republish, repurpose and otherwise add value to government information'. The point of this recommendation is that large amounts of potential value sit in Crown copyright government information, which, if harnessed by entrepreneurial individuals, could create new value and expand the public investment in the collection of this data.

While this idea may have merit, it does not emulate any of the strategies of success used by the exemplar companies of O'Reilly's list. Companies, such as Microsoft, flourished on the back of commodity hardware provided by other firms: effectively adding value to its proprietary products and services by lowering the comparative adoption costs of its platform against one with high switching costs through proprietary file formats. Google only provides its information as a service, not in machine readable raw form: its value-added database of websites is a major part of its 'secret sauce' and one it defends viciously (attacking rivals who attempt to reverse engineer Google's search results to improve their own products; Singhal, 2011). Google's release of data on trends and other statistics are commonly only provided in a form that is not machine-readable and does not provide comparative axes.

Where online firms have made the data releases that Gov 2.0 proponents call on, unanticipated problems have emerged. A good example is the release of three months of 'de-identified' search data by AOL in 2006 for researchers working on search technology (Kirk, 2006). This data was quickly analysed by members of the public and used to identify individuals from the raw material by looking at the text of successive search queries. It's not surprising that members of the taskforce (which included a representative from Google Australia) would call on the release of government data: the indexing and use of data is what has made that company successful. That these unidentified and subsidiary-use activities run counter to the general thrust of privacy debates is a subject that has gained scarce attention.

Sustaining change

Gov 2.0 presents a range of possibilities to the Australian public sector. Like previous technology and openness revolutions, it has numbers of adherents and has generated interesting and valuable outputs. The limitations of the model, however, need to be considered further, and there is ambiguity in the political assumptions built into a reform model that is based on the valorisation of one part of the US-centric ICT industry. Like the e-democracy revolution before it, Gov 2.0 needs to more closely consider the political history and context of Australia in the way it adjusts its ideas to the Australian political landscape.

Thus, we need to question the extent to which the advocates and hackers have the pragmatic political experience to ensure the sustainability of their initiatives over time.

While the Gov 2.0 community gives considerable attention to technological exemplars for emulation, more attention to the political reality of radical openness initiatives is needed. Australia's experience with its respective *Freedom of Information Acts* (FOIA) is informative. A classic 'open government' initiative of the 1970s, and imported into Australia by reformers, Rick Snell has demonstrated how the limited use of the act by Opposition MPs and journalists to embarrass governments has led to decreased commitment to the spirit of these reforms (2002). Because of the reality of the use of these initiatives for partisan purposes (Stubbs, 2008: 672–73), FOIA remains an under-funded and understaffed area of public administration, largely because governments see it as adding nothing but trouble to public administration.

All the myriad ways

The data-driven policy agenda is still in its early days and its direction is uncertain. While there are tendencies in the project towards an uncritical adoption of aspects of 'start-up' culture that are at odds with the role of the state in providing equitable services to all, the heart and soul of these projects remain up for grabs. The inclusion of a wider range of participants 'hacking away' at/in the heart of government means a more interesting mix of participants. Just as the 'femocrats' of the 1970s and 1980s saw activist bureaucrats pushing within the public sector to diversify and expand the way policy considered the issues of women in the Australian public sector (Sawer, 2007: 20), it is likely that this new group of activist–programmers will be able to expand the ways that governments think about the development and design of policy and programs to be more transparent and participative. As with the feminist infiltration, there are questions regarding whom these policies benefit and the capacity of positive technical and cultural changes to be sustained over time, particularly those democratic initiatives that significantly challenge entrenched elites. The attacks on feminist policy structures in the 2000s and beyond in Australia show that these 'wins' are not necessarily permanent, and we have seen how initiatives aimed at general openness can be perverted by partisans and undermined over time.

Epilogue – An invitation to readers

This book is provided under a liberal licence that permits the creation and distribution of derivative works. It is part of an expanding body of writing, multimedia, and teaching resources being provided in open access repositories. As public servants, academics have an obligation to ensure the highest availability of our work to the public, to ensure barriers to participation are kept as low as possible, but also that the wider community has the opportunity to see and judge our work and the investment they put into it. Repositories like ANU E Press and licensing arrangements that encourage distribution and creativity are part of this restructuring of the way in which information is made accessible.

The study of digital media in Australia in particular is an area of scholarship subject to rapid development and change due to the evolving nature of the technology and society's engagement with it, and the expanding range and diversity of scholarship in this area. As an author I have no misconceptions that the original version of this book will/has quickly, in whole and in part, become out of date. Additionally, this book suffers from a number of obvious gaps, the first being a systematic analysis of digital age policy outputs in the areas of personal privacy, state surveillance, intellectual property, and industry policy.

I invite you, under the terms of the book's licence, to correct, expand and develop this document through the creation of derivative works.

Peter John Chen
Sydney, October 2012
peterjohnchen@gmail.com

References

Aichholzer, Georg & Burkert, Herbert, 2004, *Public Sector Information In The Digital Age: Between Markets, Public Management and Citizen's Rights*, Cheltenham: Edward Elgar Publishing.

Aikens, G. Scott, 1996, 'A history of Minnesota electronic democracy 1994', *First Monday*, 1(5), 4 November, http://firstmonday.org/htbin/cgiwrap/bin/ojs/index.php/fm/rt/printerFriendly/494/415#dep6

Aitkin, Don, 1977, *Stability and Change in Australian Politics*, Canberra: Australian National University Press.

Alberici, Emma, 2007, 'Alan Jones and 2GB breached Code of Practice: ACMA', *The World Today*, 10 April, Sydney: Australian Broadcasting Corporation.

Alesina, Alberto & Tabellini, Guido, 2008, 'Bureaucrats or politicians? Part II: Multiple policy tasks', *Journal of Public Economics*, 92: 426–47.

Allen, Geoff, 2012, 'Public affairs practice in Australia', *Journal of Public Affairs*, 12(1): 77–80.

Allen, Matthew, 2009, 'Tim 0'Reilly and web 2.0: The economics of memetic liberty and control', *Communication, Politics & Culture*, 42(2): 6–23.

Almond, Gabriel & Verba, Sidney, 1963, *The Civic Culture: Political Attitudes and Democracy in Five Nations*, Princeton University Press.

Althusser, Louis, 1971, *Lenin and Philosophy, and Other Essays*, Translator: Ben Brewster, London: New Left Books.

Anderson, Lori & Bishop, Patrick, 2005, 'E government to e democracy: Communicative mechanisms of governance', *Journal of E Government*, 2: 5–26.

Arendt, Hannah, 1958, *The Human Condition*, University of Chicago Press.

Armstrong, Edward, 2001, 'Gangsta misogyny: A content analysis of the portrayals of violence against women in rap music, 1987–1993', *Journal of Criminal Justice and Popular Culture*, 8(2): 96–126.

Arnold, Bruce, 2004, *Australasian Telecommunications: The Era of Competition?*, April, http://www.caslon.com.au/austelecomsprofile2.htm, accessed: 14 June 2012.

Ash, Tim, 2008, *Landing Page Optimization: The Definitive Guide to Testing and Tuning for Conversions*, Indianapolis: Wiley Publishing.

Associated Press, 2012, 'Despite massive anti-austerity protests, Spain's leader defends the cuts', *Washington Post*, 13 May.

Aston, Heath, 2012a, 'Gillard's father died of shame: Alan Jones', *theage.com.au*, 29 September, http://www.theage.com.au/opinion/political-news/gillards-father-died-of-shame-alan-jones-20120929-26soa.html, accessed: 10 October 2012.

——, 2012b, 'Ex-lover punished for Facebook revenge', *smh.com.au*, 22 April, http://www.smh.com.au/technology/technology-news/exlover-punished-for-facebook-revenge-20120421-1xdpy.html, accessed: 22 April 2012.

Atkinson, Joe, 2005, 'Metaspin: Demonisation of media manipulation', *Political Science*, 57(2): 17–27

Australian, 2007, 'Editorial. History a better guide than bias', *Australian*, 12 July, http://www.theaustralian.com.au/news/opinion/editorial-history-a-better-guide-than-bias/story-e6frg6zo-1111113937838, accessed: 23 August 2011.

Australian Associated Press (AAP), 2007, 'Heffernan's gibe "hurt Australian women"', *theage.com.au*, 4 May, http://www.theage.com.au/news/national/heffernans-gibe-hurt-australian-women/2007/05/04/1177788348405.html, accessed: 3 June 2012.

——, 2009, 'NSW government ads suspect', *Financial Review*, 9 December, http://www.afr.com/p/national/nsw_government_ads_suspect_Egdk3NNktjiJV5ZPXzrSbK, accessed: 28 May 2012.

——, 2010a, 'Kevin Rudd defends mining ads', *news.com.au*, 29 May, http://www.news.com.au/national/kevin-rudd-defends-mining-ads/story-e6frfkvr-1225872937660, accessed: 28 May 2012.

——, 2010b, 'New government "illegitimate": Hockey', *Weekly Times Now*, 8 September, http://www.weeklytimesnow.com.au/article/2010/09/08/231545_politics-news.html, accessed: 12 August 2011.

——, 2011, 'Fifteen top brands vow to boycott Kyle in 2012', *smh.com.au*, 6 December, http://www.smh.com.au/entertainment/tv-and-radio/fifteen-top-brands-vow-to-boycott-kyle-in-2012-20111206-1ognf.html, accessed: 28 June 2012.

——, 2012a, 'Embarrassment for PM after protests', *smh.com.au*, 27 January, http://news.smh.com.au/breaking-news-national/embarrassment-for-pm-after-protests-20120127-1qkc7.html, accessed: 4 June 2012.

——, 2012b, 'Tyler Clementi case: former student guilty in US webcam suicide', *smh.com.au*, 17 March, http://www.smh.com.au/world/tyler-clementi-case-former-student-guilty-in-us-webcam-suicide-20120317-1vbrj.html, accessed: 23 April 2012.

——, 2012c, 'Burke laments parliamentary behaviour', *ninemsn*, 1 June.

Australian Broadcasting Corporation (ABC), 2006, 'Cronulla's Australia Day shines despite racist campaign', *ABC Online*, 26 January.

——, 2010, 'Audio backs tweets in editor's defamation row', *ABC News*, 29 November, http://www.abc.net.au/news/2010-11-29/audio-backs-tweets-in-editors-defamation-row/2355368, accessed: 28 May 2012.

——, 2012, 'Gillard labels Abbott a misogynist', *ABC News*, 9 October, http://www.abc.net.au/news/2012-10-09/julia-gillard-attacks-abbott-of-hypocrisy/4303634, accessed: 10 October 2012

Australian Bureau of Statistics (ABS), 2011, *6523.0 Household Income and Income Distribution*, Canberra.

Australian Communications and Media Authority (ACMA), 2009, 'Teens', *Cyber(smart:)*, http://www.cybersmart.gov.au/Teens.aspx, accessed: 22 August 2011.

Australian Electoral Commission (AEC), 2011, *Electoral Pocketbook: May 2011*, Canberra.

Australian Government, 2005, *Public Sector Management — Managing Out: The Public Sector in the Community*, Topic Eight: 'Managing the media and public relations', Canberra: Commonwealth of Australia.

Backhouse, Jennifer, 2007, 'e-Democracy in Australia: The challenge of evolving a successful model', *The Electronic Journal of e-Government*, 5(2): 107–16.

Bacon, Wendy, Loh, Michelle, Taylor, Alex & Pavey, Sasha, 2010, 'Spinning the media: Key findings in a week in the life of the media', *Crikey*, 15 March, http://www.crikey.com.au/2010/03/15/spinning-the-media-key-findings-in-a-week-in-the-life-of-the-media/, accessed: 30 August 2010.

Bahnisch, Mark, 2006, 'The political uses of blogs', in Axel Bruns & Joanne Jacobs (eds), *Uses of Blogs*, New York: Peter Lang, pp. 139–49.

————, 2008, 'Political blogging in the 2007 Australian federal election: Beyond citizen journalism and towards civic creativity', *Pacific Journalism Review*, 14(2): 8–14.

————, 2012, 'Larvatus Prodeo's last post', *Larvatus Prodeo*, 10 April, http://larvatusprodeo.net/archives/2012/04/10/larvatus-prodeos-last-post/, accessed: 10 April 2012.

Bale, Kim, 2010, 'Behind the success of 10 top Causes', *Socialbrite*, 19 May, http://www.socialbrite.org/2010/05/19/behind-the-success-of-10-top-causes/, accessed: 22 August 2011.

Bang, Henrik & Sørensen, Eva, 1999, 'The everyday maker: A new challenge to democratic governance', *Administrative Theory & Praxis*, 21(3): 325–4.

Banks, Gary, 2009, 'Evidence-based policy making: What is it and how do we get it?', in John Wanna (ed.), *Critical Reflections on Australian Public Policy: Selected Essays*, Canberra: ANU E Press, pp. 107–29.

Bannister, Frank & Connolly, Regina, 2011, 'The trouble with transparency: A critical review of openness in e-Government', *Policy & Internet*, 3(1).

Barber, Benjamin, 1999, 'Three scenarios for the future of technology and strong democracy', *Political Science Quarterly*, 113(4): 573–89.

Bard, Alexander & Soderqvist, Jan, 2002, *Netocracy: The New Power Elite and Life After Capitalism*, London: Pearson Education.

Bardsley, Anna, 2010, 'Government 2.0: The role of ambiguity in the construction of a policy', Honours thesis, University of Sydney.

Barlow, John, 1996, *A Declaration of the Independence of Cyberspace*, https://projects.eff.org/~barlow/Declaration-Final.html, accessed: 27 March 1997.

Barnes, Alison & Lafferty, George, 2010, 'The *Fair Work Act*: As good as it gets?', *The Economic and Labour Relations Review*, 21(1): 1–12.

Barnes, George, 2005, *Selling the Australian Government: Politics and Propaganda from Whitlam to Howard*, Sydney: UNSW Press.

Barrett, Pat, 2003, *Governance and Joined-up Government — Some Issues and Early Successes*, Australasian Council of Auditors- General Conference, Melbourne, 6 February.

Barry, Evonne, 2012, 'Principals tinker for Naplan test', *Herald Sun*, 16 May, http://www.heraldsun.com.au/news/more-news/principals-tinker-for-naplan/story-fn7x8me2-1226356732745, accessed: 14 June 2012.

Bass, Jeremy, 2010, 'Earnest Matilda is sent a'waltzing', 1 July, *smh.com.au*, http://www.smh.com.au/opinion/society-and-culture/earnest-matilda-is-sent-awaltzing-20100630-zmv2.html, accessed: 3 January 2012.

Baudrillard, Jean, 1988, *Selected Writings*, Mark Poster (ed.), Cambridge: Stanford University Press.

Beech, Matt, 2006, *The Political Philosophy of New Labour*, London: Tauris Academic Studies.

Beecher-Monas, Erica, 2007, *Evaluating Scientific Evidence: An Interdisciplinary Framework for Intellectual Due Process*, Cambridge.

Begg, Zanny, 1997, 'One Nation spies on anti-racist campaign', *Green Left*, 23 July, http://www.greenleft.org.au/node/14335, accessed: 27 April 2012.

Bellamy, Craig, Gibbs, Martin, Williamson, Andy & Cubit Sean (2011), *Political Issue Analysis System: Policy Deliberation in the Age of Information Abundance*, University of Melbourne.

Benjamin, Walter, 1936, *The Work of Art in the Age of Mechanical Reproduction*, http://www.marxists.org/reference/subject/philosophy/works/ge/benjamin.htm, accessed: 12 February 2012.

Benkler, Yochai, 2006, *The Wealth of Networks: How Social Production Transforms Markets and Freedom*, New Haven: Yale University Press.

Bennett, Scott, 2008, *The Rise of the Australian Greens*, Research Paper Number 8, 2008–09, Canberra: Parliamentary Library.

Berg, Lisbet & Gornitzka, Åse, 2012, 'The consumer attention deficit syndrome: Consumer choices in complex markets', *Acta Sociologica*, 55(2): 159–78.

Berkovic, Nicola, 2012, 'Lib pollsters sue Mike Kelly for tweet', *Australian*, 22 March, http://www.theaustralian.com.au/national-affairs/lib-pollsters-sue-mike-kelly-for-tweet/story-fn59niix-1226306640981, accessed: 23 March 2012.

Berry, Helen, 2007, '"Crowded suburbs" and "killer cities": A brief review of the relationship between urban environments and mental health', *NSW Public Health Bulletin*, 18(11–12): 222–27.

Best, Amy, 2009, 'Young people and consumption', in Andy Furlong (ed.), *Handbook of Youth and Young Adulthood: New Perspectives and Agendas*, Milton Park: Routledge, pp. 255–62.

Bimber, Bruce, Flanagin, Andrew & Stohl, Cynthia, 2005, 'Reconceptualizing collective action in the contemporary media environment', *Communication Theory*, 15(4): 365–88.

Birkland, Thomas, 2011, *An Introduction to the Policy Process: Theories, Concepts, and Models of Public Policy Making*, 3rd edn, New York: EM Sharpe.

Birnbauer, Bill, 2012, 'The power of investigative journalism and why it is needed more than ever', in Matthew Ricketson (ed.), *Australian Journalism Today*, South Yarra: Palgrave Macmillan, pp. 78–94.

Bishop, Patrick, Kane, John & Patapan, Haig 2002, 'The theory and practice of e-democracy: Agency, trusteeship and participation on the web', *International Review of Public Administration*, 7(2): 21–31.

Bitar, Karl, 2010, *Address to the National Press Club*, Canberra, 9 November.

Blair, Tony, 2007, *Lecture by the Prime Minister and Right Honourable Tony Blair MP on Public Life*, Routers, Canary Wharf, London, 12 June.

Blühdorn, Ingolfur, 2007, 'Sustaining the unsustainable: Symbolic politics and the politics of simulation', *Environmental Politics*, 16(2): 251–75.

Blumberg, Rhoda, 2009, 'The civil rights movement', in Jeff Goodwin & James Jasper (eds), *The Social Movements Reader: Cases and Concepts*, 2nd edn, pp. 15–23.

Blumler, Jay & Katz, Elihu, 1974, *The Uses of Mass Communications: Current Perspectives on Gratifications Research*, Beverly Hills: Sage.

Bogenschneider, Karen & Corbett, Tom, 2010, *Evidence-Based Policymaking: Insights from Policy-Minded Researchers and Research-Minded Policymakers*, New York: Taylor and Frances Group.

Bolt, Andrew, 2012, 'Day of shame shows why we must stop this racial charade', *Herald Sun*, 27 January, http://www.heraldsun.com.au/opinion/day-of-shame-shows-why-we-must-stop-this-racial-charade/story-e6frfifx-1226254760404, accessed: 4 June 2012.

Bolter, Jay & Grusin, Richard, 2000, *Remediation: Understanding New Media*, Cambridge: MIT Press.

Bonsón, Enrique, Torres, Lourdes, Royo, Sonia & Flores, Francisco, 2012, 'Local e-government 2.0: Social media and corporate transparency in municipalities', *Government Information Quarterly*, 29: 123–32.

Boorstin, Daniel, 1992, *The Image: A Guide to Pseudo-events in America*, New York: Vintage Books.

Bourdieu, Pierre, 1973, 'Cultural reproduction and social reproduction', in Richard Brown (ed.), *Knowledge, Education and Social Change: Papers in the Sociology of Education*, Tavistock Publications, pp. 71–112.

——, 1979, 'Public opinion does not exist', *Communication and Class Struggle*, in Armond Matelart & Seth Siegelaub (eds), New York: International General.

Boxill, Ian, Chambers, Claudia & Wint, Eleanor, 1997, *Introduction to Social Research: With Applications to the Caribbean*, Kingston: Canoe Press.

Boyd, Danah & Ellison, Nicole, 2007, 'Social network sites: Definition, history, and scholarship', *Journal of Computer-Mediated Communication*, 13(1), http://jcmc.indiana.edu/vol13/issue1/boyd.ellison.html

Boyd, EE, 2011, 'New Facebook timeline is about discovery and explosive revenue growth', *Fast Company*, 22 September, http://www.fastcompany.com/1781979/facebook-timeline-profile-page-f8-zuckerberg, accessed: 23 April 2012.

Bradley, Ben, 2005, *Psychology and Experience*, Cambridge University Press.

Bramble, Tom & Kuhn, Rick, 2011, *Labor's Conflict: Big Business, Workers and the Politics of Class*, Port Melbourne: Cambridge University Press.

Brent, Peter, 2011, *The Twitter Election? Yes, but … Twitter in Parliament House in 2010*, unpublished manuscript.

British Broadcasting Corporation (BBC), 2009, 'Murdoch attack on "dominant" BBC', *BBC News*, 29 August, http://news.bbc.co.uk/2/hi/8227915.stm, accessed: 30 May 2012.

——, 2010, 'WikiLeaks posts video of "US military killings" in Iraq', *BBC News*, 6 April, http://news.bbc.co.uk/2/hi/americas/8603938.stm, accessed: 18 May 2012.

——, 2011, '"SlutWalk" marches sparked by Toronto', *BBC News*, 8 May, http://www.bbc.co.uk/news/world-us-canada-13320785, accessed: 4 August 2011.

Browne, Neil, & Kubasek, Nancy, 1999, 'A communitarian green space between market and political rhetoric about environmental law', *American Business Law Journal*, 37(1): 127–69.

Browne, Peter, 2012, 'New ways of funding and supporting journalism', *Australian Journalism Today*, in Matthew Ricketson (ed.), South Yarra: Palgrave Macmillan, pp. 182–97.

Bruns, Axel, 2005, *Gatewatching: Collaborative Online News Production*, New York: Peter Lang.

——, 2006, 'The practice of news blogging', *Uses of Blogs*, in Axel Bruns & Joanne Jacobs (eds), New York: Peter Lang, pp. 11–22.

——, 2008, *Blogs, Wikipedia, Second Life, and Beyond: From Production to Produsage*, New York: Peter Lang Publishing.

——, 2011, 'A first map of Australia', *Mapping Online Publics*, 4 August, http://www.mappingonlinepublics.net/2011/08/04/a-first-map-of-australia/, accessed: 5 January 2012.

—— & Adams, Debra, 2009, 'Mapping the Australian blogosphere', *International Blogging: Identity, Politics, and Networked Publics*, in Adrienne Russell & Nabil Echchaibi (eds), New York: Peter Lang, pp. 85–110.

—— & Bahnisch, Mark, 2009, *Social Media: Tools for User-Generated Content: Social Drivers Behind Growing Consumer Participation in User-led Content Generation*, Volume 1: State of the Art, Brisbane: QUT.

—— & Burgess, Jean, 2011, '#ausvotes: How Twitter covered the 2010 Australian federal election', *Communication, Politics & Culture*, 44(2): 37–58.

——, Burgess, Jean, Highfield, Tim, Kirchhoff, Lars & Nicolai, Thomas, 2011, 'Mapping the Australian networked public sphere', *Social Science Computer Review*, 29: 277–87.

Bunn, Anthony, 2011, 'Mirabella staffer in $906 taxi storm', *Border Mail*, http://www.bordermail.com.au/news/local/news/general/mirabella-staffer-in-906-taxi-storm/2114837.aspx, accessed: 9 February 2012.

Burke, Kelly, 2009, 'Government scraps grocery price-watch scheme', *theage.com.au*, 27 June, http://www.theage.com.au/national/government-scraps-grocery-pricewatch-scheme-20090626-czxa.html, accessed: 13 June 2012.

Burstein, Paul, Einwohner, Rachel & Hollander, Jocelyn, 1995, *The Politics of Social Protest: Comparative Perspectives on States and Social Movement*, in J. Craig Jenkins & Bert Klandermans (eds), London: UCL Press, pp. 136–44.

Byron, Angela, 2011, *Tweet*, 28 September, https://twitter.com/#!/webchick/status/118797814435287040, accessed: 9 January 2012.

Campbell, James, 2011, 'Gillard's rivals should ditch the witch attack', *Herald Sun*, 27 March, http://www.heraldsun.com.au/opinion/gillards-rivals-should-ditch-the-witch-attack/story-e6frfifo-1226028789433, accessed: 3 June 2012.

Canadian e-Business Initiative, 2004, *Net Impact Canada IV: Strategies for Increasing SME Engagement in the e-Economy: Final Report*, September, Ottawa: Industry Canada.

Capling, Ann & Nossal, Kim Richard, 2001, 'Death of distance or tyranny of distance? The internet, deterritorialization, and the anti-globalization movement in Australia', *The Pacific Review*, 14(3): 443–65.

Case, Sue-Ellen, 2007, *Performing Science and the Virtual*, New York: Taylor & Francis.

Castells, Manuel, 2000, *The Rise of the Network Society*, 2nd edn, Oxford: Blackwell.

——, 2001, *The Internet Galaxy: Reflections on the Internet, Business, and Society*, Oxford University Press.

Cavalier, Rodney, 2005, 'The defeat of Labor: As bad as it gets', *Mortgage Nation: The Australian Federal Election 2004*, in Marian Simms & John Warhurst (eds), Perth: API-Bentley, pp. 349–59.

CeBIT Australia, 2011, *Tanner: Gov 2.0 about culture change, not technology*, CeBIT Australia.

Charnock, David & Ellis, Peter, 2004, 'Postmaterialism and postmodernization in Australian electoral politics', *Electoral Studies*, 23: 45–72.

Chase, Michael & Mulvenon, James, 2002, *You've Got Dissent!: Chinese Dissident Use of the Internet and Beijing's Counter-Strategies*, Washington: Rand.

Chattopadhyay, Saayan, 2011, 'Online activism for a heterogeneous time: The Pink Chaddi Campaign and the social media in India', *Proteus: A Journal of Ideas*, 27(1): 63–68.

Chen, Peter John, 2001, 'Political Big Brother site masks curious agenda', *Australia.Internet.Com*, 10 October.

——, 2003, 'Advocating online censorship', *Australian Journal of Public Administration*, 62(2): 41–64.

———, 2005a, 'Will the real ID card please stand up?', *On Line Opinion*, 23 August, http://www.onlineopinion.com.au/view.asp?article=3770, accessed: 23 August 2005.

———, 2005b, 'e-lection 2004? New media and the campaign', *Mortgage Nation: The Australian Federal Election 2004*, in Marian Simms & John Warhurst (eds), Perth: API-Bentley, pp. 117-32.

———, 2011, 'The new media and the campaign', *Julia 2010: The Caretaker Election*, in Marian Simms & John Warhurst (eds), Canberra: ANU E Press.

———, 2012, 'The news media', in R Smith & D Clune (eds), *From Carr to Keneally: Labor in office in NSW 1995–2011*, Sydney: Allen & Unwin.

———, Gibson, Rachel & Geiselhart, Karen, 2006, *Electronic Democracy? The Impact of New Communications Technologies on Australian Democracy*, Canberra: Democratic Audit of Australia.

——— & Hinton, Sam, 1999, 'Realtime interviewing using the World Wide Web', *Sociological Research Online*, 4(3), http://www.socresonline.org.uk/4/3/chen.html, accessed: 19 May 2011.

——— & Walsh, Lucas, 2010, 'E-election 2007? Political competition online', *Australian Cultural History*, 28(1): 47–54.

Chen, Te Fu, 2011, *Implementing New Business Models in For-Profit and Non-Profit Organizations: Technologies and Applications*, Hershey: Business Science Reference.

Christensen, Henrik, 2011, 'Political activities on the internet: Slacktivism or political participation by other means?', *First Monday*, 16(2), http://firstmonday.org/htbin/cgiwrap/bin/ojs/index.php/fm/article/view/3336/2767.

Christopher, Martin, Payne, Adrian & Ballantyne, David, 2002, *Relationship Marketing: Creating Stakeholder Value*, Oxford: Butterworth-Heinermann.

Clark, John & Themudo, Nuno, 2006, 'Linking the web and the street: Internet-based 'dotcauses' and the 'anti-globalization' movement', *World Development*, 4(1): 50–74.

Clune, David, 2012, 'Why Labor lost', in David Clune & Rodney Smith (eds), *From Carr to Keneally: Labor in Office in NSW 1995–2011*, Sydney: Allen and Unwin.

Cohen, Heidi, 2011, *30 Social Media Definitions*, 9 May, http://heidicohen.com/social-media-definition/, accessed: 19 August 2011.

Cohen, Noam, 2011, 'Define gender gap? Look up Wikipedia's contributor list', *The New York Times*, 30 January, http://www.nytimes.com/2011/01/31/business/media/31link.html?_r=1, accessed: 12 March 2012.

Collins, Jock, 2007, 'The landmark of Cronulla', in James Jupp, John Nieuwenhuysen & Emma Dawson (eds), *Social Cohesion in Australia*, Cambridge University Press, pp. 61–69.

Collins, Randall, 2004, *Interaction Ritual Chains*, Princeton University Press.

Considine, Mark, Lewis, Jenny & O'Sullivan, Siobhan, 2011, 'Quasi-markets and service delivery: Flexibility following a decade of employment assistance reform in Australia', *Journal of Social Policy*, 40(4): 811–33.

Coory, Michael, 2004, 'Ageing and healthcare costs in Australia: a case of policy-based evidence?', *Medical Journal of Australia*, 180(11): 581–83.

Cordell, Marni, 2010, 'Curtains For Newmatilda.com', *New Matilda*, 27 May, http://newmatilda.com/2010/05/27/new-matilda-fold/, accessed: 3 January 2012.

Costar, Brian & Curtin, Jennifer, 2004, *Rebels with a Cause: Independents in Australian Politics*, Sydney: UNSW Press.

Cowie, Tom, 2010, ''SheMarketing' — the science of selling Tony Abbott to women', *Crikey*, 5 July, http://www.crikey.com.au/2010/07/05/shemarketing-the-science-of-selling-tony-abbott-to-women/, accessed: 12 July 2010.

Cowling, David, 2011a, 'Search engine market share statistics, April 2011 — Australia', *Social Media News*, 18 April, http://www.socialmedianews.com.au/search-engine-market-share-statistics-april-2011-australia/, accessed: 16 May 2011.

——, 2011b, 'Facebook Australia infograph', *Social Media News*, 26 May, http://www.socialmedianews.com.au/facebook-australia-infograph/, accessed: 29 July 2011.

Cox, Joshua, Martinez, Eric & Quinlan, Kevin, 2008, 'Blogs and the corporation: managing the risk, reaping the benefits', *Journal of Business Strategy*, 29(3): 4–12.

Coyer, Kate, Dowmunt, Tony & Fountain, Alan, 2007, *The Alternative Media Handbook*, Oxon: Routledge.

Crabb, Annabel, 2010, 'The art of political language', *The Drum*, http://www.abc.net.au/news/2010-05-25/the-art-of-political-language/839962, accessed: 4 June 2012.

Craig, Natalie, 2011, 'A rally to find the slut in everyone', *smh.com.au*, 29 May, http://www.smh.com.au/victoria/a-rally-to-find-the-slut-in-everyone-20110528-1f9w3.html, accessed: 4 August 2011.

Crawford, Kate, 2006, *Adult Themes: Rewriting the Rules of Adulthood*, Sydney: Pan MacMillan.

Crawford, Mary & Pini, Barbara, 2010, 'Gender equality in national politics: The views of Australian male politicians', *Australian Journal of Political Science*, 45(4): 605–21.

Crespi, Irving, 1997, *The Public Opinion Process: How the People Speak*, Mahwah: Lawrence Erlbaum Associates.

Crook, Andrew, 2011, 'Labor state sec: Gillard, Rudd miss the point on membership', *Crikey*, 30 November, http://www.crikey.com.au/2011/11/30/labor-state-sec-gillard-rudd-miss-the-point-on-membership/, accessed: 25 April 2012.

——, 2012, 'Oz editor marshals eagles to halt Manne attack', *Crikey*, 8 March, http://www.crikey.com.au/2012/03/08/oz-editor-marshals-lawyers-to-halt-manne-attack/, accessed: 28 May 2012.

Cross, Mary, 2011, *Bloggerati, Twitterati: How Blogs and Twitter are Transforming Popular Culture*, Santa Barbara: Praeger.

Crowley, Kate, 1999, 'A failed greening? The electoral routing of the Tasmanian Greens', *Environmental Politics*, 8(4): 186–93.

Cunneen, Chris, 1997, 'Memory, murder and justice: holocaust denial and the "scholarship" of hate', in Chris Cunneen, David Fraser & Stephen Tomsen (eds), *Faces of Hate: Hate Crime in Australia*, Sydney: Hawkins Press, pp. 162–87.

Dahl, Robert, 1961, Who Governs? Democracy and Power in the American City, New Haven: Yale University Press.

Dahlberg, Lincoln, 2001, 'Extending the public sphere through cyberspace: The case of Minnesota E-democracy', *First Monday*, 6(3), http://www.firstmonday.org/htbin/cgiwrap/bin/ojs/index.php/fm/article/view/838/747.

——, 2007, 'Rethinking the fragmentation of the cyberpublic: From consensus to contestation', *new media & society*, 9(5): 827–47.

Danchev, Dancho, 2008, 'Coordinated Russia vs Georgia cyber attack in progress', *ZDNet*, 11 August, http://www.zdnet.com/blog/security/coordinated-russia-vs-georgia-cyber-attack-in-progress/1670, accessed: 15 May 2012.

Dann, Steven & Hughes, Andrew 2008, 'Lessons from Kevin 07 — political marketing', *Monash Business Review*, 4(1): 34–37.

Davis, Aeron, 2010, *Political Communication and Social Theory*, Oxon: Routledge.

Dean, Jodi, 2010, *Blog Theory: Feedback and Capture in the Circuits of Drive*, Cambridge: Polity.

Dearne, Karen, 2012, 'Labor's personally controlled electronic health record system blows out to $760m', *Australian*, 28 February, www.theaustralian. com.au/australian-it/labors-personally-controlled-electronic-health-record-system-blows-out-to-760m/story-e6frgakx-1226283273933, accesed: 30 June 2012.

de Brito, Sam, 2011, 'The anti-bogan', *smh.com.au*, 15 March, http://blogs. smh.com.au/executive-style/allmenareliars/2011/03/15/theantibogan.html, accessed: 12 February 2012.

De Bussy, Nigel & Wolf, Katharina, 2009, 'The state of Australian public relations: Professionalisation and paradox', *Public Relations Review*, 35(4), 376–81.

Dehne, Selena, 2008, 'Will your social networking profile get you hired or fired?', *Career Builder*, http://www.careerbuilder.com/Article/CB-916-Salaries-Promotions-Will-Your-Social-Networking-Profile-Get-You-Hired-or-Fired/, accessed: 22 August 2011.

Deitz, Melissa, 2010, *Watch This Space: The Future of Australian journalism*, Port Melbourne: Cambridge University Press.

della Porta, Donatella, 2009, 'Making the new polis: The practice of deliberate democracy in social forums', in Hank Johnston (ed.), *Culture, Social Movements, and Protest*, Surrey: Ashgate, pp. 181–208.

Denhardt, Janet & Denhardt, Robert, 2011, *The New Public Service: Serving, Not Steering*, New York: EM Sharpe.

Devine, Miranda, 2011, 'Fixing broken system is a capital idea', *Daily Telegraph*, 20 October, p. 26.

Dillow, Chris, 2007, *The End of Politics: New Labour and the Folly of Managerialism*, Hamshire: Harriman House.

Di Maio, Andrea, 2009, *Government 2.0: A Gartner Definition*, 13 November, http://blogs.gartner.com/andrea_dimaio/2009/11/13/government-2-0-a-gartner-definition/, accessed: 18 June 2011.

Doloswala, Kalika & Dadich, Ann, 2011, 'The accidental criminal: Using policy to curb illegal downloading', *First Monday*, 16(6).

Dreyfus, Suelette, 1997, *Underground: Tales of Hacking, Madness, and Obsession on the Electronic Frontier*, Melbourne: Mandarin Australia.

Dror, Yehezkel, 1971, *Design for Policy Sciences*, New York: American Elsevier.

Dryzek, John, 2002, *Deliberative Democracy and Beyond*, Oxford University Press.

Dubecki, Larissa, 2007, 'The mouse-click that roared', *theage.com.au*, 24 February, http://www.theage.com.au/news/national/the-mouseclick-that-roared/2007/02/23/1171734022013.html, accessed: 11 May 2012.

Duck, Siobhan, 2012, 'Channel 10 rescheduling news programs including *The Project* to improve ratings', *news.com.au*, 11 January, http://www.news.com.au/entertainment/television/the-project-on-the-move-again/story-e6frfmyi-1226241650380, accessed: 19 April 2012.

Dunleavy, Patrick, Margetts, Helen, Bastow, Simon & Tinkler, Jane, 2006, *Digital Era Governance: IT Corporations, the State and e-Government*, Oxford University Press.

Dunlop, Tim, 2012, 'The gatekeepers of news have lost their keys', *The Drum*, 10 October, http://www.abc.net.au/unleashed/4305220.html, accessed: 10 October 2012.

Dunn, Kevin, Forrest, James, Burnley, Ian & McDonald, Amy, 2004, 'Constructing racism in Australia', *Australian Journal of Social Issues*, 39(4): 409–30.

Dyer, Glenn, 2010, 'Rebates to TV networks just an ugly bribe', *Crikey*, 8 February, http://www.crikey.com.au/2010/02/08/rebates-to-tv-networks-just-an-ugly-bribe/, accessed: 12 March 2011.

Eaton, Marc, 2010, 'Manufacturing community in an online activist organization, information', *Communication & Society*, 13(2): 174–92.

Edwards, Kathy, Saha, Larry & Print, Murray, 2006, *Youth Electoral Study*, Report 3: Youth, The Family, and Learning about Politics and Voting, Canberra: Australian Electoral Commission.

Edy, Jill & Shawn Snidow, 2011, 'Making news necessary: How journalism resists alternative media's challenge', *Journal of Communication*, 61: 16–34.

Elliott, Geoff, 2010, 'The Australian's Chris Mitchell to sue Julie Posetti for defamation', *Australian*, 26 November, http://www.theaustralian.com.au/media/mitchell-says-posetti-defamed-him-on-twitter/story-e6frg996-1225961470219, accessed: 26 March 2012.

Elmer-Dewitt, Philip, 1993, 'First nation in cyberspace', *TIME International*, 6 December, p. 49.

Eltham, Ben, 2007, 'The young voters theory', *New Matilda*, 19 November, http://newmatilda.com/2007/11/19/young-voters-theory, accessed: 29 March 2012.

——, 2010, 'Rudd's inquiries will pave Gillard's policy pathways', *The Drum*, 16 September, http://www.abc.net.au/unleashed/30040.html, accessed: 13 June 2012.

Engelhardt, Nancy, 2011, 'Find us on Facebook: How cause marketing has embraced social media furlow', *Journal of Marketing Development and Competitiveness*, 5(6): 61–64.

Entman, Robert, 2010, 'Media framing biases and political power: Explaining slant in news of Campaign 2008', *Journalism*, 11(4): 389–408.

Erikson, Robert, Luttbeg, Norman & Tedin, Kent, 1991, *American Public Opinion*, 4th edn, New York: Macmillan.

Errington, Wayne & Miragliotta, Narelle, 2011, *Media and Politics: An Introduction*, 2nd edn, South Melbourne: Oxford University Press.

Esty, Daniel & Rushing, Reece, 2007, *Governing by the Numbers: The Promise of Data-Driven Policymaking in the Information Age*, Washington: Center for American Progress.

Evans, Raymond, 1992, '"Agitation, ceaseless agitation": Russian radicals in Australia and the Red flag riots', in John McNair & Thomas Poole (eds), *Russia and the Fifth Continent: Aspects of Russian-Australian Relations*, St Lucia: University of Queensland, pp. 126–71.

Eyerman, Ron & Jamison, Andrew, 1998, *Music and Social Movements: Mobilizing Traditions in the Twentieth Century*, Cambridge University Press.

Fan, Qiuyan, 2011, 'An evaluation analysis of e-government development by local authorities in Australia', *International Journal of Public Administration*, 34(14): 926–34.

Farber, Daniel & Frickey, Philip, 1991, *Law and Public Choice: A Critical Introduction*, University of Chicago Press.

Farnsworth, Malcolm, 2010, 'Pollie wants to Twitter?', *The Drum*, 26 May, http://www.abc.net.au/unleashed/34818.html, accessed: 28 November 2010.

Farr, Malcolm, 2012, 'Alan Jones: Women are "destroying the joint"', *news.com. au*, http://www.news.com.au/national/alan-jones-women-are-destroying-the-joint/story-fndo4eg9-1226462326339, accessed: 10 October 2012.

Farrell, David, Kolodny, Rodney & Medvic, Stephen, 2001, 'Parties and campaign professional in a digital age', *Press/Politics*, 6(4): 11–30.

—— & McAllister, Ian, 2005, 'Australia', in Michael Gallagher & Paul Mitchell (eds), *The Politics of Electoral Systems*, Oxford University Press, pp. 79–98.

Fernandes, Juliana, Giurcanu, Magda, Bowers, Kevin & Neely, Jeffrey, 2010, 'The writing on the wall: A content analysis of college students' Facebook groups for the 2008 Presidential election', *Mass Communication and Society*, 13(5): 653–75.

Ferrante, Joan, 2011, *Sociology: A Global Perspective*, 5th edn, Belmont: Wadsworth.

Fieschi, Catherine & Heywood, Paul, 2004, 'Trust, cynicism and populist anti☒ politics', *Journal of Political Ideologies*, 9(3): 289–309.

Finkelstein, Ray, 2012, *Report of the Independent Inquiry into the Media and Media Regulation*, Report to the Minister for Broadband, Communications and the Digital Economy, 28 February, Canberra: Commonwealth of Australia.

Flaye, Rob, 2012, *Online Advertising for Social Research*, Presentation at the University of Sydney, 28 May, http://www.youtube.com/watch?v=gpiE2VQk6-A.

Fleming, Andy, 2012, *Remarks at the 'Independent Media Inquiry and the Regulation of Online News' Public Forum*, 16 April, Online Media Group, University of Sydney.

Flew, Terry, 2008, *New Media: An Introduction*, London: Sage.

—— & Wilson, Jason, 2010, 'Journalism as social networking: The Australian youdecide project and the 2007 federal election', *Journalism*, 11(2): 131–47.

——, 2012, 'Wikileaks and the challenge of the "fifth estate"', in Matthew Ricketson (ed.), *Australian Journalism Today*, South Yarra: Palgrave Macmillan, pp. 168–81.

Forrest, James & Dunn, Kevin, 2006, 'Racism and intolerance in eastern Australia: A geographic perspective', *Australian Geographer*, 37(2): 167–86.

Foster, EM, 1909, 'The Machine Stops', *The Oxford and Cambridge Review*, Edinburgh: Archibald Constable.

Foucault, Michel, 1995 (1975), *Discipline and punish: The birth of the prison*, New York: Vintage Books.

Francis, Becky, 2006, 'Heroes or zeroes? The discursive positioning of 'underachieving boys' in English neo-liberal education policy', *Journal of Education Policy*, 21(2): 187–200.

Franti, Michael & Tse, Rono, 1992, 'Television, drug of the nation', *Hypocrisy is the Greatest Luxury*, sound recording, 4th & B'way/Island/PolyGram Records.

Fraser, Nancy, 1990, 'Rethinking the public sphere: A contribution to the critique of actually existing democracy', *Social Text*, 25/26: 56–80.

——, 1997, *Justice Interruptus: Critical Reflections on the 'Postsocialist' Condition*, London: Routledge.

Fray, Peter, 2012, *Remarks at the 'Who will Guard the Guardians?' Public Forum*, 20 March, Australian Centre for Independent Journalism, Sydney: UTS.

Friedland, Jamie & Rogerson, Kenneth, 2009, *How Political and Social Movements Form on the Internet and How They Change Over Time*, November, Research Triangle Park: Institute for Homeland Security Solutions.

Fuchs, Christian, 2008, *Internet and Society: Social Theory in the Information Age*, New York: Routledge.

Gaber, Ivor, 2005, 'Dumb and dumber: Does TV count?', *British Journalism Review*, 16(1): 24–28.

Gallagher, Sean, 2011, 'Anonymous takes down darknet child porn site on Tor network', *ars technica*, 23 October, http://arstechnica.com/business/2011/10/anonymous-takes-down-darknet-child-porn-site-on-tor-network/, accessed: 18 May 2012.

Gallop, Geoff, 2011, 'What price an ethical media?', *smh.com.au*, http://www.smh.com.au/opinion/society-and-culture/what-price-an-ethical-media-20110328-1ccwp.html, accessed: 4 June 2012

Gandy, Oscar, 1982, *Beyond Agenda Setting: Information Subsidies and Public Policy*, Norwood: Ablex Publishing.

Garden, Mary, 2010, 'Newspaper Blogs: The genuine article or poor counterfeits?', *Media International Australia*, 135: 19–31.

Gardiner, Stephanie, 2012, 'Alan Jones loses more advertisers', *smh.com.au*, 2 October, http://www.smh.com.au/entertainment/tv-and-radio/alan-jones-loses-more-advertisers-20121002-26w0y.html, accessed: 10 October 2012.

Garnett, Mark & Lynch, Philip, 2003, 'Introduction', in Garnett & Lynch (eds), *The Conservatives in Crisis: The Tories After 1997*, Manchester University Press, pp. 1–6.

Gauja, Anika, 2012, 'Participation and representation through parties', in Rodney Smith, Ariadne Vromen & Ian Cook (eds), *Contemporary Politics in Australia: Theories, Practices and Issues*, Port Melbourne: Cambridge, pp. 166–76.

Gensollen, Michael, 2007, 'Information goods and online communities', in Eric Brousseau & Nicolas Curien (eds), *Internet and Digital Economics*, Cambridge University Press, pp. 59–90.

George, Jim, 2009, 'Introduction: Are the culture wars over?', in Jim George & Kim Huynh (eds), *Culture Wars: Australian and American Politics in the 21st Century*, South Yarra: Palgrave Macmillan, pp. 6–8.

Gerbner, George & Gross, Larry, 1976, 'The scary world of TV's heavy viewer', *Psychology Today*, 10(4): 41–89.

GetUp!, nd a, *Terms of Service*, http://www.communityrun.org/tos, accessed: 9 May 2012.

GetUp!, nd b, *FAQ*, http://www.getup.org.au/about/faq, accessed: 11 May 2012.

Gibson, Rachel & Cantijoch, Marta, 2011, 'Comparing online elections in Australia and the UK', *Communication, Politics & Culture*, 44(2): 4–17.

Gibson, Rachel & McAllister, Ian, 2006, 'Does cyber-campaigning win votes? Online communication in the 2004 Australian election', *Journal of Elections, Public Opinion & Parties*, 16(3): 243-63.

——, 2011, 'Do online election campaigns win votes? The 2007 Australian "YouTube" election', *Political Communication*, 28(2): 227–44.

Gibson, Rachel, Römmele, Andrea & Ward, Stephen, 2004, *Electronic Democracy: Mobilisation, Organisation and Participation Via New ICTs*, London: Routledge.

Gibson, Rachel & Ward, Stephen, 2002, 'Virtual campaigning: Australian parties and the impact of the Internet', *Australian Journal of Political Science*, 37(1): 99–129.

Gibson, William, 1984, *Neuromancer*, New York: Ace.

Giddens, Anthony, 1984, *The Constitution of Society*, Cambridge: Polity Press.

Gilens, Martin & Craig Hertzman, 2000, 'Corporate ownership and news bias: Newspaper coverage of the 1996 *Telecommunications Act*', *The Journal of Politics*, 62: 369–86.

Gillespie, Tarleton, 2010, 'The politics of "platforms"', *New Media & Society*, 12(3): 347–64.

Gilmore, Heath, 2012, 'Success spreads: Push for My Uni website', *smh.com.au*, 20 February, http://www.smh.com.au/national/education/success-spreads-push-for-my-uni-website-20100219-olzd.html, accessed: 14 June 2012.

Gilpin, Dawn, Palazzolo, Edward, Downs, Hugh & Brody, Nicholas, 2010, 'Socially mediated authenticity', *Journal of Communication Management*, 14(3): 258–78.

Glenny, Leanne, 2008, 'Perspectives of communication in the Australian public sector', *Journal of Communication Management*, 12(2): 152–68.

Goggin, Gerard, 2010, 'The Internet, online and mobile communications and culture', in Stuart Cunningham & Graeme Turner (eds), *The Media and Communications in Australia*, large print edition, , Crows Nest: Allen and Unwin, pp. 412–54.

—— & Kate Crawford, 2010, 'Moveable types: The emergence of mobile social media in Australia', *Media Asia Journal*, 37(4): 224–31.

Gómez-Ibáñez, José, 2003, *Regulating Infrastructure: Monopoly, Contracts, and Discretion*, Cambridge: Harvard University Press.

Google Australia, 2010, *Think Politics with Google*, Sydney: Google Australia.

Goot, Murray, 2009, 'Political communication and the media', in Rod Rhodes (ed.), *The Australian Study of Politics*, Canberra: APSA, pp. 173–85.

Gould, Philip, 1998, *The Unfinished Revolution: How Modernisers Saved the Labour Party*, London: Little Brown.

Government 2.0 Taskforce, 2010, *Engage: Getting on with Government 2.0*, Canberra: Australian Government Information Management Office.

Grant, Will, Moon, Brenda & Grant, Janie, 2010, 'Digital dialogue? Australian politicians' use of the social network tool twitter', *Australian Journal of Political Science*, 45(4): 579–604.

Grattan, Michelle, 2011, 'Pushed to the limit, Bob goes in guns blazing', *theage.com.au*, 22 May, http://www.theage.com.au/opinion/politics/pushed-to-the-limit-bob-goes-in-guns-blazing-20110521-1exil.html#ixzz1wmjX9IYbwww.theage.com.au/opinion/politics/pushed-to-the-limit-bob-goes-in-guns-blazing-20110521-1exil.html, accessed: 4 June 2012.

Greason, David, 1997, 'Australia's racist far right', in Chris Cunneen, David Fraser & Stephen Tomsen (eds), *Faces of Hate: Hate Crime in Australia*, Sydney: Hawkins Press, pp. 188–213.

Green, Donald, & Gerber, Alan, 2008, *Get Out the Vote: How to Increase Voter Turnout*, 2nd edn, Washington: Brookings.

Green, Zach, 2011, 'Twitter campaigns — building community', *Twitter for the 2012 Election: Tools, Metrics and Strategy*, 2 October, http://140elect.com/2012-twitter-politics/twitter-campaigns-building-community/, accessed: 29 March 2012.

Greenleaf, Graham, 1988, 'Privacy', *Computer Law & Security Review*, 3(6): 6–8.

——, 2008, 'Hong Kong', in James Rule & Graham Greenleaf (eds), *Global Privacy Protection: The First Generation*, Cheltenham: Edward Elgar Publishing, 141–73.

Griffiths Emma, 2010, 'Ad rule backflip for tax campaign', *Lateline*, 28 May, http://www.abc.net.au/lateline/content/2010/s2912734.htm, accessed: 26 May 2012.

Griffiths, Mary, 2002, *Australian e-Democracy?: Its Potential for Citizens and Governments*, Presentation at Innovative e-Government for Victoria, Hotel Sofitel, Melbourne, 26 March.

Grow up Australia, 2010, *Media Release*, 22 February, http://www.growupaustralia.com/show-your-support/r18-games-submission/, accessed: 14 May 2012.

Grubb, Ben, 2010, 'Family First candidate's gay Twitter slur', *smh.com.au*, 9 August, http://www.smh.com.au/technology/technology-news/family-first-candidates-gay-twitter-slur-20100808-11q7p.html, accessed: 9 February 2012.

Gruber, Thomas, 2007, 'Ontology of folksonomy: A mash-up of apples and oranges', *International Journal on Semantic Web Information Systems*, 3(2): 1–11.

Gurstein, Michael, 2011, 'Open data: Empowering the empowered or effective data use for everyone?', *First Monday*, 16(2), http://firstmonday.org/htbin/cgiwrap/bin/ojs/index.php/fm/article/viewArticle/3316/2764.

Guthrie, Bruce, 2011, *Man Bites Murdoch: Four Decades in Print, Six Days in Court*, Melbourne University Press.

Habermas, Jürgen, 1991, *The Structural Transformation of the Bourgeois Public Sphere*, Thomas Burger & Frederick Lawrence (trans.), Cambridge: MIT Press.

Hall, Stuart, 1982, 'The rediscovery of "ideology": Return of the repressed in media studies', in Michael Gurevitch, Tony Bennett, James Curran & Janet Woollacott (eds), *Culture, Society and the Media*, London: Methuen.

Halliday, Josh, 2012, 'Sky News clamps down on Twitter use', *Guardian*, 7 February, http://www.guardian.co.uk/media/2012/feb/07/sky-news-twitter-clampdown, accessed: 30 May 2012.

Hambleton, Steve, 2012, 'Journos attacking Flannery: Like pulling teeth getting them to be fair', *The Power Index*, 1 June, http://www.thepowerindex.com.au/head-to-head/journos-attacking-flannery-like-pulling-teeth-getting-them-to-be-fair/201206011408, accessed: 4 June 2012.

Hamilton, Clive, 2006, *Who Listens to Alan Jones*, June, Canberra: Australia Institute.

——, 2012, 'When a newspaper calls in its lawyers: The chilling effect of The Australian vs Robert Manne', *The Conversation*, 8 March, http://theconversation.edu.au/when-a-newspaper-calls-in-its-lawyers-the-chilling-effect-of-the-australian-vs-robert-manne-5730, accessed: 28 March 2012.

—— & Denniss, Richard, 2005, *Affluenza: When Too Much is Never Enough*, Crows Nest: Allen and Unwin.

——, Downie, Christian & Lu, Yi-Hua, 2007, *The State of the Australian Middle Class*, Discussion Paper Number 98, October, Canberra: The Australia Institute.

Hannah, Annette & Murachver, Tamar, 2007, 'Gender preferential responses to speech', *Journal of Language and Social Psychology*, 26: 274–91.

Hannan, Daniel, 2010, 'Citizens' initiative procedures will restore our democracy', *Telegraph*, 28 December, http://blogs.telegraph.co.uk/news/danielhannan/100069827/citizens-initiative-procedures-will-restore-the-legitimacy-of-our-democratic-system/, accessed: 3 February 2012.

Hansen, Mark, 2010, 'New media', in Mark Hansen & Thomas Mitchell (eds), *Critical Terms for Media Studies*, Chicago University Press, pp. 172–85.

Hardaker, Claire, 2010, 'Trolling in asynchronous computer-mediated communication: From user discussions to academic definitions', *Journal of Politeness Research*, 6: 215–42.

Harding, Don, 2008, 'FuelWatch: Evidence-based-policy or policy based evidence?', *Economic Papers: A Journal of Applied Economics and Policy*, 27(4): 315–28.

Hardy, Keiran, 2010, 'Operation titstorm: Hacktivism or cyber-terrorism?', *UNSW Law Journal*, 33(2): 474–502.

Harker, Richard, Mahar, Cheleen & Wilks, Chris (eds), 1990, *An Introduction to the Work of Pierre Bourdieu*, Houndmills: MacMillan.

Hart, Kim & Greenwell, Megan, 2009, '"Causes" social networking may be all talk, no cash for nonprofits seeking funds', *Washington Post*, 22 April, http://www.washingtonpost.com/wp-dyn/content/article/2009/04/21/AR2009042103786.html, accessed: 22 August 2011.

Hartley, John & Green, Joshua, 2006, 'The public sphere on the beach', *European Journal of Cultural Studies,* 9(3): 341–62.

Hartwich, Oliver, 2010, 'Trivial twitter', *Australian*, 29 October, http://www.theaustralian.com.au/news/opinion/trivial-twitter/story-e6frg6zo-1225944886599, accessed: 26 March 2012.

Hatcher, Peter, 2011, 'The focus proved unfocused', *theage.com.au*, http://www.theage.com.au/opinion/politics/the-focus-proved-unfocused-20110204-1agt2.html, accessed: 31 January 2012.

Hayes, Colin, 2001, *Managing Through Organization: The Management Process, Forms of Organization and the Work of Managers*, London: Thompson.

Heberle, Rudolf, 1951, *Social Movements: An Introduction to Political Sociology*, Volume 3, New York: Appleton-Century-Crofts.

Heeks, Richard, 2005, 'e-Government as a carrier of context', *Journal of Public Policy*, 25: 51–74.

Hehmana, Eric, Gaertnera, Samuel & Dovidiob, John, 2011, 'Evaluations of presidential performance: Race, prejudice, and perceptions of Americanism', *Journal of Experimental Social Psychology*, 47(2): 430–35.

Heires, Katherine, 2007, 'Why it pays to give away the store', *CNN Money*, 15 March, http://money.cnn.com/magazines/business2/business2_archive/2006/10/01/8387115/index.htm, accessed: 11 May 2012.

Henman, Paul, 2010, *Governing Electronically: E-Government and the Reconfiguration of Public Administration, Policy and Power*, London: Palgrave Macmillan.

Herbst, Susan, 1991, 'Classical democracy, polls and public opinion: Theoretical frameworks for studying the development of public sentiment', *Communication Theory*, 1: 225–38.

Herman, Edward & Chomsky, Noam, 1988, *Manufacturing Consent: The Political Economy of the Mass Media*, New York: Pantheon Books.

Higley, John & Burton, Michael, 2006, *Elite Foundations of Liberal Democracy*, Lanham: Rowman & Littlefield Publishers.

Hilderbrand, Joe, 2011, 'Nazis attack teacher', *Daily Telegraph*, 3 August, p. 3.

Hill, Kashmir, 2012, 'How Target figured out a teen girl was pregnant before her father did', *Forbes*, 16 February, http://www.forbes.com/sites/kashmirhill/2012/02/16/how-target-figured-out-a-teen-girl-was-pregnant-before-her-father-did/, accessed: 21 March 2012.

Hill, Sally, 2010, *Models of Online Activism and their Implications for Democracy and Climate Change*, Discussion Paper, April, London: Foundation for Democracy and Sustainable Development.

Hills, Rachel, 2011, 'Meet the man behind the anti-carbon tax lobby', *Spectator Australia*, 17 September, http://www.spectator.co.uk/australia/7243323/meet-the-man-behind-the-anticarbon-tax-lobby.thtml, accessed: 2 May 2012.

Hindman, Matthew, 2008, *The Myth of Digital Democracy*, Princeton University Press.

Hobolt, Sara & Klemmemsen, Robert, 2005, 'Responsive government? Public opinion and government policy preferences in Britain and Denmark', *Political Studies*, 53: 379–402.

Hodge, Bob & Matthews, Ingrid, 2011, 'New media for old bottles: Linear thinking and the 2010 Australian election', *Communication, Politics & Culture*, 44(2): 95–111.

Hodkinson, Paul, 2006, 'Subcultural blogging? Online journals and group involvement among U.K. Goths', in Axel Bruns & Joanne Jacobs (eds), *Uses of Blogs*, New York, Peter Lang, pp. 187–98.

Holyoke, Thomas, Brown, Heath & Henig, Jeffrey, 2012, 'Shopping in the political arena : Strategic state and local venue selection by advocates', *State and Local Government Review*, 44(1): 9–20.

Hopewell, Luke, 2010, 'GetUp! court win allows online enrolment', *ZDNet*, 13 August, http://www.zdnet.com.au/getup-court-win-allows-online-enrolment-339305220.htm, accessed: 5 August 2011.

——, 2011, 'Anonymous ally "leaks" public election data', *ZDNet*, 5 July, http://m.zdnet.com.au/anonymous-ally-leaks-public-election-data-339317904.htm, accessed: 20 July 2011.

Hot House Interactive, 2010, *PR vs Social Media*, http://www.hothouse.com.au/our-services/social-media/pr-vs-social-media, accessed: 19 August 2011.

Howard, John, 2001, *Election Campaign Policy Launch Speech*, 28 October, http://museumvictoria.com.au/immigrationmuseum/discoverycentre/identity/videos/politics-videos/john-howards-2001-election-campaign-policy-launch-speech/, accessed: 8 March 2012.

Howell, Gwyneth & Da Silva, Bruce, 2010, 'New media, first time voters and the 2007 Australian federal election', *Public Communication Review*, 1: 27–36.

Hudson, Philip, 2010, 'Julia Gillard vows to take control of her election campaign', *Herald Sun*, 2 August, www.heraldsun.com.au/news/special-reports/julia-gillard-vows-to-take-control-of-her-election-campaign/story-fn5ko0pw-1225899749875, accessed: 30 January 2012.

Huesca, Robert, 2000, 'Communication for social change among Mexican factory workers on the Mexico-United States border', in Karin Wilkins (ed.), *Redeveloping Communication for Social Change: Theory, Practice, and Power*, Plymouth: Rowman & Littlefield, pp. 73–88.

Humphreys, Lee, 2005, 'Social topography in a wireless era: The negotiation of public and private space', *Journal of Technical Writing and Communication*, 35(4): 367–84.

——, 2008, 'Photos and fieldwork: Capturing norms for mobile phone use in the US', in Joachim Höflich & Maren Hartmann (eds), *Mobile Communication in Everyday Life: Ethnographic Views, Observations and Reflections*, Berlin: Frank and Timme, pp. 55–78.

Hutton, Drew & Connors, Libby, 1999, *A History of the Australian Environment Movement*, Cambridge University Press.

Information Week, 2010, 'Gov 2.0 summit: Advocate calls USA Spending data 'useless'', *Information Week — Online*, 7 September.

Institute of Public Administration Australia, 2012, *Public Policy Drift: Why Governments Must Replace 'Policy on the Run' and 'Policy by Fiat' With a 'Business Case' Approach to Regain Public Confidence*, Public Policy Discussion Paper, 4 April.

Jack the Insider, 2012, 'Twitter won't save the world', *Australian*, 8 March, http://blogs.theaustralian.news.com.au/jacktheinsider/index.php/theaustralian/comments/twitter_wont_save_the_world/P25/, accessed: 20 March 2012.

Jackman, Simon, 2005, 'Incumbency advantage and candidate quality', in Marian Simms & John Warhurst (eds), *Mortgage Nation: The Australian Federal Election 2004*, Perth: API-Bentley, pp. 335–47.

Jackson, Sally, 2010, 'Gillard a ranga, O'Farrell a twit', *Australian*, 16 July, http://www.theaustralian.com.au/national-affairs/state-politics/gillard-a-ranga-ofarrell-a-twit/story-e6frgczx-1225892373387, accessed: 19 April 2012.

Jackson, Stewart, 2011, 'The Australian Greens: Between movement and electoral professional party', PhD thesis, University of Sydney.

—— & Chen, Peter John, 2012, 'Understanding Occupy in Australia', *Journal of Australian Political Economy*, 69: 5–28.

Jacobs, David, 2005, 'Internet activism and the democratic emergency in the U.S.', *Ephemera, Theory & Politics in Organization*, 5(1): 68–77.

Jaensch, Dean, Brent, Peter & Bowden, Brett, 2004, *Australian Political Parties in the Spotlight*, Report Number 4, Canberra: Democratic Audit of Australia.

Jamieson, Amber, 2010, 'New New Matilda attempts old old media strategy', *Crikey*, 10 December, http://www.crikey.com.au/2010/12/10/new-new-matilda-attempts-old-old-media-strategy/, accessed: 3 January 2012.

——, 2012, 'Fairfax's new social network for media comment', *Crikey*, 8 February, http://www.crikey.com.au/2012/02/08/news-fairfax-social-media-site/, accessed: 12 March 2012.

Janda, Kenneth, Berry, Jeffrey & Goldman, Jerry, 2008, *The Challenge of Democracy: American Government in Global Politics*, Boston: Wadsworth.

Jenkins, Chris, 2012, 'Young people sidelined by 17% unemployment', *Green Left*, http://www.greenleft.org.au/node/49926, accessed: 21 March 2012.

Jenkins, Henry, 2004, 'The cultural logic of media convergence', *International Journal of Cultural Studies*, 7(1): 33–43.

Jenkins, Melissa, 2010, 'Victorian opposition calls for email hacking probe', *news.com.au*, 6 October, http://www.news.com.au/breaking-news/victorian-opposition-calls-for-email-hacking-probe/story-e6frfku0-1225935096223, accessed: 10 June 2011.

Jericho, Greg, 2012, *Rise of the Fifth Estate: Social Media and Blogging in Australian Politics*, Brunswick: Scribe.

John, Peter, 2003, 'Is there life after policy streams, advocacy coalitions, and punctuations: Using evolutionary theory to explain policy change?', *The Policy Studies Journal*, 31(4): 481–98.

Johnston, Jane & Forde, Susan, 2009, '"Not wrong for long": The role and penetration of news wire agencies in the 24/7 news landscape', *Global Media Journal*, 3(2).

Jones, Paul, 2005, 'Australian cross-media ownership rules and freedom of political communication', *UNSW Law Journal*, 28(3): 916–23.

Josephi, Beate, 2011, *Supporting Democracy: How Well do the Australian Media Perform?*, Australian Journalism Monographs, 13, Brisbane: Griffith University.

Jupp, James & Sawer, Marian, 2001, 'Political parties, partisanship and electoral governance', in Marian Sawer (ed.), *Elections: Full, Free & Fair*, Annandale: The Federation Press, pp. 261–333.

Juris, Jeffrey, 2012, 'Reflections on #Occupy everywhere: Social media, public space, and emerging logics of aggregation', *American Ethnologist*, 39(2): 259–79.

Kaplan, Andreas & Haenlein, Michael, 2010, 'Users of the world, unite! The challenges and opportunities of social media', *Business Horizons,* 53(1): 59–68.

Karvelas, Patricia, 2007, 'New party pushes online votes', *Australian*, 10 October, http://www.theaustralian.com.au/national-affairs/state-politics/new-party-pushes-online-votes/story-e6frgczx-1111114608622, accessed: 10 January 2012.

Katz, Elihu & Lazarsfeld, Paul, 1955, *Personal Influence: The Part Played by People in the Flow of Mass Communications*, New York: Free Press.

Katz, Richard & Mair, Peter, 1994, *How Parties Organize*, London: Sage.

Kaye, Barbara, Johnson, Thomas & Muhlberger, Paul, 2012, 'Blogs as a source of democratic deliberation', in Tatyana Dumova & Richard Fiordo (eds), *Blogging in the Global Society: Cultural, Political and Geographical Aspects*, Hershey: Information Science Reference, pp. 1–18.

Keane, Bernard, 2010, 'Who hacked Anna Bligh's wiki? ... Twitter and the UK election ...' *Crikey*, 31 March, http://www.crikey.com.au/2010/03/31/media-briefs-who-hacked-anna-blighs-wiki-apns-sunnier-ad-forecasts-twitter-and-the-uk-election/, accessed: 20 July 2011.

Kelso, Ross, Tegart, Alistair, Ryan, Annette, Singh, Supriya, Laidler, Terry & Burke, John, 2001, *The User Perspective in Government Electronic Service Delivery (ESD): Supporting Material*, Centre for International Research on Communication and Information Technologies, May, Melbourne: RMIT.

Kernohan, Andrew, 1998, *Liberalism, Equality and Cultural Oppression*, Cambridge University Press.

Kerr, Christian [writing as Hillary Bray], 2001, 'Labor belts Natasha, Howard woos Hansonites, Economist backs Labor', *Crikey!*, 7 October, http://www.crikey.com.au/2001/10/07/labor-belts-natasha-howard-woos-hansonites-economist-backs-labor/, accessed: 7 September 2010.

Kim, 2010, 'On Line opinion and the advertising and 'free speech' controversy', *Larvatus Prodeo*, 7 February, http://larvatusprodeo.net/2011/02/07/on-line-opinion-and-the-advertising-and-free-speech-controversy/, accessed: 3 January 2012.

King, Andrew, 2008, *Website Optimization: Speed, Search Engine & Conversion Rate Secrets*, Sabastopol: O'Reilly Media.

Kingdon, John, 1984, *Agendas, Alternatives, and Public Policies*, Boston: Little Brown.

Kingston, Margo, 2006, *The Webdiary Story*, http://webdiary.com.au/cms/?q=node/1326, accessed: 21 March 2012.

Kirchhoff, Lars, Nicolai, Thomas, Bruns, Axel & Highfield, Tim, 2009, 'Monitoring the Australian Blogosphere through the 2007 Australian Federal Election', *Proceedings of ANZCA 2009*, Brisbane, 8 July.

Kirk, Jeremy, 2008, 'Yahoo to scub personal data after three months', *Computerworld*, 17 December, www.computerworld.com/s/article/9123700/ Yahoo_to_scrub_personal_data_after_three_months, accessed: 8 February 2012.

Kitney, Damon, 2011, 'Business turns up the heat on ALP, criticise 'thought bubble' policies', *Australian*, 23 July, http://www.theaustralian.com. au/national-affairs/business-turns-up-the-heat-on-alp-criticise-thought-bubble-policies/story-fn59niix-1226100103024, accessed: 12 August 211.

Kivisto, Peter, 2010, 'Multiculturalism and racial democracy: State policies and social practices', in John Solomos & Patricia Hill Collins (eds), *The SAGE Handbook of Race and Ethnic Studies*, London: Sage, pp. 253–74.

Kornberg, Allan & Clarke, Harold, 1992, *Citizens and Community: Political Support in a Representative Democracy*, University of Cambridge Press.

Krebs, Valdis, 2005, *It's the Conversations, Stupid! The Link between Social Interaction and Political Choice*, Portola Valley: Commonwealth Institute.

Kreiss, Daniel & Howard, Philip, 2010, 'Political parties and voter privacy: Australia, Canada, the United Kingdom, and United States in comparative perspective', *First Monday*, 15(2), http://firstmonday.org/htbin/cgiwrap/bin/ojs/index.php/fm/article/view/2975/2627

Kriesi, Hanspeter, 1996, 'The organizational structure of new social movements in a political context', in Doug McAdam, John McCarthy & Mayer Zald (eds), *Comparative Perspectives on Social Movements: Political Opportunities, Mobilizing Structures, and Cultural Framings*, Cambridge University Press, pp. 152–84.

Krik, Jeremy, 2006, 'AOL search data reportedly released', *PCWorld*, 8 August, http://www.pcworld.com/article/126663/aol_search_data_reportedly_ released.html, accessed: 20 June 2011.

Krotz, Friedrich, 2009, 'Mediatization: A concept with which to grasp media and societal change', in Knut Lundby (ed.), *Mediatization: Concept, Changes, Consequences*, New York: Peter Lang, pp. 21–40.

Kuhn, Rick, 1997, 'The Australian left, nationalism and the Vietnam War', *Labour History*, 72: 163–84.

Kwek, Glenda, 2010, 'Abbott v Gillard at Rooty Hill: Galaxy to investigate', smh.com.au, 12 August, http://www.smh.com.au/federal-election/ abbott-v-gillard-at-rooty-hill-galaxy-to-investigate-20100812-1206t. html#ixzz2IHgNUaRm, accessed: 20 August 2010.

Lair, Daniel, Sullivan, Katie & Cheney, George, 2005, 'Marketization and the recasting of the professional self: The rhetoric and ethics of personal branding', *Management Communication Quarterly*, 18: 307–43.

Lam, Miawling, 2010, 'My School launch leads to parent frenzy', *news.com.au*, 31 January, http://www.news.com.au/national/my-school-launch-leads-to-parent-frenzy/story-e6frfkw9-1225825079749, accessed: 13 June 2012.

Larme, Anthony, 2000, 'Dangerous games? Censorship and "child protection"', BA Honours thesis, University of Queensland.

Lateline, 2007, 'Tony Jones talks to Opposition Leader Kevin Rudd', *Australian Broadcasting Corporation*, 8 November, http://www.abc.net.au/lateline/content/2007/s2085991.htm, accessed: 13 June 2012.

Latham, Mark, 2005, *The Latham Diaries*, Melbourne University Press.

Law Report, 2008, 'Database disagreement', *The Law Report*, ABC Radio National, 11 March, http://www.abc.net.au/rn/lawreport/stories/2008/2183680.htm

Lawyers Weekly, 2010, 'GetUp! wins High Court challenge', *Lawyers Weekly*, 6 August.

Lazarsfeld, Paul, Berelson, Bernard & Gaudet, Hazel, 1944, *The People's Choice: How the Voter Makes up his Mind in a Presidential Campaign*, New York: Columbia University Press.

Lee, Monle & Johnson, Carla, 1999, *Principles of Advertising: A Global Perspective*, Binghamton: Haworth Press.

Lehmbruch, Gerhard, 1983, 'Interest intermediation in capitalist and socialist systems: Some structural and functional perspectives in comparative research', *International Political Science Review*, 4(2): 153–72.

LeMay, Renai, 2010, 'Gamers 4 Croydon hails 'fantastic' Atkinson resignation', *Delimiter*, 21 March, http://delimiter.com.au/2010/03/21/gamers-4-croydon-hails-fantastic-atkinson-resignation/, accessed: 14 May 2012.

Lessig, Lawrence, ongoing, *Code and Other Laws of Cyberspace*, v2, http://code-is-law.org/, accessed: 10 June 2011.

Levine, Robert, 2011, *Free Ride: How the Internet Is Destroying the Culture Business and How the Internet is Destroying the Culture Business and How the Culture Business can Fight Back*, London: Random House.

Levinson, Jay & Gibson, Shane, 2010, *Guerrilla Marketing for Social Media: 100+ Weapons to Grow Your Online Influence, Attract Customers and Drive Profits*, Entrepreneur Media.

Liberal Party of Western Australia 2010, *Labor Milking WA to Pay for their Debt & Waste*, http://webcache.googleusercontent.com/search?q=cache: nIc6t-a9hK4J: www.wa.liberal.org.au/index.php%3Foption%3Dcom_ content%26view%3Darticle%26id%3D6: labor-weak-on-border- protection%26catid%3D5: federal-featured-news+'Labor+Milking+WA+t o+Pay+for+their+Debt+%26+Waste'&cd=1&hl=en&ct=clnk&gl=au&clie nt=firefox-a, accessed: 30 October 2010.

Lindblom, Charles, 1977, *Politics and Markets: The World's Political-Economic Systems*, New York: Basic Books.

Lindgren Simon & Lundström, Ragnar, 2011, 'Pirate culture and hacktivist mobilization: The cultural and social protocols of #WikiLeaks on Twitter', *New Media Society*, 13: 999–1019.

Lippmann, Walter, 1925, *The Phantom Public*, New York: Harcourt, Brace and Company.

Lister, Martin, Dovey, Jon, Giddings, Seth, Grant, Ian & Kelly, Kieran, 2003, *New Media: A Critical Introduction*, London: Routledge.

Lohr, Steve, 2011, 'In case you wondered, a real human wrote this column', *The New York Times*, 10 September, http://www.nytimes. com/2011/09/11/business/computer-generated-articles-are-gaining-traction. html?pagewanted=all, accessed: 30 May 2012.

London, Scott, 1995, 'Teledemocracy vs. deliberative democracy: A comparative look at two models of public talk', *Journal of Interpersonal Computing and Technology*, 3(2): 33–55.

Long, Daniel, 2011, 'Fake social media army used to sway public opinion', *Gizmodo*, 1 March, http://www.gizmodo.com.au/2011/03/fake-social-media- army-used-to-sway-public-opinion/, accessed: 19 August 2011.

Louw, Eric, 2010, *The Media and Political Process*, 2nd edn, London: Sage.

Lowi, Theodore, 1964, 'American business, public policy, case studies, and political theory', *World Politics*, 16: 677–715.

Lowndes, Vivian, 2010, 'The institutional approach', in David Marsh & Gerry Stoker (eds), *Theory and Methods in Political Science*, 3rd edn, Houndmills: Palgrave Macmillian, pp. 60–79.

Lownsbrough, Hannah, 2010, 'The progressive potential of online organising', *Renewal: A Journal of Labour Politics*, 18(3/4): 74–81.

Lundberg, Kirsten, 2011, *Friend or Foe?: WikiLeaks and the Guardian*, The Journalism School Knight Case Studies, New York: Columbia University.

Lundy, Kate, 2009, *Public Sphere 3: ICT & Creative Industry Development Briefing Paper*, 23 November.

Lupia, Arthur, 1992, 'Busy voters, agenda control, and the power of information', *The American Political Science Review*, 86(2): 390–403.

Ma, Lin, 2009, 'Slacktivism: Can social media actually cause social change?', *theage.com.au*, 1 October, http://www.theage.com.au/technology/technology-news/slacktivism-can-social-media-actually-cause-social-change-20090930-gcgk.html, accessed: 20 March 2012.

Macnamara, Jim, 2008, 'E-electioneering: Use of new media in the 2007 Australian federal election', Paper presented at ANZCA08 Conference: Power and Place, Wellington, July.

——, 2010a, *The 21st Century Media (R)evolution: Emergent Communication Practices*, New York: Peter Lang.

——, 2010b, 'Remodelling media: The urgent search for new media business models', *Media International Australia*, 137: 20–34.

—— & Kenning, Gail, 2011, 'E-electioneering 2010: Trends in social media use in Australian political communication', *Media International Australia*, 139: 7–22.

Maer, Lucinda, 2008, *Citizens' Initiatives*, Standard Note: SN/PC/04483, London: House of Commons Library.

Maguire, Tory, 2009, 'Phwoar!!! Tony Abbott's the full package. Wink wink.', *The Punch*, 9 December, http://www.thepunch.com.au/articles/phwoar-tony-abbotts-the-full-package.-wink-wink/, accessed: 4 June 2012.

Maher, Paul, 2010, 'NZ television offers exceptional value', *Think TV*, www.thinktv.co.nz/insights/opinions/exceptional-value/, accessed: 30 January 2012.

Maiden, Samantha, 2010, 'Departing Lodge is such tweet sorrow for Therese Rein and Kevin Rudd', *Australian*, 30 June, http://www.theaustralian.com.au/politics/departing-lodge-is-such-tweet-sorrow-for-therese-rein-and-kevin-rudd/story-e6frgczf-1225886125266, accessed: 5 August 2011.

——, 2012, 'Labor Whip Joel Fitzgibbon tweets support for Prime Minister Julia Gillard', *Courier Mail*, 27 May, http://www.couriermail.com.au/news/sunday-mail/labor-whip-joel-fitzgibbon-turns-back-on-julia-gillard-canvasses-support-for-kevin-rudd/story-e6frep2f-1226367873603, accessed: 30 May 2012.

Maley, Jacqueline, 2012, 'Out of touch maybe, but press galleries don't laud speeches', *National Times*, 12 October, http://www.smh.com.au/opinion/politics/out-of-touch-maybe-but-press-galleries-dont-laud-speeches-20121011-27frs.html, accessed: 12 October 2012.

Mann, Alana, 2008, 'Churnalism', *State of the News Print Media in Australia: 2008 Report*, December, Sydney: Press Council of Australia, pp. 5.2–5.3.

Manne, Robert, 2011, *Bad News: Murdoch's Australian and the Shaping of the Nation*, Quarterly Essay 43, Collingwood: Quarterly Essay.

Mansbridge, Jane, 2009, 'Ideological purity in the women's movement', in Jeff Goodwin & James Jasper (eds), *The Social Movements Reader: Cases and Concepts*, 2nd edn, Malden: Wiley-Blackwell, pp. 161–66.

Margetts, Helen, 2009, 'The internet and public policy', *Policy & Internet*, 1(1): a1.

——, John, Peter, Escher, Tobias & Reissfelder, Stephane, 2009, 'Experiments for web science: Examining the effect of the Internet on collective action', Paper presented to the 1st Web Science Conference, Athens, 18–20 March.

Margolis, Michael & Moreno-Riaño, Gerson, 2009, *The Prospect of Internet Democracy*, Farnham: Ashgate.

—— & David Resnick, 2000, *Politics as Usual: The Cyberspace 'Revolution'*, Thousand Oakes: Sage.

Marichal, José, 2010, 'Political Facebook groups: Micro-activism and the digital front stage', paper presented at Internet, Politics, Policy 2010: An Impact Assessment Conference, St Anne's College, Oxford, 16–17 September.

Mark, Craig, 2011, 'ALP National Conference: Party reform the empty seat at the table', *The Conversation*, 5 December, http://theconversation.edu.au/alp-national-conference-party-reform-the-empty-seat-at-the-table-4562, accessed: 2 February 2012.

Marks, Kathy, 2010, 'Exclamation politics: GetUp!', *The Monthly*, October, http://www.themonthly.com.au/monthly-essays-kathy-marks-exclamation-politics-getup-2788, accessed: 16 March 2011.

Marks, Matthew, 2007, 'myoppentssux.com: New media and digital campaigning', in Christian Kerr (ed.), *Crikey Guide to the 2007 Federal Election*, Brisbane: Private Media Partners.

Marsh, Ian, 1995, *Beyond the Two Party System: Political Representation, Economic Competitiveness and Australian Politics*, Cambridge University Press.

Marston, Greg & Watts, Rob, 2003, 'Tampering with the evidence: A critical appraisal of evidence-based policy-making', *The Drawing Board: An Australian Review of Public Affairs*, 3(3): 143–63.

Martin, Hugh, 2000, 'Bringing governments down: The 1999 Victorian election campaign and the net', *M/C Reviews*, 10 April, http://reviews.media-culture.org.au/modules.php?name=News&file=article&sid=1752, accessed: 7 September 2010.

Masnick, Mike, 2011, 'UK Prime Minister wants to ban suspected rioters from Facebook & Twitter', *techdirt*, 11 August, http://www.techdirt.com/articles/20110811/11531615478/uk-prime-minister-wants-to-ban-suspected-rioters-facebook-twitter.shtml, accessed: 27 April 2012.

Mason, Bruce & Thomas, Sue, 2008, *A Million Penguins Research Report*, http://www.ioct.dmu.ac.uk/documents/amillionpenguinsreport.pdf

Massola, James, 2011, 'Media round on Bob Brown over attack on News Limited', *Australian*, 20 May, http://www.theaustralian.com.au/national-affairs/media-round-on-brown-over-attack-on-news-limited/story-fn59niix-1226059243419, accessed: 4 June 2012.

Matthews, Mark, 2009, 'Fostering creativity and innovation in cooperative federalism — The uncertainty and risk dimensions', in John Wanna (ed.), *Critical Reflections on Australian Public Policy: Selected Essays*, Canberra: ANU E Press, pp. 59–70.

Mayer-Schönberger, Viktor, 2003, 'The shape of governance: Analyzing the world of internet regulation', *Virginia Journal of International Law*, 43: 626–30.

McAllister, Ian, 2011, *The Australian Voter: 50 Years of Change*, Sydney: UNSW Press.

—— & Clark, Juliet, 2008, *Trends in Australian Political Opinion: Results from the Australian Election Study, 1987–2007*, Canberra: Australian Social Science Data Archive.

—— & Pietsch, Juliet, 2011, *Trends in Australian Political Opinion: Results from the Australian Election Study, 1987–2010,* Canberra: Australian National Institute for Public Policy and ANU College of Arts and Social Sciences.

——, Bean, Clive, Gibson, Rachel & Pietsch, Juliet, 2012, *Australian Election Study, 2010: Study Documentation.*

McCarthy, John & Zald, Mayer, 1977, 'Resource mobilization and social movements: A partial theory', American Journal of Sociology, 82(6): 1212–41.

McCrone, Donald & Kuklinski, James, 1979, 'The delegate theory of representation', *American Journal of Political Science*, 23(2): 278–300.

McCullough, Michael, 1991, 'Democratic questions for a computer age', in John Downing, Rob Fasano, Patricia Friedland, Michale McCullough, Terry Mizrahi & Jeremy Shapiro (eds), *Computers for Social Change and Community Organising*, Binghamton: Haworth Press, pp. 9–18.

McGraw, Barry, 2010, 'My School site brings fair comparisons', *smh.com.au*, 28 January, http://www.smh.com.au/opinion/politics/my-school-site-brings-fair-comparisons-20100127-mz0x.html, accessed: 14 June 2012.

McKee, Alan, 2005, *An Introduction to the Public Sphere*, Cambridge University Press.

McKnight, David, 2012, *Rupert Murdoch: An Investigation of Political Power*, Sydney: Allen & Unwin.

McLuhan, Marshall & Fiore, Quentin, 1968, *War and Peace in the Global Village: An Inventory of Some of the Current Spastic Situations that Could be Eliminated by More Feedforward*, New York: McGraw-Hill.

McNealy, Jasmine, 2012, 'The realm of the expected: Redefined the public and private spheres in social media', in Hana Noor Al-Deen & John Hendricks (eds), *Social Media: Usage and Impact*, Plymouth: Lexington Books, pp. 255–70.

Media Report, 2007, 'The power of blogging', *Media Report — ABC Radio National*, 8 November, http://www.abc.net.au/rn/mediareport/stories/2007/2081805.htm, accessed: 12 November 2007.

Media Watch, 2010, 'Breaking news is hard to do, ABC, 28 June, www.abc.net.au/mediawatch/transcripts/s2939110.htm, accessed: 30 May 2012.

——, 2011, 'Biting the hand that feeds', ABC, 11 September, http://www.abc.net.au/mediawatch/transcripts/s3315985.htm, accessed: 9 January 2012.

Meikle, Graham, 2004, 'Networks of influence: Internet activism in Australia and beyond', in Gerard Goggin (ed.), Virtual Nation: The Internet in Australia, Sydney: UNSW Press, pp. 73–87.

Mendonça, David, Jefferson, Theresa & Harrald, John, 2007, 'Emergent interoperability: Collaborative adhocracies and mix and match technologies in emergency management', Communications of the ACM, 50(3): 44–49.

Mill, John Stuart, 2009 (1869), On Liberty, http://ebooks.adelaide.edu.au/m/mill/john_stuart/m645o/

Millar, Royce & McKenzie, Nick, 2010, 'Revealed: How the ALP keeps secret files on voters', theage.com.au, 22 November, http://www.theage.com.au/victoria/state-election-2010/revealed-how-the-alp-keeps-secret-files-on-voters-20101122-1845e.html#ixzz1leLe8EZS, accessed: 7 February 2012.

Mills, Elinor, 2012, 'Will LulzSec arrests stop high-profile hacks? Don't bet on it', CNET, 6 March, http://news.cnet.com/8301-27080_3-57391872-245/will-lulzsec-arrests-stop-high-profile-hacks-dont-bet-on-it/, accessed: 15 May 2012.

Miragliotta, Narelle, Errington, Wayne & Barry, Nicholas, 2009, The Australian Political System in Action, South Melbourne: Oxford University Press.

Missingham, Roxanne, 2010, 'The Australian Parliament in the Twitterverse', Australasian Parliamentary Review, 25(1): 3–16.

——, 2011, 'E-parliament: Opening the door', Government Information Quarterly, 28: 426–34.

Mitchell, Susan, 2011, Tony Abbott: A Man's Man, Brunswick: Scribe.

Moffit, Mary, 1994, 'Collapsing and integrating concepts of "public" and "image" into a new theory', Public Relations Review, 20(2): 159–70.

Moore, Mark, 1995, Creating Public Value: Strategic Management in Government, Cambridge: Harvard University Press.

Moral, Michel & Abbott, Geoffrey (eds), 2009, Routledge Companion to International Business Coaching, Oxon: Routledge.

Morieson, Lucy, 2011, 'Reconsidering interactivity in online journalism: Two Australian case studies', Altitude: An e-journal of Emerging Humanities Work, 9: 1–11.

Morley, Deborah & Parker, Charles, 2009, Understanding Computers: Today and Tomorrow, 12th edn, Boston: Course Technology.

Morozov, Evgeny, 2009, 'The brave new world of slacktivism', *Foreign Policy*, 18 May, http://neteffect.foreignpolicy.com/posts/2009/05/19/the_brave_new_world_of_slacktivism, accessed: 12 August 2011.

Morris, Kieran, 2011, 'Inside GetUp and the new youth politics', *Quadrant Online*, III(3), http://www.quadrant.org.au/magazine/issue/2011/3/inside-getup-and-the-new-youth-politics, accessed: 21 March 2012.

Moses, Asher, 2007, 'Online party hopes to click with voters', *smh.com.au*, 18 October, http://www.smh.com.au/news/web/online-party-hopes-to-click-with-voters/2007/10/18/1192300920221.html, accessed: 10 January 2012.

———, 2009a, 'Social not-working: Facebook snitches cost jobs', *smh.com.au*, 8 April, http://www.smh.com.au/articles/2009/04/08/1238869963400.html, accessed: 22 August 2011.

———, 2009b, 'MySpace tanks as social networks soar', *smh.com.au*, 14 October, http://www.smh.com.au/technology/technology-news/myspace-tanks-as-social-networks-soar-20091014-gwxj.html, accessed: 9 February 2012.

Muehlenberg, Bill, 2010, 'Whose rights are they anyway? The children's?', *On Line Opinion*, www.onlineopinion.com.au/view.asp?article=10923, accessed: 13 October 2011.

Muir, Kathie, 2008, *Worth Fighting For: Inside the 'Your Rights at Work' Campaign*, Sydney: UNSW Press.

Mulé, Rosa, 2001, *Political Parties, Games and Redistribution*, Cambridge University Press.

Mulgan, Richard, 1998, *Politicising the Australian Public Service?*, Research Paper No. 3 1998–99, Department of the Parliamentary Library, Canberra: Parliament of Australia.

Muncaster, Phil, 2012, 'Patriotic hackers face off in South China Sea', *The Register*, 27 April, http://www.theregister.co.uk/2012/04/27/philippine_china_hack_stand_off/, accessed: 15 May 2012.

Murphy, Damien, 2007, 'Meet Family First's member for nowhere', *smh.com.au*, 29 October, http://www.smh.com.au/articles/2007/10/28/1193555533377.html, accessed: 9 February 2012.

Murphy, Mathew & Burgess, Guy, 2004, 'Keys to power', *theage.com.au*, 30 September, http://www.theage.com.au/articles/2004/09/29/1096401641244.html, accessed: 4 October 2004.

Murphy, Padraic, 2011, 'Police raid the *Age* over ALP database hacking allegations', *Herald Sun*, 15 December, http://www.heraldsun.com.au/news/breaking-news/police-raid-the-age-over-alp-database-hacking-allegations/story-e6frf7jx-1226222717591, accessed: 7 February 2012.

Murphy, Samantha, 2011, 'Geek war: Women overtaking men as early adopters', *TechNewsDaily*, http://www.technewsdaily.com/2689-geek-war-women-overtaking-men-as-early-adopters.html, accessed: 27 April 2012.

Murray, Andrew, 2010, *Information Technology Law: The Law and Society*, Oxford University Press.

Murthy, Dhiraj, 2011, 'Twitter: Microphone for the masses?', *Media, Culture & Society*, 33(5): 779–89.

Myers, Courtney, 2011, '5 Reasons why open source will shake the CMS establishment', *The Next Web*, 2 June, http://thenextweb.com/insider/2011/06/02/5-reasons-why-open-source-will-shake-the-cms-establishment/, accessed: 1 January 2012.

Nash, Chris, 2008, 'Playing possum: Straws in the wind of the blogosphere', *Pacific Journalism Review*, 14(2): 15–36.

National Forum, 2011, *Annual Report National Forum 2011*, Brisbane: National Forum.

Negrine, Ralph & Papathanassopoulos, Stylianos, 1996, 'The 'Americanisation' of political communication: A critique', *Press/Politics*, 1(2): 45–62.

Negroponte, Nicholas, 1996, *Being Digital*, New York: Alfred A. Knopf.

Neighbour, Sally, 2011, 'The united states of Chris Mitchell', *The Monthly*, August: 16–28.

Newman, Jay, 1997, *Inauthentic Culture and its Philosophical Critics*, Quebec: McGill-Queen's University Press.

news.com.au, 2007, 'Did hackers post lewd message on Liberal Party website?', *Adelaide Now*, 9 October, http://www.adelaidenow.com.au/news/was-howards-website-hacked/story-e6freo8c-1111114610756, accessed: 9 June 2011.

Ngai, Sianne, 2005, *Ugly Feelings*, Cambridge: Harvard University Press.

Nielsen, 2009, *Nielsen Online Internet and Technology Report 2008-09*, Sydney: Nielsen Online.

——, 2010a, 'Social networks/blogs now account for one in every four and a half minutes online', *nielsenwire*, 15 June, http://blog.nielsen.com/nielsenwire/global/social-media-accounts-for-22-percent-of-time-online/, accessed: 19 August 2011

——, 2010b, *Nielsen 2010 Internet & Technology Report*, Sydney: Nielsen Online.

——, 2010c, 'Australia getting more social online as Facebook leads and Twitter grows', *nielsenwire*, 23 March, http://blog.nielsen.com/nielsenwire/global/australia-getting-more-social-online-as-facebook-leads-and-twitter-grows/, accessed: 29 July 2011.

Ninemsm, 2010, 'Gillard's earlobes shift attention from debate', *ninemsm*, 25 July.

Noell-Neuman, Elizabeth, 1984, *The Spiral of Silence: Public Opinion — Our Social Skin*, University of Chicago Press.

Nonnecke, Blair & Preece, Jenny, 2001, 'Why lurkers lurk', paper presented at the Americas Conference on Information Systems.

Norris, Pippa, 2000, *A Virtuous Circle: Political Communication in Postindustrial Societies*, Cambridge University Press.

NSW Council for Civil Liberties, 2010, *Peaceful Assembly: Your Right to Protest, Demonstrate and to Hold Rallies*, www.nswccl.org.au/issues/protest.php, accessed: 23 March 2011.

NSW Police Force, 2011, 'Police continue to monitor protest activity — Sydney CBD', *Media Release*, 6 November.

O'Donnell, Penny, 2009, 'Journalism, change and listening practices', *Continuum: Journal of Media & Cultural Studies*, 23(4): 503–17.

O'Reilly, Tim, 2009a, 'Gov 2.0: The promise of innovation', *Forbes.com*, 10 August, http://www.forbes.com/2009/08/10/government-internet-software-technology-breakthroughs-oreilly.html, accessed: 10 June 2011.

——, 2009b, 'Gov 2.0: It's all about the platform', *TechCrunch*, 4 September, http://techcrunch.com/2009/09/04/gov-20-its-all-about-the-platform/, accessed: 10 June 2011.

——, 2010, 'Government as a platform for greatness', *gov 2.0 expo*, 25–27 May, Washington Convention Centre.

Organisation for Economic Co-operation and Development (OECD), 2009, *Rethinking e-Government Services: User-Centred Approaches*, Paris.

Ortega, Felipe & González-Barahona, Jesús, 2007, *Quantitative Analysis of the Wikipedia Community of Users*, paper presented at WikiSym'07, 21–23 October, Montreal, Quebec.

Pager, Devah, 2003, 'The mark of a criminal record', *American Journal of Sociology*, 108(5): 937–75.

Palser, B, 2002, 'Journalistic blogging: mainstream news organizations could steal an idea or two from blogs', *American Journalism Review*, 24(6): 58–60.

Parmelee, John & Bichard, Shannon, 2012, *Politics and the Twitter Revolution: How Tweets Influence the Relationship between Political Leaders and the Public*, Plymouth: Lexington Books.

Pascoe, CJ, 2011, 'Resource and risk: Youth sexuality and new media use', *Sexuality Research and Social Policy*, 8: 5–17.

Pass, Steven & Hornsby, David, 2006, *CSIRAC*, 4 April, http://ww2.csse.unimelb.edu.au/dept/about/csirac/, accessed: 18 June 2012.

Pauli, Darren, 2009, 'Racial hate groups erupt on Facebook', *Computerworld*, 12 June, http://www.computerworld.com.au/article/307289/racial_hate_groups_erupt_facebook/, accessed: 24 April 2012.

——, 2011, 'Anonymous DDoS charges too weak: AFP', *ZDNet*, http://m.zdnet.com.au/anonymous-ddos-charges-too-weak-afp-339310749.htm, accessed: 9 June 2011.

Pearson, Mark & Patching, Roger, 2008, *Government Media Relations: A 'Spin' Through the Literature*, Humanities & Social Sciences papers, Paper 228, http://epublications.bond.edu.au/hss_pubs/228.

Perry, Barbara & Olsson, Patrik, 2009, 'Cyberhate: The globalization of hate', *Information & Communications Technology Law*, 18(2): 185–99.

Petray, Theresa, 2011, 'Protest 2.0: Online Interactions and Aboriginal Activists', *Media, Culture & Society*, 33(6): 923–40.

Phillips, Gail, 2008, *Media Analysis Report: Australian Television Current Affairs*, Reporting Diversity.

Phillips, Sara, 2010, 'Who are the Greens voters?', ABC, http://www.abc.net.au/environment/articles/2010/08/06/2976030.htm, accessed: 2 April 2012.

Phillips, Tim & Smith, Philip, 2001, 'Popular understandings of "UnAustralian": An investigation of the un-national', *Journal of Sociology*, 37(4): 323–39

——, 2003, 'Everyday incivility: Towards a benchmark', *The Sociological Review*, 51(1): 85–107.

Pickerill, Jenny, 2001, 'Strengthening cohesion, networking cells: Environmental activists on-line', in Hugh Brown, Geert Lovink, Helen Merrick, Ned Rossiter, David Teh & Michele Willson (eds), *Politics of a Digital Present*, Melbourne: Fibreculture Publications, pp. 69–78.

——, 2006, 'Radical politics on the net', *Parliamentary Affairs*, 59(2): 266–82.

Pilkington, Ed, 2011, 'SlutWalking gets rolling after cop's loose talk about provocative clothing', *Guardian*, 6 May, http://www.guardian.co.uk/world/2011/may/06/slutwalking-policeman-talk-clothing, accessed: 13 February 2012.

Pini, Barbara, Brown, Kerry & Previte, Josephine, 2004, 'Politics and identity in cyberspace: A case study of Australian women in agriculture online', in Wilm van de Donk, Brian Loader, Paul Nixon & Dieter Rucht (eds), *Cyberprotest: New Media, Citizens and Social Movements*, London: Routledge, pp. 259–75.

Plasser, Fritz & Plasser, Gunda, 2000, *Global Political Campaigning: A Worldwide Analysis of Campaigning Professionals and their Practices*, Westport: Praeger.

PM, 2010, 'Sydney sociologist warns Australians ignore race hate groups at their peril', *Radio National*, 19 April, Sydney: ABC.

Pocock, Barbara & Brown, Karen, 2009, 'Gender politics in Australian unions: Gender equality meets the struggle for union survival', in Janice Foley & Patricia Baker (eds), *Unions, Equity, and the Path to Renewal*, Vancouver: UBC Press, pp. 157–76.

Poole, Fiona, 2012, 'PM wants the ear of "mommy bloggers"', *702 ABC Sydney*, 18 June, http://blogs.abc.net.au/nsw/2012/06/pm-wants-the-ear-of-mommy-bloggers.html, accessed: 30 June 2012.

Poplin, Alenka, 2011, 'Playful public participation in urban planning: A case study for online serious games', *Computers, Environment and Urban Systems*, 36: 195–206.

Poster, Mark, 1995, CyberDemocracy: Internet and the Public Sphere, http://www.hnet.uci.edu/mposter/writings/democ.html.

Potter, Will, 2011, *Green is the New Red: An Insider's Account of a Social Movement Under Siege*, San Francisco: City Lights Books.

Poulsen, Kevin & Zetter, Kim, 2010, 'U.S. intelligence analyst arrested in WikiLeaks video probe', *Wired*, 6 June, http://www.wired.com/threatlevel/2010/06/leak/, accessed: 18 May 2012.

Power Inquiry, 2006, *Power to the People: The Report of Power: An Independent Inquiry into Britain's Democracy*, March, London: York Publishing Distribution.

Poynting, Scott, 2006, 'What caused the Cronulla riot?', *Race & Class*, 48 (1): 85–92.

Public Relations Institute of Australia (PRIA), 2011, About Public Relations, http://www.pria.com.au/aboutus/what-is-public-relations/, accessed: 26 May 2012.

Pusey, Michael & McCutcheon, Marion, 2011, 'From the media moguls to the money men? Media concentration in Australia', Media International Australia, 140: 22–34.

Putnam, Robert, 1995, 'Tuning in, tuning out: The strange disappearance of social capital in America', *PS: Political Science & Politics*, 28(4): 664–83.

——, 2000, Bowling Alone: *The Collapse and Revival of American Community*, New York: Simon & Schuster.

Qizilbash, Mozaffar, 2008, 'Amartya Sen's capability view: Insightful sketch or distorted picture?', in Flavio Comim, Mozaffar Qizilbash & Sabina Alkire (eds), *The Capability Approach: Concepts, Measures and Applications*, Cambridge University Press, pp. 53–81.

Quiggin, John, 2006, 'Blogs, wikis and creative innovation', *International Journal of Cultural Studies*, 9(4): 481–96.

Radio Adelaide, 2004, *The History of Australian*, Radio Adelaide.

Rainie, Lee & Smith, Aaron, 2012, *Social Networking Sites and Politics*, Washington: Pew Internet.

Ramadge, Andrew, 2008, 'Scientology protests start across Australia', 10 February, *news.com.au*, http://www.news.com.au/technology/scientology-protests-start-across-australia/story-e6frfro0-1111115518342, accessed: 18 May 2012.

Rana, Norman, 2009, *E-Marketing Intelligence: Transforming Brand and Increasing Sales Using Digital Channels*, Self-Help Publishers.

Rasmussen, Sarah, 2007, 'Building a decentralised machine: The new grassroots politics', *The Kennedy School Review*, 7: 81–91.

Readfearn, Graham, 2012, '"You overpaid, overeducated parasite": ANU climate scientist emails', *Crikey*, 10 May, http://www.crikey.com.au/2012/05/10/you-overpaid-overeducated-parasite-anu-climate-scientist-emails/, accessed: 21 May 2012.

Reeve, David, 1988, *Philosopher-Kings: The Argument of Plato's Republic*, Indianapolis: Hackett.

Resnick, David, 1999, 'The normalization of cyberspace', in Chris Toulouse & Timothy Luke (eds), *The Politics of Cyberspace*, London: Routledge.

Rheingold, Howard, 2002, *Smart Mobs: The Next Social Revolution*, Cambridge: Basic Books.

Rhodes, Rod, 1997, *Understanding Governance*, Buckingham: Open University Press.

Rice, Benno, 2010, 'Where's your Senate vote flowing? Go below the line …', *Crikey*, 3 August, http://www.crikey.com.au/2010/08/03/wheres-your-senate-vote-flowing-go-below-the-line/, accessed: 3 February 2012.

Roberts, Hal & Etling, Bruce, 2011, 'Coordinated DDoS attack during Russian Duma elections', *Internet & Democracy Blog*, 8 December, https://blogs.law.harvard.edu/idblog/2011/12/08/coordinated-ddos-attack-during-russian-duma-elections/, accessed: 16 May 2012.

Robinson, Sue, 2006, 'Journalism and the internet', *New Media & Society*, 8(5): 843–49.

——, 2011, '"Beaming up" traditional journalists: The transition of an American newspaper into cyberspace', in David Domingo & Chris Paterson (eds), *Making Online News: Newsroom Ethnographies in the Second Decade of Internet Journalism*, Volume 2, New York: Peter Lang, pp. 31–44.

Rodan, Debbie & Balnaves, Mark, 2010, 'Media activist websites: The nature of e-participation spaces', *Australian Journalism Review*, 32(1): 27–39.

Rodgers, Emma, 2009, 'Senior Liberals desert Turnbull', *ABC News*, 26 November, http://www.abc.net.au/news/2009-11-26/senior-liberals-desert-turnbull/1158164, accessed: 30 January 2012.

Rohlinger, Deana & Brown, Jordan, 2009, 'Democracy, action, and the internet after 9/11', *American Behavioral Scientist*, 53(1): 133–50.

Rolfe, Peter, 2010, 'Melton Liberal candidate Braidy Kean's insult to police chief commissioner Simon Overland', *Herald Sun*, http://www.heraldsun.com.au/news/special-reports/melton-liberal-candidate-braidy-keans-insult-to-police-chief-commissioner-simon-overland/story-fn5kmqy2-1225953240482, accessed: 9 February 2012.

Rosen, Devan, Lafontaine, Pascale & Hendrickson, Blake, 2011, 'CouchSurfing: Belonging and trust in a globally cooperative online social network', *New Media & Society*, 13(2): 1–18.

Rosenberg, Mark, Hayes, Elisabeth, McIntyre, Margaret & Neill, Nancy, 2010, *Real Collaboration: What It Takes for Global Health to Succeed*, Berkeley: University of California Press.

Rosenberg, Shawn, Ward, Dana & Chilton, Stephen, 1988, *Political Reasoning and Cognition: A Piagetian View*, Durham: Duke University Press.

Rosenbloom, Henry, 2012, 'The press under pressure', *Henry's Blog*, 24 May, http://scribepublications.com.au/news-and-events/post/the-press-under-pressure/, accessed: 24 May 2012.

Rosenfeld, Michel, 2010, 'Should constitutional democracies redefine emergencies and the legal regimes suitable for them?', in Austin Sara (ed.), *Sovereignty, Emergency, Legality*, Cambridge University Press, pp. 240–72.

Rouke, Francis & Schulman, Paul, 1989, 'Adhocracy in policy development', *The Social Science Journal*, 26(2): 131–42.

Rout, Milanda, 2011, 'Gillard was concerned schools prepared for NAPLAN tests', *Australian*, 13 April, http://www.theaustralian.com.au/national-affairs/gillard-was-concerned-schools-prepared-for-naplan-tests/story-fn59niix-1226038104285, accessed: 14 June 2012.

Rucht, Dieter, 2004, 'Movement allies, adversaries and third parties', in David Snow, Sarah Soule & Hanspeter Kriesi (eds), *The Blackwell Companion to Social Movements*, Malden: Blackwell, pp. 197–216.

Rudd, Kevin, 2009, 'The global financial crisis', *The Monthly*, 42, http://www.themonthly.com.au/monthly-essays-kevin-rudd-global-financial-crisis--1421, accessed: 13 June 2012.

Rutherford, Jennifer, 2001, 'One love too many: The undoing of Pauline Hanson', *Australian Journal of Politics & History*, 47(2): 192–208.

Ryan, Stephen, 2010, 'Internet filter protest 'computer terrorism'', *Newcastle Herald*, 23 October, http://www.theherald.com.au/news/local/news/general/internet-filter-protest-computer-terrorism/1976743.aspx, accessed: 9 June 2011.

Sabatier, Paul & Jenkins-Smith, Hank, 1993, *Policy Change and Learning: An Advocacy Coalition Approach*, Boulder: Westview Press.

———, 1999, 'The advocacy coalition framework: An assessment', in Sabatier (ed.), *Theories of the Policy Process*, Boulder: Westview Press.

Salvatore, Armando, 2007, *The Public Sphere: Liberal Modernity, Catholicism, Islam*, New York: Palgrave Macmillan.

Sanders, Karen, 2009, *Communicating Politics in the Twenty-First Century*, Houndmills: Palgrave.

Sandvig, Christian, 2008, 'Wireless play and unexpected innovation', in Tara McPherson (ed.), *Digital youth, innovation, and the unexpected*, Cambridge: MIT Press.

Sawer, Marian, 2006. 'Above-the-line voting: How democratic?', Representation, 41(4): 286–90.

———, 2007, 'Australia: the fall of the femocrat', in Joyce Outshoorn & Johanna Kantola (eds), *Changing state feminism*, Basingstoke: Palgrave Macmillan, pp. 20–40.

———, 2009, *Making Women Count: A History of the Women's Electoral Lobby in Australia*, Sydney: UNSW Press.

Scalmer, Sean, 2002, *Dissent events: Protest, the Media and the Political Gimmick in Australia*, Sydney: UNSW Press.

Scammell, Margaret, 1998, 'The wisdom of the war room: US campaigning and Americanisation', *Media, Culture and Society*, 20(2): 251–75.

Schattschneider, Elmer, 1960, *The Semi-Sovereign People: A Realist's View of Democracy in America*, New York: Holt, Rhinehart & Winston.

Scheufele, Dietram & Patricia Moy, 2000, 'Twenty-five years of the spiral of silence: A conceptual review and empirical outlook', *International Journal of Public Opinion Research*, 12(1): 3–28.

Scholz, Trebor, 2010, 'Infrastructure: Its transformation and effect on digital activism', in Mary Joyce (ed.), *Digital Activism Decoded: The New Mechanics of Change*, New York: International Debate Association, pp. 17–32.

Schroth, Christoph & Janner, Till, 2007, 'Web 2.0 and SOA: Converging concepts enabling the internet of services', *IT Pro*, May/June: 36–41.

Schudson, Michael, 1998, *The Good Citizen: A History of American Civic Life*, New York: Martin Kessler.

Schuler, Douglas, 2004, 'Towards civic intelligence: Building a new sociotechnological infrastructure', in Andrew Feenberg & Darin Barney (eds), *Community in the Digital Age: Philosophy and Practice*, Lanham: Rowman and Littlefield, pp. 263–86.

Scott, Mark, 2010, *The Quest for Truth: Quality Journalism and a 21st Century ABC*, Sydney: ABC.

Semetko, Holli, Blumler, Jay, Gurevitch, Michael & Weaver, David, 1991, *The Formation of Campaign Agendas: A Comparative Analysis of Party and Media Roles in Recent American and British Elections*, Hillsdale: Lawrence Erlbaum.

Senator Online, Undated, SOL FAQ, http://senatoronline.org.au/faq/, accessed: 10 January 2012.

Shade, Leslie, Porter, Nikki & Sanchez, Wendy, 2005, '"You can see anything on the internet, you can do anything on the internet!": Young Canadians talk about the internet', *Canadian Journal of Communication*, 30(4): 503–26.

Shannon, Claude, 1948, 'A mathematical theory of communication', *Bell System Technical Journal*, 27: 379–23, 623–56.

Shapira, Rina & Navon, David, 1991, 'Alone together: Public and private dimensions of a Tel-Aviv cafe', *Qualitative Sociology*, 14(2): 107–25.

Sharman, Campbell, 1994, 'Political parties', in Judith Brett, James Gillespie & Murray Goot (eds), *Developments in Australian Politics*, South Melbourne: MacMillan, pp. 332–33.

Shaw, Frances, 2011, '(Dis)locating feminisms: Blog activism as crisis response', *Outskirts: Feminisms Along the Edge*, 24.

Sheales, Ryan, 2012, *Remarks to the Australasian Study of Parliament Group (Victorian Chapter)*, 5 June, Parliament of Victoria.

Shearman, Sachiyo & Yoo, Jina, 2007, '"Even a penny will help!": Legitimization of paltry donation and social proof in soliciting donation to a charitable organization', *Communication Research Reports*, 24(4): 271–82.

Shiel, Fergus, 2003, 'Legal web snares Crikey publisher', *Age*, 7 May, http://www.theage.com.au/articles/2003/05/06/1051987702129.html, accessed: 30 May 2012.

Shirky, Clay, 2008, *Here Comes Everybody: The Power of Organising without Organisations*, London: Allen Lane.

Sievers, Bruce, 2010, *Civil Society, Philanthropy, and the Fate of the Commons*, Lebanon: Tufts University Press.

Sifry, David, 2006, 'State of the blogosphere, April 2006, Part 1: On blogosphere growth', *Sifry's Alerts*, 17 April, http://www.sifry.com/alerts/archives/000432.html, accessed: 6 February 2012.

Silverman, Craig, 2007, *Regret the Error: How Media Mistakes Pollute the Press and Imperil Free Speech*, New York: Stirling.

Simms, Marian, 1981, 'Australia', in Joni Lovenduski & Jill Hills (eds), *Politics of the Second Electorate: Women and Public Participation*, London: Routledge and Kegan Paul, pp. 83–111.

Simons, Margaret, 2007, *The Content Makers: Understanding the Media in Australia*, Camberwell: Penguin.

——, 2010, 'Post-New Matilda … where to, and what are the lessons?', *Crikey*, 31 May, http://www.crikey.com.au/2010/05/31/post-new-matilda-where-to-and-what-are-the-lessons/, accessed: 3 January 2012.

—— & Fraser, Malcolm, 2010, *Malcolm Fraser: The Political Memoirs*, Carlton: Miegunyah Press.

Sinclair, Lara, 2010, 'Crikey! Publisher Eric Beecher lashes the ABC', *Australian*, 11 October, http://www.theaustralian.com.au/media/crikey-publisher-eric-beecher-lashes-the-abc/story-e6frg996-1225936854078, accessed: 4 January 2012.

Singhal, Amit, 2011, 'Microsoft's Bing uses Google search results — and denies it', *The Official Google Blog*, 1 February, http://googleblog.blogspot.com/2011/02/microsofts-bing-uses-google-search.html, accessed: 20 June 2011.

Small, Tamara, 2008a, 'The Facebook effect? On-line campaigning in the 2008 Canadian and US elections', *Policy Options*, November: 85–87.

——, 2008b, 'Equal access, unequal success — major and minor Canadian parties on the net', *Party Politics*, 14(1): 51–70.

Smith, Kerry, 2011, 'Occupy Sydney marches, re-occupies', *Green Left*, 5 November, www.greenleft.org.au/node/49344, accessed: 21 November 2011.

Snell, Rick, 2002, 'Freedom of Information and the delivery of diminishing returns or how spin doctors and journalists have mistreated a volatile reform', *The Drawing Board: An Australian Review of Public Affairs*, 3(2): 187–207.

Solly, Ross, Isbister, Helen & Birtles, Bill, 2007, *Journalism: Jobs that Make News*, Ultimo: Career FAQs.

Sperti, Teresa, 2010, 'End of financial year performance — digital style', *Digital Marking Lab*, 18 July, http://digitalmarketinglab.com.au/index. php/2010/07/18/end-of-financial-year-performance---digital-style/, accessed: 5 January 2012.

Stafford, Patrick, 2010, 'Hitwise data shows Google dominates Australian search, Bing nowhere to be seen', *Smart Company*, 25 March, http://www. smartcompany.com.au/internet/20100325-hitwise-data-shows-google-dominates-australian-search-bing-nowhere-to-be-seen.html, accessed: 16 May 2011.

Stanyer, James, 2001, *The Creation of Political News: Television and British Party Political Conferences*, Brighton: Sussex Academic Press.

Stauber, John, 2009, 'Beyond MoveOn: Using the internet for real change', *PR Watch*, 27 April, http://www.prwatch.org/node/8350, accessed: 9 May 2012.

Stephey, MJ, 2008, 'Sarah Palin's e-mail hacked', *Time*, 17 September, http:// www.time.com/time/politics/article/0,8599,1842097,00.html, accessed: 10 June 2011.

Sterling, Greg, 2007, 'Happy birthday, Flickr: Web 2.0 pioneer turns three', *search engine land*, 27 February, http://searchengineland.com/happy-birthday-flickr-web-20-pioneer-turns-three-10620, accessed: 16 June 2011.

Stone, Adrienne, 2011, '"Insult and emotion, calumny and invective": Twenty years of freedom of political communication', *University of Queensland Law Journal*, 30(1): 79–97.

Stone, Deborah, 1998, *Policy Paradox: The Art of Political Decision Making*, Revised Edition, New York: WW Norton.

Stoppard, Tom, 1967, *Rosencrantz and Guildenstern are Dead*, London: Faber and Faber.

Strolovitch, Dara, 2006, 'Do interest groups represent the disadvantaged? Advocacy at the intersections of race, class, and gender', *The Journal of Politics*, 68(4): 894–910.

Stubbs, Rhys, 2008, 'Freedom of information and democracy in Australia and beyond', *Australian Journal of Political Science*, 43(4): 667–84.

Sunstein, Cass, 1993, 'On analogical reasoning', *Harvard Law Review*, 106(3): 741–91.

Swanson, David & Mancini, Paolo (eds), 1996, *Politics, Media and Modern Democracy: An International Study of Innovations in Electoral Campaigning and their Consequences*, Westport: Praeger.

Swinburne University of Technology, 2010, *The Brumby Dump*, 21 October, http://www.swinburne.edu.au/chancellery/mediacentre/hawthorn/news/2010/10/the-brumby-dump, accessed: 21 May 2012.

Taft, Ronald & Walker, Kenneth, 1958, 'Australia', Arnold Rose (ed.), *The Institutions of Advanced Societies*, Minneapolis: Lund.

Tanner, Lindsay, 1999, *Open Australia*, Annandale: Pluto Press.

——, 2011, *Sideshow: Dumbing Down Democracy*, Melbourne: Scribe.

Tate, Ryan, 2010, 'Steve Jobs offers world "freedom from porn"', *Gawker*, 15 May, http://gawker.com/5539717/steve-jobs-offers-world-freedom-from-porn, accessed: 10 June 2011.

Taylor, JA, 1998, *Telematics and the Scottish Parliament: Transferable Democratic Innovations*. A Report Prepared at the Centre for the Study of Telematics and Governance Faculty of Business, Glasgow Caledonian University.

Taylor, Paul, 2011, *Žižek and the Media*, Cambridge: Polity.

Technorati, 2011, *State of the Blogosphere 2011*, http://technorati.com/blogging/article/state-of-the-blogosphere-2011-introduction/.

Tell 'em Australia, 2011, *About Us*, http://www.tellem.net.au/about-us/, accessed: 6 January 2012.

Tham, Joo-Cheong, 2010, *Money and Politics: The Democracy we Can't Afford*, Sydney: UNSW Press.

The Science Show, 2011, 'The conversation', *ABC Radio National*, 9 April, http://mpegmedia.abc.net.au/rn/podcast/2011/04/ssw_20110409_1238.mp3

Thomas, Julian, 2004, 'Horizons of expectation: Imaginary trajectories of electronic government', in Gerard Goggin (ed.), Virtual Nation: The Internet in Australia, Sydney: UNSW Press, pp. 258–72.

Thomson, Craig, 2012, *Proof Statements — House of Representatives*, 21 May, Canberra: Parliament of Australia.

Thorp, Holden & Goldstein, Buck, 2010, *Engines of Innovation: The Entrepreneurial University in the Twenty-First Century*, Chapel Hill: University of North Carolina Press.

Tiffen, Rodney, 1989, *News and Power*, Sydney: Allen & Unwin.

——, 2012, 'Spin doctors, news values and the public interest — the Bermuda Triangle of policy debate', in Matthew Ricketson (ed.), *Australian Journalism Today*, South Yarra: Palgrave Macmillan, pp. 16–27.

Tindal, Suzanne, 2009, 'NSW follows Lundy's public sphere', *ZDNet*, http://www.zdnet.com.au/nsw-follows-lundys-public-sphere-339297501.htm, accessed: 20 April 2012.

Tobin, Hugh, 2006, 'Fear of txt', *Review*, April, Melbourne: Institute of Public Affairs, p. 51.

Trewhella, Damian, 2005, 'How can information and communication technologies (ICT) support the peace movement? An investigation into the resurgence of the peace movement in Australia', Paper Presented at the Engaging Communities Conference, Brisbane Convention & Exhibition Centre, 14–17 August.

Truman, David, 1951, *The Governmental Process: Political Interests and Public Opinion*, New York: Alfred A. Knop.

Tucker, Kerry, 2004, 'A matter of content — The unauthorised diversion and receipt of a member's e-mails', paper presented at the Australian Electronic Governance Conference, 14-15 April, Centre for Public Policy, University of Melbourne.

Turnbull, Malcolm, 2012, 'Politics, journalism and the 24/7 news cycle', *More or Less: Democracy & New Media*, Sydney: Future Leaders, pp. 50–67.

Turow, Joseph, 2006, *Niche Envy: Marketing Discrimination in the Digital Age*, Boston: Massachusetts Institute of Technology.

United Nations, 2005, *UN Global E-government Readiness Report 2005: From E-government to E-inclusion, Department of Economic and Social Affairs, Division for Public Administration and Development Management*, New York: United Nations.

Ubayasiri, Kasun, 2006, 'Internet and the public sphere: A glimpse of YouTube', *ejournalist*, 6(2),

Valverde, Francisco & Pastor, Oscar, 2009, 'Facing the technological challenges of web 2.0: A RIA model-driven engineering approach', in Gottfried Vossen, Darrell Long & Jeffrey Xu Yu (eds), *Web Information Systems Engineering — WISE 2009*, Berlin: Spinger, pp. 131–44.

van de Donk, Wim, Loader, Brian, Nixon, Paul & Rucht, Dieter (eds), 2004, *Cyberprotest: New Media, Citizens, and Social Movements*, London: Routledge.

van Onselen, Ainslie & van Onselen, Peter, 2008, 'On message or out of touch? Secure web sites and political campaigning in Australia', *Australian Journal of Political Science*, 43(1): 43–58.

van Onselen, Peter, 2009, 'Nationals face up to primary challenge', *Australian*, 17 January, http://www.theaustralian.com.au/news/nationals-face-up-to-primary-challenge/story-e6frg6q6-1111118584339, accessed: 25 April 2012.

—— & Wayne Errington, 2004, 'Voter tracking software: The dark side of technology and democracy', in Peter John Chen & Winsome Roberts (eds), *Proceedings of the Australian Electronic Governance Conference 2004*, multimedia CDROM, 14–15 April.

——, 2007, *John Winston Howard: The Definitive Biography*, Melbourne University Press.

VanSlyke Turk, Judy, 1985, 'Information subsidies and influence', *Public Relations Review*, 11(3): 10–25.

Vascellaro, Jessica, 2009, 'Why email no longer rules … And what that means for the way we communicate', *The Wall Street Journal*, 12 October, http://online.wsj.com/article/SB10001424052970203803904574431151489408372.html, accessed: 29 March 2012.

Vasek, Lanai, 2012, 'Tony Abbott has labelled Aboriginal rioters "un-Australian"', *Australian*, 27 January, http://www.theaustralian.com.au/national-affairs/mob-doesnt-speak-for-us-say-indigenous-leaders/story-fn59niix-1226254996811, accessed: 4 June 2012.

Vine, Josie, 2009, 'The larrikin paradox: An analysis of larrikinism's democratic role in Australian journalism', PhD thesis, RMIT University.

Vitak, Jessica, Zube, Paul, Smock, Andrew, Carr, Caleb, Ellison, Nicole & Lampe, Cliff, 2011, 'It's complicated: Facebook users' political participation in the 2008 Election', *Cyberpsychology, Behavior and Social Networking*, 14(3): 107–14.

Vromen, Ariadne, 2007, 'Australian young people's participatory practices and internet use', *Information, Communication & Society*, 10(1): 48–68.

——, 2008, 'Building virtual spaces: Young people, participation and the Internet', *Australian Journal of Political Science*, 43(1): 79–97.

—— & William Coleman, 2011, 'Online movement mobilisation and electoral politics: The case of GetUp!', *Communication, Politics & Culture*, 44(2): 76–94.

Vultee, Fred, 2007, 'Securitization: A new approach to framing and media portrayals of the "War on Terror"', paper presented at the Annual Meeting of the Association for Education in Journalism and Mass Communication, December 8, The Renaissance, Washington.

Wainwrigh, Robert, 2009, 'Australian Holocaust denier arrested', *smh.com.au*, 2 October, http://www.smh.com.au/news/world/australian-holocaust-denier-arrested/2008/10/02/1222651205020.html, accessed: 24 April 2012.

Walsh, Kerry, 2008, 'Note to Steve: Forget the stunts', *smh.com.au*, http://www.smh.com.au/news/opinion/note-to-steve-forget-the-stunts/2008/09/06/1220121597553.html, accessed: 3 February 2012.

Walsh, Lucas, 2007, *Darebin eForum Evaluation Report*, 8 August, Centre for Citizenship and Human Rights, Deakin University.

Ward, Ian, 2003, 'An Australian PR state?', *Australian Journal of Communication*, 30(1): 25–42.

——, 2008, 'Kevin07. Labor's pitch to generation YouTube', *Social Alternatives*, 27(2): 11–16.

—— & James Cahill, 2007, 'Old and new Media: Blogs in the third age of political communication', paper presented at the Australasian Political Studies Association Annual Conference, 24–6 September, Melbourne: Monash University.

Warner, Michael, 2002, *Publics and Counterpublics*, Cambridge: Zone Books.

Waters, Cara, 2012, 'ACCC investigates petrol price collusion', *Smart Company*, 4 May, http://www.smartcompany.com.au/legal/049510-accc-investigates-petrol-price-collusion.html, accessed: 18 June 2012.

Watson, Tom, 2009, *CauseWired: Plugging In, Getting Involved, Changing the World*, New Jersy: John Wiley and Sons.

Weaver, Anne, 2011, 'Gamification — Time for an epic win?', *Access*, 25(3): 20–23.

Wei, Ran & Leung, Louis, 1999, 'Blurring public and private behaviors in public space: policy challenges in the use and improper use of the cell phone', *Telematics and Informatics*, 16: 11–25.

West, Darrell & Orman, John, 2003, *Celebrity Politics*, Upper Saddle River: Prentice Hall.

White, Micah, 2011, 'A vision of post-clicktivist activism', *AdBusters*, 26 July, http://www.adbusters.org/blogs/blackspot-blog/vision-post-clicktivist-activism.html, accessed: 20 March 2012.

Whitelaw Towers, 2011, 'Andy Slackbastard AKA Andy Flemming fulls a favor', *Whitelaw Towers*, 5 June, http://whitelawtowers.blogspot.com.au/2011/06/ndy-slackbastard-aka-andy-flemming.html, accessed: 25 April 2012.

Whittaker, Zack, 2011, 'Royal phone hacking scandal: New investigating email hacks', *ZDNet*, 10 June, http://www.zdnet.com/blog/igeneration/royal-phone-hacking-scandal-now-investigating-email-hacks/10656, accessed: 10 June 2011.

Whyte, Sarah, 2011, 'Beware getting off your Facebook', *theage.com.au*, 2 January, http://www.theage.com.au/technology/technology-news/beware-getting-off-your-facebook-20110101-19cj7.html, accessed: 2 March 2012.

Wicks, Robert, 2001, *Understanding Audiences: Learning to use the Media Constructively*, New Jersey: Lawrence Erlbaum Associates.

Wilkins, Georgia, 2012, '"Rude" reporter apologises to PM', 23 February, *theage.com.au*, http://www.theage.com.au/opinion/political-news/rude-reporter-apologises-to-pm-20120223-1tpy5.html, accessed: 4 June 2012.

Wilkinson, Dennis & Huberman, Bernardo, 2007, 'Cooperation and quality in Wikipedia', paper presented at WikiSym'07, 21–23 October, Montreal, Quebec.

Williams, Chuck, 2008, *Management*, Mason: South-Western Cengage Learning.

Williamson, Andy, 2010, 'Politicians get their clicks', *theworldtoday.org*, February, London: Chatham House.

Wilson, Jason, 2011, 'Playing with politics: Political fans and Twitter faking in post-broadcast democracy', *Convergence*, (17): 445–61.

Wilson, Shaun & Spies-Butcher, Benjamin, 2011, 'When labour makes a difference: Union mobilisation and the 2007 federal election in Australia', *British Journal of Industrial Relations*, 49: s306–31.

Winn, Jane & Wright, Benjamin, 2001, *The Law of Electronic Commerce*, 2004–2 Supplement, New York: Aspen.

Winner, Langdon, 1986, *The Whale and the Reactor: A Search for Limits in an Age of High Technology*, University of Chicago Press.

Wlezien, Christopher, 2010, 'Election campaigns', in Lawrence LeDuc, Richard Niemi & Pippa Norris (eds), *Comparing Democracies 3: Elections and Voting in the 21st Century*, London: Sage.

Woll, Thomas & Raccah, Dominique, 2010, *Publishing for Profit: Successful Bottom-Line Management for Book Publishers*, 4th edn, Chicago Review Press.

Wordsworth, Matt, Binnie, Kerrin, Burgess, Sam & Barry, Siobhan, 2012, 'Qld Labor candidate expelled after homophobic rant', *7 News Sydney*, 21 February, http://www.abc.net.au/news/2012-02-20/queensland-labor-candidate-peter-watson-quits/3841192, accessed: 21 February 2012.

Wring, Dominic, 2005, *The Politics of Marketing the Labour Party*, Basingstoke: Palgrave Macmillian.

Young, Graham, 2011, 'Wanted — new financial backers', *On Line Opinion*, 7 February, http://www.onlineopinion.com.au/view.asp?article=11583&page=0, accessed: 23 August 2011.

——— & Brown, Hugh, 2003, 'Interview: Graham Young and Hugh Brown of On Line Opinion 2003', *YouTube*, 15 December, http://www.youtube.com/watch?v=gSaeoC8drSM, accessed: 15 December 2011.

Young, Sally, 2007a, 'Political and parliamentary speech in Australia', *Parliamentary Affairs*, 60(2): 234–52.

———, 2007b, 'Following the money trail: Government advertising, the missing millions and the unknown effects', *Public Policy*, 2(2): 104–18.

———, 2011a, *How Australia Decides: Election Reporting & the Media*, Port Melbourne: Cambridge University Press.

——, 2011b, 'Disclosure, accountability and the role of the media', Joo-Cheon Tham, Brian Costar & Graeme Orr (eds), *Electoral Democracy: Australian Prospects*, Melbourne University Press, pp. 209–31.

Zajko, Mike, 2011, 'The shifting politics of climate science', *Society*, 48(6): 457–61.

Zappala, Gianni, 1998, 'Clientelism, political culture and ethnic politics in Australia', *Australian Journal of Political Science*, 33(3): 381–97.

Zittrain, Jonathan, 2008, *The Future of the Internet And How to Stop It*, New Haven: Yale University Press.

Zoch, Lynn & Molleda, Juan-Carlos, 2009, 'Building a theoretical model of media relations using framing, information subsidies, and agenda-building', Carl Botan & Vincent Hazleton (eds), *Public Relations Theory II*, New Jersey: Lawrence Erlbaum, pp. 245–72.

www.ingramcontent.com/pod-product-compliance
Lightning Source LLC
LaVergne TN
LVHW071357070326
832902LV00028B/4631